Taxation of Loan Relationships and Derivative Contracts Supplement to the 10th edition

Taxation of Loan Relationships and Derivative Contracts: Supplement to the 10th edition

David Southern QC
MA, DPhil, MPhil (Oxon), CTA (Fellow)
One of Her Majesty's Counsel
A Master of the Bench of Lincoln's Inn
A member of Temple Tax Chambers
Visiting Professor and Director of the School of Tax Law,
Queen Mary, University of London

Bloomsbury Professional
LONDON · DUBLIN · EDINBURGH · NEW YORK · NEW DELHI · SYDNEY

BLOOMSBURY PROFESSIONAL

Bloomsbury Publishing Plc

41–43 Boltro Road, Haywards Heath, RH16 1BJ, UK

BLOOMSBURY and the Diana logo are trademarks of Bloomsbury Publishing Plc

First published in Great Britain 2020

Copyright © Bloomsbury Professional, 2020

Reprinted 2020

All rights reserved. No part of this publication may be reproduced or transmitted in any form or by any means, electronic or mechanical, including photocopying, recording, or any information storage or retrieval system, without prior permission in writing from the publishers.

While every care has been taken to ensure the accuracy of this work, no responsibility for loss or damage occasioned to any person acting or refraining from action as a result of any statement in it can be accepted by the authors, editors or publishers.

All UK Government legislation and other public sector information used in the work is Crown Copyright ©. All House of Lords and House of Commons information used in the work is Parliamentary Copyright ©. This information is reused under the terms of the Open Government Licence v3.0 (http://www.nationalarchives.gov.uk/doc/open-government-licence/version/3) except where otherwise stated.

All Eur-lex material used in the work is © European Union, http://eur-lex.europa.eu/, 1998–2020.

British Library Cataloguing-in-Publication Data

A catalogue record for this book is available from the British Library.

ISBN: 978 1 52650 706 8

Typeset by Compuscript Ltd, Shannon
Printed and bound by CPI Group (UK) Ltd, Croydon, CR0 4YY

To find out more about our authors and books visit www.bloomsburyprofessional.com. Here you will find extracts, author information, details of forthcoming events and the option to sign up for our newsletters

Preface

When I completed the 10th edition of *Taxation of Loan Relationships and Derivative Contracts* in the middle of 2017, the proposed new rules on carried-forward losses and the corporate interest restriction were threats which had not yet materialised.

I unwisely hazarded the guess that these extensive new codes would not be introduced for the time being. I was wrong. Amongst other things, I had underestimated the political pressure, partly generated by globalisation, which the OECD's Base erosion and profit shifting (BEPS) project has both generated and reflected. This results in a tendency to regard all multinationals as being engaged in various forms of undesirable tax avoidance.

This does not represent the full picture and it seems to me that the concern is overdone. Large corporate organisations, like governments, can be instruments both of benevolence and malevolence; a force for good and a force for ill. More commonly than not, the benevolent, responsible impulse predominates and it is important to have a balanced perspective. Moreover, the two sets of rules apply to a broad swathe of companies as well as MNEs.

The new rules present a considerable challenge in terms of confining the content of the book to its original core subject matter, namely, loan relationships and derivative contracts. When I wrote the first edition of the work back in 1996, both these areas were governed by specific and focused legislation. This legislation has now expanded into areas of general corporation tax, and general corporation tax itself has fragmented into a number of specialist areas. Hence, there is a tension between focus and inclusiveness.

I have been regularly promising and regularly failing to deliver this supplement for over two years. Its completion would not have been possible without the inexhaustible patience and encouragement of David Wright of Bloomsbury.

I am greatly indebted to the knowledge and insights of Sarah Squires of Old Square Tax Chambers and Heather Self of Blick Rothenberg, both of whom have a command of the subject which is awesome.

Preface

My daughter Ruth undertook the proofreading and produced the artwork.

The errors and confusions remain my own, to lament over on winter evenings. This is intended to provide technical guidance and practical help in challenging areas of law and practice. This is a collaborative venture. Please send corrections, comments, criticisms and suggestions to me (David.SouthernQC@templetax.com) or Bloomsbury (info@bloomsburyprofessional.com).

David Southern QC
Temple Tax Chambers
June 2020

Contents

Preface	v
Table of statutes	xi
Table of statutory instruments	xxi
Table of cases	xxiii
Abbreviations	xxvii

1 Introduction: New Currents in Corporation Tax — 1
- Section A: Can more be had? — 1
- Section B: UK and international tax — 2
- Section C: The purpose of double taxation treaties — 3
- Section D: The BEPS project — 4
- Section E: The BEPS Action Plan — 6
- Section F: BEPS and its UK implementation — 7
- Section G: Policy background — 8
- Section H: Tax avoidance — 10
- Section I: The taxation of companies — 12
- Section J: The debt-equity distinction — 13
- Section K: Conclusion — 15

2 Corporate Interest Restriction (CIR) — 16
- Section A: BEPS Action 4 — 17
- Section B: History of UK rules — 19
- Section C: The interaction rules — 21
- Section D: Outline of the corporate interest restriction (CIR) rules — 24
- Section E: Steps in applying the legislation — 28
- Section F: Diagram — 31
- Section G: The key rules — 33
- Section H: Accounts adjustments — 38
- Section I: The worldwide group (WWG) — 42
- Section J: Rule 1 — 49
- Section K: Rule 2 — 50
- Section L: Rule 3 — 53
- Section M: Rule 4 — 56
- Section N: Rule 5 — 59
- Section O: Rule 6 — 59
- Section P: Rule 7 — 63
- Section Q: Rule 8 — 65

Contents

Section R: Rule 9	69
Section S: Rule 10	71
Section T: Rule 11	71
Section U: Rule 12	72
Section V: Rule 13	74
Section W: Rule 14	78
Section X: Rule 15	83

3 Loss Relief — **86**

Section A: History of the UK rules	87
Section B: Compliance costs	91
Section C: The legislation	92
Section D: Outline of the system	93
Section E: Carried on on a commercial basis	96
Section F: In-year and carry back loss relief	98
Section G: Current year group and consortium relief	99
Section H: Transitional accounting periods	104
Section I: Interaction with the CIR	107
Section J: Current year losses	108
Section K: Flexible relief	109
Section L: Banks and insurance companies	110
Section M: Carried-forward losses, post-1 April 2017	112
Section N: Carried-forward losses post-1 April 2017 (single company/within relevant maximum)	113
Section O: Group relief for carried-forward losses	118
Section P: Definition of group	120
Section Q: Carried-forward losses available to be group relieved	121
Section R: The loss cap	124
Section S: The key concepts in the loss cap	125
Section T: Relevant profits	130
Section U: Relevant maximum	136
Section V: The cap on relievable carried-forward losses	145
Section W: Corporate capital loss restriction	148
Section X: Corporate acquisitions followed by transfer of trades and assets	155

4 Capital Instruments — **160**

Section A: Capital instruments rules	160
Section B: Hybrid mismatches	161
Section C: BEPS Action Points 2 and 15	164
Section D: Conditions for D/NI mismatch	165
Section E: Other types of mismatch	167
Section F: Regulatory capital	170
Section G: Hybrid capital instruments rules	173

5 Transfer Pricing — **176**
   Section A: The ALP and separate entity principle — 176
   Section B: Passive association — 180
   Section C: The transfer pricing hypothesis — 180
   Section D: Incorporation of BEPS — 182
   Section E: Thin capitalisation — 184
   Section F: The EU context — 185
   Section G: The UK rules — 188
   Section H: Application to financing arrangements — 191
   Section I: Securities — 194
   Section J: Guarantees — 196
   Section K: Economic substance re-characterisation — 197
   Section L: Corresponding adjustments — 198
   Section M: Balancing payments — 200
   Section N: Withholding tax — 200
   Section O: Centrally provided services — 201
   Section P: Exemptions — 203
   Section Q: Compliance aspects — 204
   Section R: Diverted profits tax — 205

6 Controlled Foreign Companies — **212**
   Section A: BEPS — 212
   Section B: The UK rules — 213
   Section C: Definition of CFC — 215
   Section D: The control test — 215
   Section E: The exemptions — 217
   Section F: The CFC gateways — 219
   Section G: Computation of CFC profits — 223

Index — 225

Table of statutes

[All references are to paragraph number.]

C

Capital Allowances Act 2001
s 260(3)	2.185

Companies Act 2006 .... 2.92
s 136	2.91
260	2.94
399	2.91, 2.95, 2.174
405	2.95
678	2.91
679	2.91
1159	2.93, 2.95
1160	2.93, 2.94, 2.95
1161	2.94
1162	2.94
Sch 7	2.93, 2.94
Sch 10A	2.93, 2.94
para 4(1), (2)	2.94

Corporation Tax Act 2009 .... 5.81
s 2	3.3
(1)	3.33
5	1.11
(1), (2)	5.99
14–18	6.16
15–15E	3.89
18A	2.237, 16.17
21	1.11, 2.76, 5.10, 5.40
22	1.11, 2.76, 5.10, 5.40
45A	3.131
45A–45H	3.145
46	2.18
62(5A)	3.112
180–182	2.62
261	2.62
262	2.62
297, 298	3.80
299	3.82, 6.5, 6.42
302	4.52
303	4.52
(1)(a)	4.48

Corporation Tax Act 2009 – *contd*
s 306A	2.124
307	2.18
320	2.109
320B	2.152, 2.153, 4.1, 4.50, 4.58
322(2)	2.152
(3)	4.54
(4)	4.38
323A	2.152
330A(7)	3.47
331(3), (4)	3.47
415	4.36
420A	4.50, 4.55
420B	4.1
442	2.30
443	2.30
444	4.4
455B–455D	2.30
455B(1)	2.18
456–463	3.20, 3.48
457(3)	3.98, 3.159, 3.171, 3.185, 3.195, 3.197
(5)	3.36
458(1)	3.11
463A–463I	3.20, 3.82
463B(1)(a)–(c)	3.114
463G	3.21, 3.99, 3.114, 3.131, 3.171, 3.195, 3.198
(7)	3.112
(10)	3.113
(11)	3.88
(13)	3.95
463H	3.36, 3.99, 3.114
(4)	3.185
(5)	3.98, 3.159, 3.171, 3.195, 3.197
463I	3.114
464	2.23

Table of statutes

Corporation Tax Act 2009 – *contd*
s 464(1) 2.23, 2.25
   (2) 2.23
  465 .... 2.23
  475C 4.1, 4.50, 4.52, 4.53
   (1)(c) 4.52
   (8), (9) 4.52
  476(1) 4.48
  479 .... 4.52
  480 .... 4.52
  499 .... 2.110
  571 .... 2.23
  573 .... 3.82
  574 .... 3.82
  577 .... 4.36
  585 .... 4.36, 4.52
  595 .... 2.18
  597(1) 2.190
  598(1)(b) 2.59
  640 .... 4.36
  652 .... 4.36
  653 .... 4.36
  670 .... 4.36
  690 .... 4.4
  698B(1) 2.18
  753 .... 3.21, 3.83, 3.99, 3.112,
               3.171, 3.195, 3.198
   (2) 3.113
   (3) 3.131
  Pt 9A (ss 931A–931W) 3.185
  s 906(1) 2.109
   1210(5A) 3.185
   1211(7A) 3.185
   1216DA(3) 3.185
   1216DB(5A) 3.185
   1216DC(7A) 3.185
   1217DA(3) 3.185
   1217DB(5A) 3.185
   1217MA(3) 3.185
   1217MC(9) 3.185
   1217SA(3) 3.185
   1217SC(9) 3.185
   1218 .... 3.84
   1218B 3.114
   1218ZDA(3) 3.185
   1218ZDC(9) 3.185
   1219 .... 3.21, 3.99
   1223 ...... 3.21, 3.84, 3.99, 3.123, 3.131
    (3B) 3.84, 3.112
    (3D) 3.113

Corporation Tax Act 2010
s 4 .... 3.33
  (2) 2.19, 2.100, 2.121,
                2.122, 3.35
  (3) 3.33, 3.34
 37 .... 3.36, 3.45, 3.104
  (3)(a) 3.46, 3.209
  (b) 3.46
 37–45 .... 3.20
 38 .... 3.46
 39 .... 3.45, 3.46
 44(1) 3.37
 45 .... 3.45, 3.95, 3.99, 3.109
  (4) 3.73
  (a) 3.74
  (b) 3.73, 3.159, 3.195
  (4A)–(4C) 3.73
 45A 3.21, 3.99, 3.101, 3.103,
        3.104, 3.105, 3.106, 3.107,
        3.109, 3.115, 3.171, 3.195,
          3.198, 3.209, 3.237
  (1)(c) 3.104
  (2) 3.88
  (3) 3.97, 3.99, 3.100,
               3.104, 3.107
  (a), (c) 3.104
  (4) 3.102, 3.104
  (5) 3.102, 3.104, 3.112
  (6) 3.102, 3.104
  (7) 3.104, 3.113
 45A–45F 3.79, 3.99
 45A–45H 3.20
 45B 3.73, 3.99, 3.100, 3.107,
          3.108, 3.109, 3.113,
            3.171, 3.195
  (4) 3.113, 3.159
 45C 3.99, 3.105, 3.106,
              3.108, 3.195
  (1)(d) 3.104
  (2) 3.106
  (a), (b) 3.104
  (3) 3.104, 3.105
 45D 3.99, 3.108, 3.195
  (2) 3.105, 3.113
  (5) 3.113
 45E 3.99, 3.108
  (2) 3.113
 45ED 3.99
 45F 3.99, 3.109, 3.110,
              3.224, 3.237

Table of statutes

Corporation Tax Act 2010 – *contd*
s 45G	3.109, 3.110
45H	3.109
46	3.45
62	3.21, 3.99, 3.131
(3)	3.171, 3.195, 3.198
(5C)	3.113
62–67	3.85
63	3.21, 3.99, 3.131
(4)	3.21, 3.99
(6)	3.113
65(4B)	3.185
67A(5A)	3.185
97–156	3.122
99	3.45, 3.46, 3.48
(1)(c)	3.114
(e)	3.85
102	3.85
131	3.122
132	3.54, 3.58
133	3.54
(1)	3.59
(2)	3.60
134	3.61
139	3.63
142	3.63
143(2), (3)	3.64
146B	3.65
150	3.124
151	3.51, 3.124
152	3.51, 3.124
153	3.124
154	3.51
155	3.51
155A, 155B	3.51
157–182	3.50, 3.125
162	4.55
(1B)	4.55
169–182	3.127
185(2)	3.55
188	3.118
188AA–188CK	3.145
188AA–188FD	3.20, 3.115
188BB	3.114, 3.119, 3.144
(1)	3.131
(3)–(5)	3.96
(6)	3.96, 3.132
188BC	3.118
188BD	3.132
188BE	3.120, 3.140

Corporation Tax Act 2010 – *contd*
s 188BF	3.140
188BG	3.96
188BH	3.141
188BI	3.142
188CA–188EK	3.238
188CB	3.119, 3.134, 3.143, 3.144
188CC	3.119, 3.138, 3.143
188CD	3.119
188CE	3.122, 3.134, 3.135
188CF	3.134, 3.136, 3.138
188CG	3.134, 3.137
188CH	3.138, 3.139
188CI	3.138
188CJ	3.122
188CK	2.123, 3.143
188DB	3.206
188DC	3.206
188DD	3.206
188ED	3.208
188FA	3.133
246	3.85
247	3.85
Pt 7ZA (ss 269ZA–269ZZB)	3.19, 3.20, 3.145
s 269ZA–269ZO	3.189
269ZB	3.31, 3.35, 3.89, 3.92, 3.94, 3.98, 3.99, 3.151, 3.162, 3.198, 3.219
(3)	3.95, 3.151, 3.169, 3.198
(a)	3.73
(b)	3.159
(4)	3.151, 3.159, 3.169
(5)	3.195, 3.196
(7)	3.129, 3.152, 3.158, 3.162, 3.167, 3.205
(a)	3.213
(8)	3.166
269ZBA(2)	3.212
(5)	3.213
269ZC	3.31, 3.35, 3.92, 3.94, 3.98, 3.99, 3.151, 3.161, 3.163, 3.198, 3.219
(2)	3.151, 3.169, 3.198
(3)	3.195, 3.196
(5)	3.152, 3.158, 3.163, 3.167, 3.205

Table of statutes

Corporation Tax Act 2010 – *contd*
s 269ZC(5)(a)............................ 3.213
269ZD............. 3.31, 3.35, 3.92, 3.93,
3.94, 3.98, 3.99,
3.151, 3.161, 3.172
  (2).............................. 3.172
  (3)........................ 3.21, 3.151,
3.169, 3.171
    (j) 3.120
  (4)........................ 3.195, 3.208
  (5).............. 3.31, 3.95, 3.151,
3.173, 3.176, 3.178,
3.185, 3.206
  (6)............................ 3.155
269ZE................................ 3.92, 3.94
  (2), (7)........................ 3.93
269ZF 3.30, 3.31,
3.151, 3.173, 3.177, 3.179,
3.180, 3.181, 3.184, 3.186,
3.187, 3.208, 3.218
  (1).............. 3.30, 3.173, 3.176,
3.180, 3.185
  (2)............. 3.176, 3.180, 3.185
  (3)............. 3.32, 3.180, 3.181,
3.183, 3.185, 3.188
  (4)........................ 3.180, 3.185
  (5)........................ 3.180, 3.185
269ZFA................... 3.30, 3.31, 3.32,
3.151, 3.173, 3.177, 3.179,
3.180, 3.181, 3.186,
3.187, 3.208
  (1), (2) 3.187
269ZFB–269ZQ 3.177
269ZFC(5)(a)........................ 3.213
269ZG................... 3.94, 3.104, 3.106
  (6) 3.92
269ZH................................ 3.94
269ZI 3.94
  (1)............................ 3.185
269ZJ–269ZN...................... 3.95
269ZK............................... 3.95
269ZR 3.153, 3.155,
3.168, 3.205
  (2) 3.207
269ZS 3.168, 3.202, 3.203
  (1)............................ 3.202
  (2)–(4)....................... 3.201
  (9)............................ 3.204
269ZT 3.168, 3.202
  (1) 3.204

Corporation Tax Act 2010 – *contd*
s 269ZT(4), (5)........................ 3.202
269ZU................................ 3.202
269ZV................................ 3.202
  (2).............................. 3.204
  (3)(e)........................... 3.204
  (5).............................. 3.204
  (7).............................. 3.204
269ZW.................. 3.19, 3.31, 3.151,
3.153, 3.155
  (2).............................. 3.157
269ZWA 3.221
269ZX............................... 3.157
269ZY............................... 3.157
269ZYA 3.221
269ZYB 3.221
269ZZ 3.19, 3.205
  (1) 3.152, 3.166
  (2) 3.152, 3.165
269ZZA 3.208
269ZZB 3.19, 3.124, 3.126
  (1), (2) 3.126
  (3)...................... 3.124, 3.126
  (4)............................ 3.126
  (5)...................... 3.125, 3.127
  (6)............................ 3.124
  (7)(a)–(c)..................... 3.128
Pt 7A (ss 269A–269DO) 3.20, 3.90
s 269B 3.161
269CA 3.90
269CA–269CN.................... 3.91
Pt 8 (ss 270–356JB) 3.88
s 303A–327 .... 3.20
303B(4)............... 3.159, 3.185, 3.195
303C 3.123
303D(5) 3.159, 3.185, 3.195
304(7) 3.185
Pt 8ZA (ss 356K–356NJ) 3.88
356NE–356NJ 3.20
375 .... 3.104
534 .... 2.233
541 .... 2.233
Pt 14 (ss 672–730) 3.210
s 672................................ 3.230
672–691 .... 3.20
673–676....................... 3.231, 3.232
Pt 14 Ch 2A
  (ss 676AA–676AL)............. 3.210
s 676AA–676ED............... 3.231, 3.234
676AC............................. 3.235

Table of statutes

Corporation Tax Act 2010 – *contd*
  s 676AD 3.236
    676AE 3.236, 3.237
    676AF 3.237
    676BA–676BE 3.238
    676CA–676CI 3.239
    676DA–676DE 3.240
    676EA–676EE 3.241
    677–691 .... 3.231, 3.233
    724A 2.140
  Pt 14A (ss 730A–730D) 3.210
  s 730F 3.210
    882 .... 6.25
    940A–943 .... 3.20, 3.223, 3.230
    1000(1) 2.11, 3.50
         E 2.11, 2.30
         F 2.11, 2.30, 3.50
    1005 .... 2.11, 2.30, 3.50
    1015 .... 2.11, 2.30, 4.55, 3.50
         (1A) 4.55
         (4), (6) 4.48
    1119 .... 3.34, 3.51
    1122 .... 2.175, 6.25
    1124 .... 5.54
    1154 .... 3.50, 3.51, 3.125
    1172 .... 3.70, 3.77
    1219 .... 3.171, 3.195, 3.198

F

Finance Act 1951
  s 37 .... 5.51
Finance Act 1996 .... 2.11
  s 84(1) 2.18
Finance Act 1998
  Sch 18 .... 2.207
    para 2(1) 2.203
    67, 68 .... 3.119
    70 .... 3.119, 3.132
    71, 71A 3.119
Finance Act 1993 .... 2.18
Finance Act 1994 .... 2.18
Finance Act 1996 .... 2.11, 2.18
Finance Act 2004 .... 1.48
Finance (No 2) Act 2005 .... 2.17
Finance Act 2007
  Sch 24 .... 2.217
  Sch 23
    para 1 .... 5.68
Finance Act 2008
  Sch 36 .... 2.216

Finance Act 2009
  Sch 15 .... 2.13
Finance Act 2011
  s 7 .... 3.71
    (5) 3.71
Finance Act 2012
  s 68 .... 3.92, 3.93
    123–127 .... 3.20
    124B 3.195
    124A(2) 3.123
    124C(3) 3.123
Finance Act 2014 .... 5.122
  s 214–233 .... 5.110
Finance Act 2015
  s 77 .... 1.26
    77–116 .... 5.105
    (1) 5.104
    79(2)(i) 5.104
    80 .... 5.106, 5.109
    (1)(d), (f) 5.106
    81 .... 5.106, 5.109
    82 .... 5.109, 5.112
    (5) 4.9
    83 .... 5.109, 5.112
    84 .... 5.109, 5.112
    85 .... 5.109, 5.112
    86 .... 5.106
    92 .... 5.111, 5.120
    93 .... 5.111
    96(2) 5.112
    101 .... 5.115
    102 .... 5.115, 5.119
    107, 108 .... 5.106, 5.107
    109 .... 5.108
    110 .... 5.106
    (4)–(9) 5.106
  Sch 2 .... 3.90
Finance (No 2) Act 2015
  s 31 .... 5.51
Finance Act 2016
  Sch 10 .... 1.26
Finance (No 2)
  Act 2017 .... 1.3, 2.10
  s 20 .... 2.16
    30 .... 2.16
  Sch 4 .... 1.26
    para 190(1) 3.69
         (2) 3.69
         (b) 3.69, 3.70
    191 .... 3.76

Table of statutes

Finance (No 2) Act 2017 – *contd*
  Sch 5...................................... 1.26, 2.16
    para 11(1)............................. 2.16
Finance Act 2018 .... 1.26
Finance Act 2019 .... 3.186
  Sch 10
    para 8................................... 3.187
        32................................... 3.187
  Sch 4
    para 19.................................. 2.62
  Sch 20...................................... 4.1, 4.50
Financial Services and Markets
  Act 2000............................... 4.40

I

Income and Corporation Taxes
  Act 1970
  s 204....................................... 5.102
Income and Corporation Taxes
  Act 1988
  s 212(1) 5.47
    209(2)(da)........................... 5.47
    343..................................... 3.229
Income Tax Act 1977
  s 770....................................... 5.51
Income Tax Act 2007
  s 66(1), (2)............................. 3.38
    874..................................... 4.49
    889..................................... 4.49
    987..................................... 4.56
Income Tax (Trading and Other
  Income) Act 2005
  s 863(1) 3.38

P

Partnership Act 1890
  s 1(1) 3.38

T

Taxation (International and Other
  Provisions) Act 2010........... 1.6
  s 2... 1.7, 1.8
    6.. 4.24
    18...................................... 2.114
    116.................................... 4.38
    126–132............................. 4.38
  Pt 4 (ss 146–217) 2.30, 5.52
  s 146–217.............................. 2.30
    147.................................... 5.77, 5.83
      (1) 5.53, 5.57

Taxation (International and Other
  Provisions) Act 2010 – *contd*
  s 147(3) 5.23, 5.53, 5.69, 5.93
      (5) 5.53, 5.93
    148..................................... 5.52
      (3) 5.54
    151..................................... 5.21
    152................... 5.69, 5.70, 5.83, 5.84
      (2) 5.70, 5.72
      (5) 5.72, 5.74, 5.77, 5.78
      (6) 5.72
    153.................... 5.69, 5.73, 5.75
      (1) 5.77
    154(3) 5.63
      (4) 5.76
      (6) 5.71
    155..................................... 5.53, 5.71
    157..................................... 2.175, 5.54
    158..................................... 2.175, 5.54
    159..................................... 2.175, 5.54
    160..................................... 2.175, 5.55
    164..................................... 1.10
      (1) 5.8
      (4) 5.56
    165..................................... 5.96
    166..................................... 5.58
      (1) 5.93
    167..................................... 5.58
      (1), (3)........................... 5.94
    168..................................... 5.58, 5.95
    169..................................... 5.95
    170..................................... 5.95
    172..................................... 5.93, 5.108
    173..................................... 5.94
    174..................................... 5.69, 5.83
    175..................................... 5.69
    179..................................... 5.96
    181..................................... 5.84, 5.85
    182(3) 5.84
    187..................................... 5.89
    192..................................... 5.73, 5.77
    195..................................... 5.86
    217(1) 5.54
    218–230............................. 5.98
    231–259............................. 4.2
  Pt 6A (ss 259A–259NF)...... 2.24, 2.30
  s 259A(1)–(3)........................ 4.7
      (7) 4.13
    259A–259E....................... 4.1
    259A–259NF..................... 2.30

Taxation (International and Other Provisions) Act 2010 – *contd*

s 259B	4.6
259BA(2)	4.21
259BB	4.14
259BE	4.16
259C	4.25, 4.31
259C–259CE	4.34
259CA	4.25
(4)	4.29
(6), (7)	4.27
259CB	4.25, 4.28
(3)	4.3
(6)	2.24, 4.4
259CC	4.25
259CD	4.25, 4.29
(3)(a)	4.29
259CE	4.30
259D–259DG	4.34
259DB	4.32
259DD	4.33
259E–259ED	4.34
259F–259FC	4.34
259G–259GE	4.34
259H–259HC	4.34
259I–259ID	4.34
259IC(10)	4.12, 4.17
259J–259JC	4.34
259K–259KD	4.34
259N	4.5, 4.15
259NB	4.26
259NC	4.26
259ND	4.26, 6.23
259NEA	4.3
260–353B	1.26
308	2.48
371AA–371VJ	1.26, 6.11
371AA(3)	6.12
(4)(a)	6.11
371AH	6.54
371BA(3)	6.56
371BB	6.35
371BC	6.12
371BD	6.12
371CA	6.37
(11)	6.6
371CC	6.44
371CD	6.44
371CF	6.53
371DA–371DL	6.37

Taxation (International and Other Provisions) Act 2010 – *contd*

s 371DA(3)(a), (f)	6.38
371DB	6.38
371IA	6.46
371IB(6), (7)	6.48
(10)(c)	6.48
371JA–371JG	6.31
371KA–371KJ	6.26
371KC	6.16
371LA–371LC	6.32
371MA–371MC	6.33
371NA–371NE	6.34
371OA–371OE	6.15
371PA	6.58
371SB	6.56
371SC–371SK	6.58
371TA–371TC	6.15
371VG	6.42
371VI	6.6
Pt 10 (ss 372–382)	2.16
s 372(1)(a)	2.25
(7)(i)	2.118
(ii)	2.119
372–498	2.16
373–377	2.203
373(1)	2.101, 2.104
(3)	2.198
374	2.208
375	2.203, 2.237
(2)	2.35, 2.102, 2.213
376	2.203
(6)	2.35
377	2.237
378(2)	2.35
379	2.35
380	2.35, 2.196, 2.237
381	2.196
382	2.52, 2.104, 2.232
(1)	2.24, 2.106
(2)–(5)	2.106
(11)	2.24
382–391A	2.105
383	2.106
384	2.106, 2.107, 2.232
(4)	2.107
385	2.111
(1)–(5)	2.111
(6)	2.106, 2.111
386	2.111

Table of statutes

Taxation (International and Other Provisions) Act 2010 – *contd*

s 387	2.111
388	2.114
389	2.113
390(1), (2)	2.104
(3)	2.113, 2.115
(4)	2.115
(5)	2.106
391	2.109
391A	2.109
392	2.52
(1)	2.134
(2), (3)	2.137, 2.138
393	2.135
(3), (4)	2.52
394	2.135
395	2.135
395A	2.140
396	2.39, 2.48, 2.52, 2.115, 2.129
(1)	2.129, 2.130
(2)	2.129, 2.130
(a)	2.130
(b)	2.130, 2.159
397	2.37, 2.39, 2.52, 2.132, 2.142
(1)	2.142
398	2.37, 2.39, 2.52, 2.132, 2.159, 2.160
(1)	2.162
(2)	2.191
399	2.160, 2.161
(1)	2.47, 2.161
400	2.52, 2.192
(1)	2.52
(2)	2.191
(3)	2.155, 2.199
(4)	2.191, 2.199
400A	2.199
401–404	2.224, 2.237
405	2.52, 2.127
(a)	2.120
406	2.117, 2.120, 2.121, 2.190
(1), (2)	2.121
(3)(a)	2.121, 2.122
(7)	2.118
407(1), (2)	2.123
(3)	2.124
408	2.124
409	2.125
410	2.52, 2.144, 2.165

Taxation (International and Other Provisions) Act 2010 – *contd*

s 410(1)	2.144
(2)–(6)	2.147
411	2.165
(1)	2.146
(d)	2.148
(e)	2.148
(iii)	2.148
(2)	2.149
(3), (4)	2.154
412	2.148, 2.165
413	2.52, 2.150, 2.165
(1)	2.150
(3)	2.152
(a), (d)	2.152
(4)	2.153
(d), (e)	2.153
414	2.48, 2.52, 2.165, 2.168
(1)	2.168
(3)	2.170, 2.173
(b)	2.170
(4)	2.173
415	2.48, 2.168
(4)–(6), (8)	2.170
415–443	2.184
416	2.48, 2.52, 2.181, 2.183
(5)	2.185
417	2.186
(5)	2.147, 2.186
(6)	2.147
418	2.187
419	2.188
420	2.56, 2.57, 2.237
421	2.56, 2.57, 2.237
(1)(c), (d)	2.59
422	2.189, 2.237, 2.238
(7)	2.189, 2.238
423–426	2.237
427–429	2.222, 2.237
430	2.223, 2.237
(6)	2.223
432–449	2.226
433	2.227, 2.237
(5)	2.227
434	2.237
435	2.237
436	2.228
(5)	2.229
437(2)	2.228

xviii

Table of statutes

Taxation (International and Other Provisions) Act 2010 – *contd*	
s 438	2.230
(4)–(6)	2.231
440	2.230
441	2.230
442	2.230
(3)	2.230
443	2.230
444	2.237
450	2.232
452	2.233
453	2.72, 2.232
454A	2.73
456	2.112, 2.232, 2.237
457	2.112, 2.237
459	2.110
461	2.234
462	2.174
463	2.174, 6.23
(1)(c)	2.179
464	2.174, 2.175
(1)	2.179
465	2.174, 2.175
(1)	2.175
(3)–(5)	2.179
466	2.176
467	2.176
468	2.177
473	2.70
(1)	2.70
(2)	2.70
(3)	2.70
(4)(d)	2.70
(c)	2.76
(5)	2.71
474	2.70, 2.75
475	2.72
475A	2.70
475C(9)	4.60
476	2.83
477	2.74
480	2.77
481	2.77
482	2.77
483	2.77
484	2.77, 2.79
485	2.77
(1), (2)	2.80
486	2.80

Taxation (International and Other Provisions) Act 2010 – *contd*	
s 487	2.77
490	2.81, 2.118
492	2.46
Sch 7A	2.203, 2.213
para 1	2.203, 2.204
4	2.206
(2)	2.215
7(2)	2.208
8	2.208
10	2.205
(1)–(3)	2.204
11	2.205
12(3)(a)–(g)	2.237
12–19	2.210
13	2.237
14	2.237
15	2.189, 2.237, 2.238
16	2.237
17	2.237
18	2.237
19	2.237
20(3)	2.196
20–26	2.211
22	2.102
23(2)	2.212
24	2.203, 2.215
29–37	2.217
40–44	2.217
49	2.217
(2)(b)	2.217
52	2.217
54	2.189, 2.238
56	2.216
60–66	2.216
Taxation of Chargeable Gains Act 1992	
s 2A(1)(b)	3.218
18(3)	3.220
(9)–(12)	3.220
136	3.223
139	3.223
171	3.220, 3.238
204–213A	3.214
286(5)	3.220
Sch 7A	3.222
Taxes Management Act 1970	2.207
s 108(3)	3.204

Table of statutory instruments

[All references are to paragraph number.]

A

Authorised Investment Funds (Tax) Regulations 2006, SI 2006/964
- reg 18(2A) 2.110
- 19 .... 2.110
- 23 .... 2.110
- 69Z16(2A) 2.110
- 69Z17 .... 2.110

C

Controlled Foreign Companies (Excluded Banking Business Profits) Regulations 2012, SI 2012/3041 .... 6.52

Controlled Foreign Companies (Excluded Territories) Regulations 2012, SI 2012/3024 .... 6.27
- reg 5 .... 6.29

Corporate Interest Restriction (Financial Statements: Group Mismatches) Regulations 2017, SI 2017/1224,
- reg 1, 2 .... 2.61

D

Double Taxation Relief (Base Erosion and Profit Shifting) Order 2018, SI 2018/630 ..... 4.24

F

Financial Services and Markets Act 2000 (Regulated Activities) Order 2001, SI 2001/544
- Sch 1
  - Part 1 .... 3.92

L

Loan Relationships and Derivative Contracts (Disregard and Bringing into Account of Profits and Losses) Regulations 2004, SI 2004/3256 .... 2.56
- reg 3 .... 2.56, 2.57
  - (5)(c) 4.58
- 4 .... 2.56, 2.57
- 6A 2.56, 2.57
- 7 .... 2.56, 2.57, 2.59
- 7A 2.56
- 8 .... 2.56, 2.57
- 9 .... 2.56, 2.57, 2.58, 2.60
  - (2), (4) 2.59

T

Taxation of Regulatory Capital Securities Regulations 2013, SI 2013/3209 .... 4.49, 4.50

Taxation of Securitisation Companies Regulations 2006, SI 2006/3296
- reg 22 .... 2.110

Taxes (Base Erosion and Profit Shifting) (Country-by-Country Reporting) (Amendment) Regulations 2017, SI 2017/497 .... 5.31

Taxes Base (Base Erosion and Profit Shifting) (Country-by-Country Reporting) Regulations 2016, SI 2016/237 .... 5.31

Table of cases

[*All references are to paragraph number.*]

A

Abbey National Treasury Services Plc v HMRC [2015] UKFTT 341 (TC), [2015] 7 WLUK 388, [2015] SFTD 929.. 5.58

B

Beacon v HMRC [2018] UKFTT 104 (TC), [2018] 2 WLUK 635, [2018] SFTD 846, [2018] STI 786 .... 3.42
Bosal Holding BV v Staatssecretaris van Financien (C168/01) [2003] All ER (EC) 959, [2003] STC 1483, [2003] ECR I-9409, [2003] 3 CMLR 22, [2003] BTC 513, 6 ITL Rep 105, [2003] STI 1638, ECJ 5.43
Bulmer Ltd v J Bollinger SA (No 2) [1974] Ch 401, [1974] 3 WLR 202, [1974] 2 All ER 1226, [1974] 5 WLUK 97, [1974] 2 CMLR 91, [1974] FSR 334, [1975] RPC 321, (1974) 118 SJ 404, CA 1.5

C

Cadbury Schweppes Plc v IRC (C-196/04) [2007] Ch 30, [2006] 3 WLR 890, [2006] STC 1908, [2006] ECR I-7995, [2006] 9 WLUK 144, [2007] 1 CMLR 2, [2007] All ER (EC) 153, [2006] CEC 1026, [2008] BTC 52, 9 ITL Rep 89, [2006] STI 2201, ECJ... 6.9
Chevron Australia Holdings Pty Ltd v Commissioner of Taxation (No 4) [2015] FCA 1092.. 5.18
Clark (Inspector of Taxes) v Oceanic Contractors Inc [1983] 2 AC 130, [1983] 2 WLR 94, [1983] 1 All ER 133, [1983] STC 35, [1982] 12 WLUK 161, 56 TC 183, (1982) 13 ATR 901, (1983) 133 NLJ 62, (1983) 127 SJ 54, HL 5.101

F

Falmer Jeans Ltd v Rodin (Inspector of Taxes) [1990] STC 270, [1990] 1 WLUK 707, 63 TC 55... 3.228
Fowler v HMRC (2018) STC 2041 .... 4.19

G

General Electric Canada Inc v The Queen [2010] FCA 344 .... 5.18
Gillette Safety Razor Ltd v IRC [1920] 3 KB 358, [1920] 6 WLUK 34............ 5.51
Glencore Energy UK Ltd v HMRC [2017] EWHC 1476 (Admin), [2017] STC 1824, [2017] 6 WLUK 625, [2017] BTC 20, QBD..................... 5.105, 5.117

H

HMRC v South Eastern Power Networks Plc [2019] UKUT 367 (TCC), [2020] STC 298, [2019] 12 WLUK 458, [2020] STI 99 .... 3.65

Table of cases

HMRC v Total E & P North Sea UK Ltd [2019] UKUT 133 (TCC), [2019] STC 1110, [2019] 4 WLUK 479.. 3.71

I

Ingenious Games LLP v HMRC [2019] UKUT 226 (TCC), [2019] STC 1851, [2019] 7 WLUK 509, [2019] STI 1466 .... 3.43
Irish Bank Resolution Corp Ltd (In Special Liquidation) v HMRC [2019] UKUT 277 (TCC), [2019] STC 2286, [2019] 10 WLUK 118, 22 ITL Rep 224, [2019] STI 1684 .... 1.13, 6.30

L

Lankhorst-Hohorst GmbH v Finanzamt Steinfurt (C-324/00) [2003] STC 607, [2002] ECR I-11779, [2003] 2 CMLR 22, [2003] BTC 254, 5 ITL Rep 467, [2002] STI 1807, ECJ 5.44
Laycock (Inspector of Taxes) v Freeman, Hardy & Willis Ltd [1939] 2 KB 1, [1938] 4 All ER 609, (1939) 55 TLR 218, [1938] 12 WLUK 4, 22 TC 288, CA... 3.228
Leekes Ltd v HMRC [2018] EWCA Civ 1185, [2018] 1 WLR 3837, [2018] 4 All ER 504, [2018] STC 1245, [2018] 5 WLUK 421, [2018] BTC 21, [2018] STI 1043 .... 3.229
Liverpool & London Globe Insurance Co v Bennett (Surveyor of Taxes) [1913] AC 610, [1913] 7 WLUK 135, HL 3.90

M

Metallgesellschaft Ltd v IRC (C-397/98); Hoechst AG v IRC (C-410/98) (2001) STC 452, [2001] Ch 620, [2001] 2 WLR 1497, [2001] STC 452, [2001] ECR I-1727, [2001] 3 WLUK 256, [2001] 2 CMLR 32, [2001] All ER (EC) 496, [2001] BTC 99, 3 ITL Rep 385, [2001] STI 498, ECJ 5.42

R

R v IRC [1996] STC 681, [1996] 2 WLUK 205, 68 TC 205, [1996] COD 421, CA... 3.2
R (on the application of Cobalt Data Centre 2 LLP) v HMRC [2019] UKUT 342 (TCC), [2020] STC 23, [2019] 11 WLUK 257, [2019] STI 1880 .... 3.44
R (on the application of Rowe) v HMRC [2017] EWCA Civ 2105, [2018] 1 WLR 3039, [2018] STC 462, [2017] 12 WLUK 250, [2018] BTC 4... 5.110, 5.118
Reed International v HMRC [1976] AC 336, [1975] 3 WLR 413, [1975] 3 All ER 218, [1975] STC 427, [1975] 7 WLUK 144, [1975] TR 197, (1975) 119 SJ 794, HL.. 4.48

S

Samarkand Film Partnership Nos 3 v HMRC [2017] EWCA Civ 77, [2017] STC 926, [2017] 2 WLUK 645, [2017] BTC 4, CA...................................... 3.41
Societe de Gestion Industrielle SA (SGI) v Belgium (C-311/08) [2010] 1 WLUK 387, [2010] 2 CMLR 38, [2010] CEC 1130, [2011] BTC 123, ECJ 5.45

Table of cases

T

Test Claimants in the Thin Cap Group Litigation v IRC (C-524/04) [2007] STC 906, [2007] ECR I-2107, [2007] 2 CMLR 31, [2008] BTC 348, 9 ITL Rep 877, [2007] STI 538, ECJ.. 5.47, 5.49

U

Union Castle Mail Steamship Co Ltd v HMRC [2018] UKUT 316 (TCC), [2018] STC 2034, [2018] 10 WLUK 8 .... 5.58

W

Wannell v Rothwell (Inspector of Taxes) [1996] STC 450, [1996] 3 WLUK 472, 68 TC 719, Ch D 3.38

Abbreviations

ACB	Amortised cost basis
ALP	Arm's-length principle
ANGIE	Adjusted net group interest expense
ANTIE	Aggregate net tax-interest expense
ANTII	Aggregate net tax-interest income
AOA	Authorised OECD approach
APA	Advance pricing agreement
ATCA	Advance thin capitalisation
ATED	Annual tax on enveloped dwellings
BEPS	Base erosion and profit shifting
BLABAG	Basic Life Assurance and General Annuity Business
CA	Companies Act
CBCR	Country by country reporting
CCLR	Corporate capital loss restriction
CFC	Controlled foreign company
CILR	Corporate income loss restriction
CIR	Corporate interest restriction
CT	Corporation tax
CTA	Corporation Tax Act
CTSA	Corporation tax self-assessment
DA	Deductions allowance
DEMPE	Development, enhancement, maintenance, protection and exploitation
DPT	Diverted profits tax
DR	Disregard Regulations: Loan Relationships and Derivative Contracts (Disregard and Bringing into Account of Profits and Losses Regulations, SI 2004/3256
DTA	Deferred tax asset
DTR	Double taxation relief
DTT	Double taxation treaty

Abbreviations

EATR	Effective average tax rates
EBITDA	Earnings before interest, tax, depreciation and amortisation
EEA	European Economic Area
EU	European Union
FA	Finance Act
FCPE	Finance company partial exemption
FRL	Flexible relief losses
FRR	Fixed ratio rule
FV	Fair value
GAAP	Generally Accepted Accounting Principles
GRR	Group ratio rule
IAS	International Accounting Standards
IFRS	International Financial Reporting Standards
IP	Intellectual property
IRR	Interest restriction return
ITA	Income Tax Act 2007
ITTOIA	Income Tax (Trading and Other Income) Act 2005
JV	Joint venture
KERT	Key entrepreneurial risk-taking function
MDF	Modified debt cap
MLI	Multi-lateral instrument
MNE	Multi-national enterprise
MTP	Modified total profits
NTIE	Net tax-interest expense
NTLRD	Non-trading loan relationship deficit
NTPDA	Non-trading profits deduction allowance
OBR	Office of Budget Responsibility
OECD	Organisation for Economic Co-operation and Development
OECD MC	OECD Model Convention
PE	Permanent establishment
PFE	Private finance initiative
PIE	Public infrastructure election
QIC	Qualifying infrastructure company
QNGIE	Qualifying net group-interest expense

Abbreviations

QNTP	Qualifying non-trading profit
QTP	Qualifying trading profit
REIT	Real Estate Investment Trust
RM	Relevant maximum
RRL	Restricted relief losses
Sch	Schedule
SCT	Corporation tax surcharge
SFTD	*Simon's First-tier Tax Decisions*
SI	Statutory instrument
SME	Small or medium-sized enterprise
SPF	Significant people function
STC	Simon's Tax Cases
SWTI	Simon's Weekly Tax Intelligence
TAAR	Targeted anti-avoidance rule
TCGA	Taxation of Chargeable Gains Act 1992
TIOPA	Taxation (International and Other Provisions) Act 2010
TP	Transfer pricing
TPDA	Trading profits deduction allowance
TPG	Transfer Pricing Guidelines for Multinational Enterprises and Tax Administrations approved by the OECD
UP	Ultimate parent
WWDC	Worldwide debt cap
WWG	Worldwide group

Chapter 1

Introduction: New Currents in Corporation Tax

Chapter Contents

Section	Topic	Paragraphs
A	Can more be had?	1.1–1.4
B	UK and international tax	1.5–1.11
C	Purpose of double taxation treaties	1.12–1.13
D	The BEPS project	1.14–1.21
E	The BEPS Action Plan	1.22–1.25
F	BEPS and its UK implementation	1.26
G	Policy background	1.27–1.39
H	Tax avoidance	1.40–1.48
I	The taxation of companies	1.49–1.53
J	The debt-equity distinction	1.54–1.60
K	Conclusion	1.61–1.63

Section A: Can more be had?

1.1 In 1085, William the Conqueror sent out commissioners to record the ownership and value of all the land in England. With a speed, thoroughness and exactitude which the modern computerised civil service can only envy, the results of their enquiries were recorded and compiled within a year in the Great Domesday Book and Little Domesday Book (1086). The returns for the Abbey of Ely included the standard list of questions the commissioners were required to ask, and those to whom they directed their enquiries were required to answer. The last question was always: 'If more (tax) can be had than at present?'

1.2 *Introduction: New Currents in Corporation Tax*

1.2 That is the spirit which animates the changes which have led to new currents in corporation tax. The predominant motive has been at international level rather than at domestic level. However, the result has been a wide-reaching transformation of UK rules on corporate taxation.

1.3 As was observed by Julius von Kirchmann in 1847: *'three amending words of the legislator and whole libraries becomes waste paper'*. Changes introduced by Finance (No 2) Act 2017 (F(No 2)A) had the effect of making, if not whole libraries into waste paper, certainly rendering out of date sections of the 10th edition of *Taxation of Loan Relationships and Derivative Contracts* published in March 2017.

1.4 These changes stemmed almost entirely from the Organisation for Economic Co-operation and Development's (OECD) Base Erosion Profit-Shifting (BEPS) project and its UK implementation. They were developed by separate, but related, initiatives of the UK Parliament. They go considerably further than the specific changes to the loan relationships and derivative contracts rules, important though those are, and alter the taxation of corporate profits generally.

Section B: UK and international tax

1.5 Until recently, international tax was a separate area of tax, confined to a select band of specialists. That has all changed. Like EU law, in Lord Denning's classic formulation, international tax has become *'an incoming tide, flowing up the estuaries and entering into the rivers'* of domestic law: *Bulmer v Bollinger* [1974] 2 All ER 1226 at 1231. As a result, because of OECD initiatives, major and far-reaching changes have been made to UK domestic taxation.

1.6 The main UK legislation on international tax is the Taxation (International and Other Provisions) Act 2010 ('TIOPA 2010').

1.7 Section 2 of TIOPA 2010 states that if the UK enters into a double taxation agreement with another state, and the Queen by Order in Council *'directs that it is expedient that those arrangements should have effect'*, then the provisions of the double taxation treaty take effect as part of UK domestic tax law and override any inconsistent domestic tax rule.

1.8 Treaties form part of international public law. The subjects of public international law are states, not persons actual or legal. The UK has a dualist system of international law, which only takes effect if it is transformed into domestic law. Alternative terms are 'converted' or 'received'. Double taxation treaties link the domestic tax systems of the two contracting states concerned. So, if they are to perform that function, they must be converted into UK internal law. Section 2 of TIOPA 2010 is a transformation clause, which enables double taxation treaties to be given effect as part of UK domestic law.

1.9 Such a clause was traditionally known as a *non obstante* clause because it meant that once a double taxation treaty was received into domestic law, it prevailed over inconsistent domestic law. In other words, it took effect notwithstanding – *non obstante* – domestic law with which it was inconsistent.

1.10 The other key section is TIOPA 2010, s 164, which states that the UK transfer pricing rules are to be interpreted in accordance with the OECD *Transfer Pricing Guidelines for Multinational Enterprises and Tax Administrations*. TIOPA 2010, s 164 does not incorporate the OECD Transfer Pricing Guidelines into UK law. They are to be regarded as guidance, having the status of soft international law.

1.11 The Corporation Tax Act (CTA) 2009, s 5 says that a non-resident company is only subject to corporation tax if it carries on a trade in the UK through a permanent establishment, or carries on a trade of dealing in or developing land in the UK other than through a permanent establishment. Section 21, following Article 7 of the OECD Model Convention, states that the profits attributable to the permanent establishment are those that the establishment would have made if it were a distinct and separate enterprise. It thus incorporates into UK law the distinct and separate enterprise hypothesis. Following on from that, section 22 then states that, in accordance with the separate enterprise principle, transactions between the permanent establishment and any other parts of the non-UK resident company shall be treated as taking place in accordance with the arm's-length principle (ALP).

Section C: The purpose of double taxation treaties

1.12 Three principles have hitherto governed national and international taxation:

(a) income and gains are taxed on the basis of either residence or source;

(b) residence basis is in general unlimited (worldwide) taxation; and

(c) source taxation is on a limited basis.

So, if a person is resident in State A, but has income in State B, he may suffer economic double taxation.

1.13 *Introduction: New Currents in Corporation Tax*

1.13 The classic functions of double taxation treaties have been:

(a) to produce a fair and rational allocation of tax revenues between states; and

(b) to prevent economic double taxation.

As the Upper Tribunal observed in *Irish Bank Resolution Corporation Ltd v R & C Comrs* [2019] UKUT 277 (TCC) at [7]:

> 'The purpose of a double taxation convention between two states is to ensure that a person ... does not pay tax twice on the same income.'

However, given the assumptions and direction of the OECD's BEPS project, a third object has been added, namely:

(c) to prevent tax avoidance by multinational enterprises (MNEs).

Section D: The BEPS project

1.14 The OECD took the view that, in consequence of the integration of national economies and markets (globalisation), the established rules of international taxation created opportunities for MNEs to shift profits from high-tax countries (base erosion) to low-tax countries (profit shifting). In particular, the OECD took the view that user-generated value is not captured under the existing international framework.

1.15 The common thread running through the changes set out in Chapters 2–6 is that they constitute, directly or indirectly, the UK's response to the OECD's BEPS project. Base Erosion and Profit Shifting refers to the means, thought to be adopted by MNEs, of reducing tax liabilities in high-tax countries (base erosion) and moving value-generating activities to low-tax countries (profit shifting). The BEPS project seeks to align taxation with genuine economic activity and value generation.

1.16 This was considered in outline in paragraphs 20.2–20.7 of the 10th edition, drawing attention to the tension between tax cooperation and tax competition amongst states. Like all successful research projects, the BEPS project established in advance the conclusions which it was going to reach. BEPS is concerned with *'tax avoidance arrangements that exploit gaps and mismatches in tax rules to artificially shift profits to low or non-tax locations'* (OECD.org/tax/beps). Such strategies may include placing debt in high-tax jurisdictions, the use of hybrid entities and instruments (whose fiscal treatment differs between tax jurisdictions), transfer pricing, avoidance of permanent establishments and intangible assets. BEPS is directed against regime-based

Introduction: New Currents in Corporation Tax **1.21**

measures, leaving states free to reduce general rates. The BEPS Final Report was released on 15 October 2015.

1.17 On 29/30 January 2020, in its Two Pillars document, the OECD produced proposals to take the BEPS project forward. Pillar 1 is concerned with (a) how economic activity generated by the digital economy should be taxed, and (b) how taxing rights on profits generated from cross-border digital activity should be allocated. Pillar 1 seeks to articulate a unified approach to the allocation of tax according to market jurisdictions. It is scoped at consumer-facing services. Pillar 1 seeks a consensus agreement (the Inclusive Framework). The nexus between taxation and economic activity should be based on sales, abandoning or hollowing out the PE concept. This will ensure taxation, at a minimal effective rate, in the country where economic value is generated. It is scoped at consumer-facing services. This may involve significant modifications in this area to ALP, overlying the ALP with a formula-based approach. What is proposed is a three-tier profit allocation system. Pillar 2 focuses on the remainder of BEPS issues.

1.18 Accordingly, the OECD Inclusive Framework/Two-Pillar approach makes radical proposals which would lead to the replacement of transfer pricing by formulary apportionment (ie, where states carve out shares of tax revenues amongst themselves rather than requiring enterprises to modify the pricing on their controlled transactions by reference to ALP).

1.19 On 25 April 2019, the OECD published the full text of the latest version of the OECD Model Convention as it read on 21 November 2017. This reflects the development of international taxation in the wake of BEPS. The changes to transfer pricing are now incorporated into the 2017 OECD Transfer Pricing Guidelines. The OECD has also issued *OECD Transfer Pricing Guidance on Financial Transactions, Inclusive Framework on BEPS Actions 4, 8–10* (February 2020). The focus is on the balance of debt and equity in a MNE. The theme of the paper is *'the process of accurate delineation of the actual transaction'* (§10.16).

1.20 There are 43 OECD members. There are a further 68 BEPS associates committed to the BEPS package and its implementation. The BEPS programme functions through 'best practice guidelines'.

1.21 The sort of situation with which the OECD was concerned was illustrated by the Luxembourg tax ruling for McDonalds restaurants: [2018] SWTI 1762. A Luxembourg tax-resident company, McDonald's Europe Franchising, had, having regard to the terms of the United-States–Luxembourg double taxation treaty, a United States permanent establishment. The company's profits were not taxed in Luxembourg if they were attributable to the United States PE. The United States did not regard the operation in question as a PE

1.22 *Introduction: New Currents in Corporation Tax*

of the Luxembourg company. Hence, the profits were not taxed either in the United States or in Luxembourg. The result was double non-taxation of the Luxembourg company's franchising income.

Section E: The BEPS Action Plan

1.22 The BEPS Action Plan was published on 19 July 2013. This consisted of a package of 15 Actions which members and associates of the OECD would need to undertake in order to give effect to the OECD's recommendations. These have led to widespread changes in national taxation. The UK has taken the lead in implementing BEPS Actions.

1.23 The Actions re-appeared in the Final Report of 5 October 2015, which outlined 15 'Action Items':

- Action 1 concerns the digital economy.
- Action 2 is on 'neutralising the effects of hybrid mismatch arrangements'.
- Action 3 is on controlled foreign company rules.
- Action 4 recommends that an entity's net deduction for interest and economically equivalent payments should be limited to a percentage of the earnings before interest, taxes, depreciation, and amortisation (EBITDA) in a corridor of 10–30%.
- Action 5 applies to countering harmful tax practices. These include IP regimes. The recommendation is that there should be a nexus between income-receiving benefits and expenditure contributing to that income.
- Action 6 seeks to prevent the granting of treaty benefits in inappropriate circumstances (treaty shopping).
- Action 7 is concerned with preventing artificial avoidance of the PE status.
- Actions 8–10 deal with changes to the Transfer Pricing Guidelines.
- Action 11 deals with the monitoring and reporting of BEPS.
- Action 12 is mandatory tax disclosure rules.
- Action 13 is concerned with 'transfer pricing documentation and country-by-country reporting (CBCR). For groups with annual revenues of more than €750 million, this requires the filing of information on activities and tax paid in particular countries.
- Action 14 seeks to make dispute resolution procedures more effective.
- Action 15 seeks to develop a multilateral instrument to facilitate the modification of bilateral tax treaties

1.24 The BEPS actions are designed to be implemented via changes in domestic law and practice and via treaty amendment, facilitated by the negotiation of the multilateral instrument (Action 15).

1.25 The Actions correspond to the aims of the BEPS project, namely:

- greater transparency (Actions 11, 12, 13);
- better alignment of taxation with substantial economic activity, i.e. separating reward from legal ownership (Actions 1, 6, 7, 8, 9, 10);
- ensuring the coherence of the tax system (Actions 2, 3, 4, 5); and
- the implementation and co-ordination of Actions (Actions 14, 15).

Section F: BEPS and its UK implementation

1.26 BEPS has had a major effect on UK legislation. These changes fall into five groups, which are considered in Chapters 2 to 6:

(1) BEPS Action 4 (Limiting Base Erosion Involving Interest Deductions and Other Financial Payments). This has produced the Corporate Interest Restriction (CIR) Rules. Schedule 5 of the Finance (No 2) Act 2017 took effect from 16 November 2017 and replaced the worldwide debt cap (10th edition, Chapter 21) with the CIR rules. This is considered in Chapter 2. The CIR rules supplement the transfer pricing rules based on the ALP.

(2) Carried-forward loss relief. With effect from 1 April 2017, Sch 4 of F(No 2)A 2017 introduced an entirely different system of relief for carried-forward losses. This is dealt with in Chapter 3. This legislation is indirectly BEPS-inspired, because it applies broadly to the same groups of companies as the CIR; the separation out of finance costs under CIR made necessary a general revision of the carried-forward loss rules.

(3) BEPS Action 2: The hybrid mismatch rules were introduced by FA 2016, Sch 10. Further new rules on hybrid capital instruments were brought in by FA 2018, with effect from 1 January 2019. These are considered in Chapter 4.

(4) BEPS Actions 10–12 (Aligning transfer pricing outcomes and value creation); Action 13 (Transfer pricing documentation and CBCR); Action 14 (Making dispute resolution procedures more effective); Action 15 (Multilateral instrument for amending DTTs). All these Actions, together with the issue of revised Transfer Pricing Guidelines, have resulted in extensive changes to the UK transfer pricing rules. This is dealt with in Chapter 5. Alongside the transfer pricing rules are the

1.27 *Introduction: New Currents in Corporation Tax*

Diverted Profits Tax (DPT) rules, introduced by FA 2015, s 77 with effect from 1 April 2015. These are also considered in Chapter 5.

(5) BEPS Action 3: The code for the taxation of Controlled Foreign Companies (CFCs) in TIOPA 2010, ss 371AA–371VJ was substantially revised. This is considered in Chapter 6.

Section G: Policy background

1.27 These are all, in part, a response to globalisation. The initial reaction of BEPS-compliant jurisdictions was to lower rates of corporation tax. Loss of revenue is compensated for by the removal of reliefs from corporation tax generally, such as carried-forward loss relief and interest deductions. Any overall fall in tax revenues from companies has to be made good either from non-mobile sources of tax (land, employment or savings), by reductions in public spending per se, by increased borrowing and, when investors will no longer purchase national debt, by the printing of money by the central bank, as occurred in the German hyperinflation of 1923.

1.28 BEPS was founded on the assumption that financial resources were limited and that there was a trade-off between taxation and public benefits. These financial calculations were overthrown by the economic and social disruption resulting from measures adopted by the UK and other western governments in response to the outbreak of COVID 19. If a government decides to print money, its power to command resources is only limited by the readiness of currency holders to accept the state's currency in exchange for goods and services, and as a store of wealth.

1.29 From one point of view, national governments are seeking to fight back Canute-like against the process of globalisation. States can rarely be of uniform disposition in this area, because in tax terms, one state's gain will often be another state's loss. States seek to protect their own tax base not only against the efforts of individuals and businesses to reduce their tax burden and increase their economic freedom, but also against the efforts of other states to attract the same.

1.30 The CIR rules, transfer pricing changes and DPT all reflect a common endeavour to protect or renationalise the UK tax base by placing obstacles in the way of the removal from the UK of people, assets and business activities. Taxation is territorial in that tax revenues flow to and are expended by national governments. The essential problem of the corporate tax base is that it straddles taxing jurisdictions and move between them. Economic boundaries and national boundaries do not coincide. As Marx observed in the *Communist Manifesto* (1848) 'capitalism is international'.

1.31 Three principal mechanisms are used internationally to determine the jurisdiction to tax companies and the division of the corporate tax basis between jurisdictions:

- corporate residence;
- arm's-length pricing; and
- permanent establishment.

1.32 Until the 1980s, MNEs remained essentially national. Producers were organised along national lines. Economic change has modified this: MNEs and their supply chains are now organised along transnational, divisional lines. Some 70% of world trade is conduct by MNEs and emerging economies have a particular dependence on the corporate income tax paid by them as a source of tax revenue. These corporations are international, not national.

1.33 This has led to concern that national democracies cannot control a transnational market economy. There is a loss of control of the tax agenda by any single state. States seek to resist the unwarranted depletion or displacement of a country's tax base. The common concerns of national governments were summed up by Margaret Hodge MP, as Chairman of the Public Accounts Committee of the UK House of Commons:

> '… international companies are able to exploit national and international tax structures to minimise corporation tax on the economic activity they conduct in the UK. The outcome is that they do not pay their fair share'.

On this view, the notorious ingenuity of the tax adviser is always a step ahead of the plodding policeman, with the result that some taxpayers – corporate and individual – do not pay their 'fair share' of tax, with the result that, if government resources are assumed to be a zero-sum game, other taxpayers bear an unfair burden.

1.34 Private provision, in turn, competes with state provision, so that taxation constantly chisels away at private savings. Higher taxes in one state to afford improved public provision, in turn may be undermined by lower taxation in other states seeking to attract savings, investment and employment from the higher-tax state.

1.35 There have been two reactions: (a) unilateral tax competition, whereby individual states seek to attract investment and tax revenue on the basis that higher effective average tax rates (EATR) deters investment and lower EATRs increases investment; and (b) international co-operation, whereby states seek to harmonise tax measures so as to limit tax competition.

1.36 Conventional economic theory suggests that unrestrained tax competition will lead to the under provision of public goods. In short, governments will be able to raise less in tax revenues than they require to finance public expenditure. An older view is that this is simply the product of popular democracy, where politicians competing for office are bound to promise more in terms of social provision that the economy can produce. This was given classic expression in Joseph Schumpeter's *The Crisis of the Tax State* (1920). However, it does not follow that a redistribution of the tax burden will necessarily produce better overall distributional outcomes. Moreover, the state's ability to resort to the printing presses to create money means that it always has the ability to shift resources from the private to the public sector.

1.37 There is a tension between globalisation and national democracy and accountability. This has led, in the 2010s, to a populist upsurge on both the political left and the political right against international organisations and what, in the 1970s and 1980s, would have been called 'international finance capitalism' or in older Leninist terms 'imperialism'. Both right and left, for different ideological reasons, espouse economic nationalism in which everyone will pay their fair share of tax. The right takes the view that there is nothing wrong with tax, except that it is too high. The left takes the view that there is nothing wrong with tax, except that it is too low. One side wants capitalism without welfare. The other wants welfare without capitalism. Both are convinced that by 'taking back control' at national level, the tax basis and wider economy can be reshaped in accordance with political ideology.

1.38 Socialism in one country and capitalism in one country are equally illusory. The real question is, what forms of international co-operation best serve the national interest?

1.39 Consistent with this overall approach, the UK has sought to attract Foreign Direct Investment (FDI) by lowering general rates of corporation tax. The fall in the tax yield may need to be made good by cutting relief. The rules restricting the carry forward of losses for tax purposes and CIR are of this genre, as well as owing their justification to BEPS, and are, in essence, revenue-generating measures. However, this involves replacing a relatively simple and well-understood systems with systems of great complexity which create greater levels of uncertainty.

Section H: Tax avoidance

1.40 There is also a tension between tax competition and tax avoidance. On the one hand, states compete to secure internationally mobile investments and profits. On the other hand, they seek to prevent the transfer of what they regard as part of 'their' tax revenues to other jurisdictions.

1.41 Tax competition is based both on 'rate-based' and 'regime-based' measures. The former comprises lowering rates of corporation tax generally, the latter consists in establishing specific preferential regimes. States call their own measures 'non-harmful tax competition' and those adopted by other states 'harmful tax competition'.

1.42 Tax avoidance has been given very considerable prominence by many tax authorities in recent years, partly spurred on by the impulses coming from BEPS. However, an over-intensive concern with tax avoidance may end up frustrating both the purposes for which tax systems are established and the sources of tax. As the OECD has observed (*International Tax Avoidance and Evasion*):

> 'It is possible to reduce or remove tax liability by perfectly acceptable tax planning (e.g. choosing among tax reliefs and incentives the most advantageous route consistent with normal business transactions) or even by refraining from consuming a taxed product, and it is clearly not the intention of governments to combat activities of this kind. To describe tax planning or abstention from consumption as 'tax avoidance' is, however, to strain the meaning of language as ordinarily used, and governments tend to take an operational approach towards tax avoidance to cover those forms of tax minimization which are unacceptable to governments.'

1.43 The BEPS project revolves round attaining the proper balance between tax competition and tax avoidance. The new legislation gives a clear priority to opposing tax avoidance, deference to international standards and the confining of tax competition to rate-based as opposed to regime-based measures.

1.44 The pressures and policy of BEPS have, in turn, been echoed and reinforced in an EU context by the Council Directive of 12 July 2016 laying down rules against tax avoidance practices that directly affect the functioning of the internal market (2016/1164/EU) ('the EU Anti-Avoidance Directive', ATAD). Along with a Commission Recommendation of 25 January 2016 on the implementation of measures against tax treaty abuse (2016/136/EU), it was adopted on 12 July 2016, and modified on 29 May 2017 (ATAD2).

1.45 The Commission Recommendation encourages Member States to include a principal purpose test (PPT) in double taxation agreements, in accordance with BEPS Action 6, whereby treaty benefits will be withheld *'if it is reasonable to conclude, having regard to all the relevant facts and circumstances, that obtaining that benefit was one of the principal purposes of any arrangement or transaction ... unless it is established that it reflects a genuine economic activity ...'.*

1.46 *Introduction: New Currents in Corporation Tax*

1.46 The directive is more wide-ranging:

(i) It repeats the BEPS mantra that *'the current political priorities in international taxation highlight the need for ensuring that tax is paid where profits are value are generated'*.

(ii) It expresses concerns about the erosion of national tax sovereignty in these terms: *'It is thus imperative to restore trust in the fairness of tax systems and allow government to effectively exercise their tax sovereignty.'*

(iii) It welcomes BEPS Actions as means of promoting fair and efficient taxation.

1.47 Article 4(1) introduces the 'exceeding borrowing costs' limitation rule. *'Exceeding borrowing costs'* means *'the amount by which the deductible borrowing costs of a taxpayer exceed taxable interest revenues'*: art 2(3). The rule is that borrowing costs shall only be deductible in the period in which they are incurred up to 30% of the taxpayer's EBITDA. This is subject to a right to deduct borrowing costs up to €3 million. The borrowing costs of long-term public infrastructure projects may be excluded from the limitation rule. As an alternative, the limitation may be determined by the equivalent group ratio of borrowing costs to EBITDA. These principles have been adopted in the UK in the form of the CIR.

1.48 This legislation has been reinforced by the EU Mandatory Disclosure Directive, adopted on 25 May 2018 and which came into force in the UK on 31 December 2019. This requires 'intermediaries' who design or promote tax-planning arrangements to report arrangements and transactions that are considered by the EU to be potentially aggressive. That information is then exchanged amongst EU Members. This is very similar to the DOTAS scheme under FA 2004. Certain hallmarks are subject to a main benefit test (ie, the purpose of a feature is only reportable if the main benefit which can reasonably be anticipated is to obtain a particular tax advantage (eg, the round-tripping of funds using conduits or entities without substance)). Other hallmarks are not subject to the filter of a main benefit test (eg, non-transparent legal or beneficial ownership chains).

Section I: The taxation of companies

1.49 A company is a legal fiction. It is simply a piece of paper – or nowadays an electronic entry – on a register. When the formation of companies by registration became commonplace in the nineteenth century, a residence, a directing mind and actions were ascribed to companies on the analogy of individuals. However, companies can neither suffer, act by themselves nor be imprisoned. Companies are fictitious persons.

1.50 Companies do not pay taxes. Taxes are paid by their employees, shareholders, suppliers and customers. Companies are legal instruments for raising funds to establish and carry on a business activity, owned through the medium of shares. A large part of personal savings is drawn into companies, directly or indirectly (through bank deposits, collective investment schemes and pension schemes), which through the profits which companies generate, provide the return to savers which they require both to compensate them for the sacrifice of immediate enjoyment, and to provide for longer-term and unplanned requirements (unemployment, retirement, ill-health, social care, death, lockdown and all the ills that flesh is heir to).

1.51 Companies raise funds through equity (own funds) and debt (borrowed funds). When a company needs to fund a major project, it borrows the great part of the cost. The interest costs would be eliminated by a corresponding reduction in taxation for the corporate profits. Interest on debt is generally a deductible expense of the paying company for company law, accounting and tax purposes, and taxable in the hands of the payer. Interest is thus untaxed at company level (see 10th edition, para 9.2).

1.52 By contrast, dividends and equity returns are generally not deductible in computing company profits, and obtain tax relief in the hands of the shareholder. This led to concerns that companies could eliminate their tax liabilities by raising their finance through debt rather than equity. In practice, this tendency was limited because investors would not provide finance to companies which did not pay dividends. This is because the retention of funds by companies which they could distribute to shareholders constitutes a financial risk, namely, that the money may be lost.

1.53 The business must produce a rate of return which exceeds that available on the deposit of funds in a bank or in the holding of government bonds. The investor's purpose in investing in a business is to secure a higher rate of return than that offered by a bank deposit or government securities. If the business cannot achieve a superior return to that offered by these lower risk investments, then it should be closed down so that the investors' funds can be put to alternative use or simply invested risk-free.

Section J: The debt-equity distinction

1.54 There are four fundamental distinctions between equity and debt:

(1) The loan creditor has a legal entitlement to be repaid during the life of the company. The shareholder has no legal right to the return of his capital prior to the winding up of the company.

1.55 *Introduction: New Currents in Corporation Tax*

(2) For accounting purposes, interest on debt is an expense in earning profits, whereas dividends on shares are a distribution out of profits.

(3) Interest is untaxed in the company, and taxed on the lender, whereas dividends are taxed in the company and tax free when paid to other companies.

(4) Interest and gains on bonds are taxed and relieved on an accruals basis, whereas dividends and gains on shares are taxed on a realisations basis.

1.55 The reason for the beneficial tax treatment of debt is this. If debt interest and dividends were alike non-deductible for tax purposes, this would significantly increase the rate of profit which a business would have to return in order to make investment in the business attractive to investors, as compared with bank deposits and government loans. The result would be that many businesses would become unviable and many business start-ups would never take place. Tax revenues would correspondingly be reduced rather than enhanced. If on the other hand dividends and debt interest were alike deductible in computing taxable profits, no company need ever pay tax.

1.56 The profit which businesses earn over and above the risk-free rate of interest (the 'economic rent') goes partly to the government in taxes and partly to investors.

1.57 Most businesses do not hold cash beyond the need for working capital, because the purpose of most businesses is to use cash to earn higher returns that are obtained on risk-free cash investments. The exceptions are banks, insurance companies and certain investment businesses, all of which exist to buy and sell money. Most business are, therefore, loan debtors rather than loan creditors.

1.58 The tax advantages of debt have, in turn, led to related party (shareholder) debt, whereby shareholders themselves lent money to the company in which they held shares, so receiving an assured return in the form of interest on debts. Tax authorities reacted by classifying related party debt as quasi-equity and, in an international context, disallowing deductions or increasing taxable profits by reference to transfer pricing guidelines.

1.59 These different treatments in corporate law, accountancy and tax reflect economic reality, in that the risk structure of equity and debt is fundamentally different. Debt is tax advantaged and lower risk. Equity is tax disadvantaged and high risk. In the case of companies, debt-type profits and losses are taxed and relieved through the loan relationship rules. Equity-type gains and losses are taxed and relieved through corporation tax on capital gains.

1.60 The tax advantages of debt are, in turn, curtailed by restrictions on interest deductibility, such as the US rule preventing the use of carry forward net operating losses to 80% of taxable income. The CIR pursues the same objective by different means, based on Action 4.

Section K: Conclusion

1.61 The commercial decision as to how to a group finances its activities is overridden by a legislative-bureaucratic fiat as to how it should finance itself by reference to a normative standard. As a result of these rules, the cost of debt finance relative to equity finance is increased; to that extent it cannot be said that corporation tax taxes the profit of the equity shareholders.

1.62 Whatever the legislative purpose may be, the effect is to maintain or increase the corporate tax charge (ie, the tax on savers, employees and customers). Thus, the corporation tax rate is reduced by the front door but increased by the back door, so that a lower rate of tax is applied to a higher amount of taxable profit. This is to deliver the form but not the substance of rate reduction. Moreover, the reduction in relief for capital expenditure, to pay for the cuts in headline rates, makes investment by companies more expensive. The increase in compliance burdens and responsibilities is severe. At the same time, corporate offences of facilitating tax avoidance and personal liabilities of finance directors are piled on companies. Meanwhile efforts continue with unabated enthusiasm to raise the drawbridge to the UK's principal market for goods and services.

1.63 For the tax gatherer, the question is, can indeed more be had? For the tax adviser, the question is how they can steer their clients through these new and contiguous minefields. The object of this book is to assist in the endeavours of both.

Chapter 2

Corporate Interest Restriction (CIR)

Chapter Contents

Section	Topic	Paragraphs
A	BEPS Action 4	2.1–2.10
B	History of UK rules	2.11–2.21
C	The interaction rules	2.22–2.30
D	Outline of the corporate interest restriction (CIR) rules	2.31–2.46
E	Steps in applying the legislation	2.47–2.48
F	Diagram	2.49
G	The key rules	2.50–2.53
H	Accounts adjustments	2.54–2.63
I	The worldwide group (WWG)	2.64–2.98
J	Rule 1: The interest deduction restriction	2.99–2.102
K	Rule 2: Aggregate net tax-interest expense (ANTIE)	2.103–2.115
L	Rule 3: Ratio of ANTIE to aggregate tax-EBITDA	2.116–2.127
M	Rule 4: The basic interest allowance	2.128–2.140
N	Rule 5: Fixed ratio rule	2.141–2.142
O	Rule 6: Fixed ratio debt cap	2.143–2.157
P	Rule 7: Group ratio rule	2.158–2.165
Q	Rule 8: Qualifying net group interest expense (QNGIE)	2.166–2.179
R	Rule 9: Group-EBITDA	2.180–2.190
S	Rule 10: Group ratio debt cap	2.191
T	Rule 11: Interest allowance	2.192–2.193
U	Rule 12: Interest allowance and ANTIE	2.194–2.201
V	Rule 13: Allocation of disallowances	2.202–2.218
W	Rule 14: Special rules	2.219–2.234
X	Rule 15: The 15 elections	2.235–2.238

Section A: BEPS Action 4

2.1 Debt financing is prevalent (i) due to risk transfer to the providers of finance, and (ii) the fact that interest on debt is generally deductible whereas dividends constitute a division of profits instead of an expense of earning profits, and share appreciation does not give rise to a realised profit. However, the providers of debt are often also shareholders. Related party debt does not economically correspond to third-party debt, as investors may take their return in the form of interest. In that case, profits will be depressed, corporation tax yield will fall, the existence of distributable reserves may be of importance primarily to external creditors and the company may move into a loss-making situation, which conceals its true profitability.

2.2 The aim of the corporate interest restriction (CIR) is to strip out 'excessive' debt funding on the grounds that it distorts economic performance by depressing profits for accounting and tax purposes below their true level. The CIR seeks to reduce the tax advantage of debt by focusing on earnings before interest, tax, depreciation and amortisation (EBITDA) as a more reliable measure of profitability and disregarding related party interest payments.

2.3 The means adopted to achieve this end are straightforward:

(i) First, in a departure from the general practice of UK corporation tax, the tax is based on the consolidated group accounts of all companies in the group, rather than the individual entity accounts, because items which appear as assets of one group company and liabilities of another will be cancelled out, leaving only third-party liabilities ('true' liabilities). In practice, this largely means the consolidated accounts of the UK sub-group within an international group. Indeed, all the members of the worldwide group (WWG) may be UK resident companies.

(ii) By this means, interest liabilities are computed leaving out of account intra-group obligations, which cancel each other out.

(iii) Interest is added back to profits to give EBITDA, as if interest were a distribution.

(iv) The tax-deductible proportion of interest is found by reference to the ratio of interest payments to profits.

(v) Where the fixed ratio rule is used, the deductible proportion is 30%. Otherwise the proportion is obtained by dividing interest by profits and expressing the result as a percentage.

(vi) The difference between the numerator and the denominator of the fraction gives rise to leverage, so that the alteration of one or the other gives rise to a disproportionate effect.

2.4 *Corporate Interest Restriction (CIR)*

2.4 While this scheme is simple in outline, its realisation is more complex. The CIR, like all such legislative schemes, starts from the premise that the actual arrangements adopted are artificial, and it is necessary to construct a further set of artificial arrangements for tax purposes in order to penetrate to the 'real' situation. The legislator must pattern reality for the participants better than they can do it for themselves. Real artifice is to be used to drive out assumed artifice and to get to reality. This is a dangerous path to go down, in politics as in taxation, and may end in the search for some sort of Rousseauean natural man.

2.5 The Organisation for Economic Cooperation and Development (OECD) was concerned that international groups would structure their financing arrangements to minimise tax by allocating greater use of debt in high-tax jurisdictions to gain relief from tax for interest payments and other equivalent financing costs made on external borrowings and intra-group loans. Action 4 is concerned with limiting the deductibility of finance costs for tax purposes. This has traditionally been the role of thin capitalisation rules, operating within the framework of the arm's length principle (ALP). The OECD's framework on Action 4 barely mentions ALP-based thin capitalisation. Instead it is to be largely supplanted by an elaborate code of interest-deduction restrictions, intended to operate in a mechanical fashion. Transfer pricing adjustments on financing transactions are made on an entirely different basis to CIR. An international group will be subject both to transfer pricing adjustments on financial transactions, and restrictions on corporate interest deductions, which aim to be entirely mechanical. Moreover, the CIR applies to groups which are entirely UK based.

2.6 The BEPS working group on deductibility of finance costs concluded that transfer-pricing adjustments for intra-group debt based on the arm's-length principle (ALP) were not sufficient to limit potential base erosion. Accordingly, it proposed a system-wide limit on net financing deductions, using either fixed ratio or as an alternative a group ratio.

2.7 These concerns are particularly marked in a cross-border context. In the view of the OECD: *'The use of third party and related party interest is perhaps one of the most simple of the profit-shifting techniques available in international tax planning'*: OECD, *Limiting Base Erosion Involving Interest Deductions and Other Financial Payments Action 4 – 2016 Update*, p 19.

2.8 BEPS Action 4 rules are intended to apply in three situations.

(i) *Inbound situation*: Groups placing third-party debt in high-tax countries (inbound financing). Lending to a UK company by a related company to shelter UK profits, so that there is no tax charge on the lender corresponding to the tax saving in the borrower.

Corporate Interest Restriction (CIR) **2.13**

(ii) *Outbound situation*: Groups using third-party or intra-group financing to fund the generation of tax-exempt income. A UK company borrows money, thus securing current interest deduction and invests abroad to obtain tax-exempt income in the form of dividends.

(iii) *Domestic situation*: UK company uses third-party or intra-group financing to generate interest deductions in excess of the company's actual or notional third-party interest expense.

2.9 The CIR rules are also designed to implement art 4 of the EU Anti-Tax Avoidance Directive (2016/1164), which Member States were required to implement by 1 January 2019.

2.10 BEPS Action 4 was adopted in the UK at a speed, with an enthusiasm and in a comprehensive fashion which its progenitors may scarcely have anticipated. A new system for tax relief for carried-forward losses was also introduced by Finance (No 2) Act 2017 (Chapter 3). The combined effect of the CIR and the carried-forward loss rules has been to produce a veritable tsunami of corporate tax legislation.

Section B: History of UK rules

2.11 The UK introduced a comprehensive and separate code for the taxation of corporate debt and interest in the loan relationships rules set out in FA 1996. The UK's ALP-based thin capitalisation rules became applicable to wholly UK transactions as part of the general transfer pricing rules introduced with effect from 1 April 2004 and take effect in priority to the loan relationship rules. Until 2009, the thin capitalisation rules provided the core rules to tackle excessive interest deductions. Where they applied, they provided for interest payments to be disregarded for tax purposes. Certain more specific rules provided for interest to be re-characterised as distributions: CTA 2010, ss 1000(1)E, F, 1005, 1015.

2.12 The foreign profits reform of 2009 introduced an exemption for foreign dividends received in the UK. The decision was taken to maintain interest deductions for the financing of overseas investments, giving rise to tax exempt income in the form of foreign dividends. In 2011, the foreign branch exemption was introduced, allowing all profits from non-UK branches to be excluded from the charge to UK corporation tax.

2.13 These changes made the UK a popular choice for regional holding companies. This popularity in turn gave rise to the worldwide debt cap (WWDC) introduced by the Finance Act 2009, Sch 15. These rules had bedded down, and companies affected by them had developed appropriate compliance systems. Though not based on the BEPS fixed ratio/group ratio,

2.14 *Corporate Interest Restriction (CIR)*

the rules were an acceptable alternative to specific measures implementing BEPS Action 4.

2.14 The WWDC was explained in Chapter 21 of the 10th edition of this work. This capped the amount of UK deductible interest by reference to the amount of interest paid by the WWG to third parties. The WWDC rules adopted a situation-based approach, allowing the group to deduct interest in the UK up to the group's overall gross external interest cost. Interest relief in the UK was restricted by comparing the level of UK debt to the level of WWG debt. Where the ratio of UK debt to worldwide debt exceeded a defined limit, the finance cost of the excess debt was disallowed as a deduction for tax purposes. The WWDC allowed the worldwide external interest expense to be fully deductible in each territory rather than allocated according to a fixed or global apportionment formula.

2.15 The WWDC adopted the gross concept for the available amount of finance costs deduction. By contrast, the CIR is based on the net concept, applying the restriction to the UK group's interest expense and other equivalent finance costs.

2.16 Finance (No 2) Act 2017, s 30 and Sch 5, introduced a new code of restrictions on interest deductibility for tax purposes (the CIR). They impose a limit on the amount of finance costs that groups can deduct for tax. These wholly replace the WWDC, formerly contained in TIOPA 2010, ss 260–353B. The WWDC was repealed by F(No 2)A 2017, s 20, Sch 5, para 11(1) in relation to accounting periods beginning on or after 1 April 2017. The replacement legislation is contained in TIOPA 2010, Part 10, ss 372–498 and Sch 7A. The replacement system (CIR) radically differs from the WWDC and affects many more groups.

2.17 The tax arbitrage provisions in Finance (No 2) Act 2005 (replaced by the hybrid mismatch rules considered in Chapter 4) prohibited interest deduction from transactions that had no business purpose, and used hybrid entities or hybrid instruments to gain double deduction from the same interest expense, or double non-taxation of the same interest receipt.

2.18 Finance Act 1993 (foreign exchange differences), FA 1994 and FA 1996 all embodied a policy decision that tax should follow the commercial accounts. This policy is now embodied in CTA 2009, ss 307, 595. However, this policy is subject to not only to specific statutory overrides (CTA 2009, s 46) but also to a general override that the commercial accounts must 'fairly represent' the profits of the business for tax purposes (FA 1996, s 84(1)) or in its current articulation may be counteracted to ensure a result which is 'just and reasonable' for tax purposes (CTA 2009, ss 455B(1), 698B(1)). In the latter form, the override is restricted by requiring as a yardstick the presence as a precedent fact of 'relevant avoidance arrangements', but these are defined in very wide terms, so as to make the yardstick a cosmetic rather than a substantive restriction.

2.19 The transfer pricing rules are a specific override to the policy that tax follows the accounts. The scope of the departure is limited by two factors: (i) the rules only apply to transactions between connected companies; and (ii) the application of ALP. The CIR constitutes an extensive, detailed and specific override to this policy because, for the purpose of applying the CIR, the *taxable total profits* (CTA 2010, s 4(2)) have to be extensively modified to produce profits corresponding to the ALP.

2.20 It is necessary to deconstruct the commercial accounts, the consolidated accounts and the tax accounts to extract different sets of information figures for the purposes of the CIR, transfer pricing, DPT and carried-forward loss calculations. Moreover, there is no exclusion for domestic groups, so wholly UK groups are equally within the CIR as multinational groups. There is a £2m *de minimis* threshold intended to exclude smaller groups.

2.21 The same groups which are affected by the CIR are likely to be affected by the restrictions on carried-forward loss. Accordingly, these changes raise questions about the competitiveness of the UK corporate tax system. In 2016, the Office for Budget Responsibility estimated that the increased corporate tax yield from the CIR would be £4 billion over four years (2017–2021).

Section C: The interaction rules

2.22 There is a high degree of overlap between the loan relationship and derivative contracts rules, the CIR rules, transfer pricing for financial transactions and rules for capital instruments, so it is necessary to delineate clearly between the respective spheres of application and the priorities of these different sets of rules with common subject matters. The general legal maxim is *lex specialis legibus generalibus derogat* ('special laws override general laws'). So, a rule with a narrower subject matter will take precedence over a rule of more general application.

2.23 In accordance with this principle, the loan relationship and derivative contacts override general corporation tax rules but take effect subject to any express provisions to the contrary: CTA 2009, ss 464, 465 and 571:

'464 (1) The amounts which are brought into account in accordance with this Part in respect of any amount are the only amounts

2.24 *Corporate Interest Restriction (CIR)*

which may be brought into account for corporation tax purposes in respect of it.

(2) Subsection (1) is subject to any express provision to the contrary.'

2.24 The hybrid mismatch rules (Chapter 4) (TIOPA 2010, Part 6A) take precedence over the transfer pricing, the CIR and the loan relationship rules: TIOPA 2010, ss 259CB(6), 382(10)(11). These are, in any event, specialised and narrow in their scope.

2.25 TIOPA 2010, s 372(1)(a) states:

'This Part contains provision that –

(a) disallows certain amounts that a company would (apart from this Part) be entitled to bring into account for the purposes of corporation tax in respect of interest and other financing costs …'

This is an '*express provision to the contrary*' within CTA 2009, s 464(1), so the CIR rules override the loan relationship rules.

2.26 Like the transfer pricing rules, the CIR rules are a one-way street. They can increase but never reduce the tax charge. Both sets of rules also adopt a wide test of connection. Both sets of rules make substantial modifications to the commercial accounts for tax purposes.

2.27 There, however, the similarities end. The transfer pricing rules operate in a quite different way to the CIR rules. The transfer pricing rules are applied at entity level, whereas the CIR provisions operate at group level, and the disallowance of interest deduction is then apportioned on a discretionary basis amongst the UK group members. The transfer pricing rules are applied on a case-by-case basis, taking account of all the circumstances, whereas the CIR rules adopt a formulaic approach and are applied in a mechanical fashion. Hence, the transfer pricing rules may influence but will not displace the CIR rules.

Example 1

A UK subsidiary, Universal plc, borrows £50m from its South African parent, Rand Inc at 5%. On transfer pricing analysis, the annual interest-expense is adjusted to 3.5% so, for tax purposes, the accounts figure of £2.5m is replaced by a tax-interest expense of £1.75m. The CIR does not apply, because Universal's interest capacity is > £2m.

Example 2

A UK subsidiary, Universal plc, borrows £100m from its South African parent, Rand Inc at 5%. On transfer pricing analysis, the annual interest-expense is adjusted to 3.5% so, for tax purposes, the accounts figure of £5m is replaced by an interest expense of £3.5m. Universal's ANTIE includes this interest liability at £3.5m, not £5m. Applying CIR, the UK members of the WWG have an interest capacity of (say) £2.5m, but a tax-interest expense of £4m. Of the disallowed interest expense of £(4m − 2.5m) = 1.5m, £1m is apportioned by the reporting company to Universal plc. So, applying the combined effect of the transfer pricing and CIR rules, Universal plc's finance cost of £5m is, for tax purposes, reduced to £2.5m, causing additional corporation tax on profits of £2.5m to be payable:

	£
Interest (per accounts)	5,000,000
Transfer pricing adjustment	(1,500,000)
CIR disallowance	(1,000,000)
Loan relationship debit	2,500,000
Additional CT (19%)	475,000

2.28 Rules relating to the taxation of distributions take precedence over the CIR, so that, for example, preference share dividends are excluded in the computation of adjusted net group income expense (ANGIE). The key distinction between debt and equity is that interest is a cost of making profits, and so deductible for accounting and tax purposes, whereas dividends are an application of taxed profits, and so non-deductible. The fundamental aim of the distinction is to tax interest in the hands of the lenders (though classically enforcing this liability through withholding tax as source taxation), and to tax equity profits in the hands of the shareholders over the life of the business.

2.29 In practice, there are numerous exceptions to this principle. For accounting purposes, dividends on fixed-rate redeemable preference shares are treated as interest: IAS 32, paras 18 and 36. Paragraph 18 states:

> 'Substance and form are commonly consistent, but not always. Some financial instruments take the legal form of equity but are liabilities in substance and others may combine features associated with equity instruments and features associated with financial liabilities. For example:
>
> (a) A preference share that provides for mandatory redemption by the issuer for a fixed or determinable amount at a fixed or

2.30 *Corporate Interest Restriction (CIR)*

determinable future date, or gives the holder the right to require the issuer to redeem the instrument at or after a particular date for a fixed or determinable amount, is a financial liability.'

However, for loan relationship purposes, such preference share dividends remain non-deductible distributions.

2.30 For tax purposes, interest may be made non-deductible or re-characterised as a dividend. The restrictions include in order of precedence:

(i) hybrid mismatch rules (TIOPA 2010, ss 259A–259NF);

(ii) interest re-characterisation of 'non-commercial securities' or 'special securities' (CTA 2010, ss 1000(1)E, (1) F, 1005, 1015);

(iii) transfer pricing based on ALP (TIOPA 2010, ss 146–217);

(iv) CIR;

(v) unallowable purpose (CTA 2009, ss 442–443); and

(vi) targeted anti-avoidance rules (CTA 2009, ss 455B–455D).

Section D: Outline of the corporate interest restriction (CIR) rules

2.31 Unlike both ALP-based transfer pricing and the WWDC, the CIR adopts a prescriptive approach, limiting interest deductibility to a fraction of the group's pre-tax profits after adding interest and depreciation back to the profits. The CIR rules apply more widely than the WWDC by limiting corporation tax deductions for net financing costs to a percentage of tax-EBITDA, given by two alternative rules, instead of by reference to a group's external funding costs. Deductions for net 'tax interest' are limited to the external net accounting costs (as compared with the gross costs under WWDC).

2.32 The CIR applies for accounting periods beginning on or after 1 April 2017. Accounting periods which straddle 1 April 2017 are divided into two notional accounting periods for the period up to 1 April and the period following 1 April. Though the rules applied from 1 April 2017, they were only legally enacted on 16 November 2017. Successive amendments have been passed since then, coming into force on different dates.

2.33 According to the HMRC Guidance, the CIR is *'designed to combat attempts by multinational enterprises (MNEs) and other companies to obtain excessive tax relief for net interest and similar financing costs. The aim ... is to ensure relief on financing costs is commensurate with the extent to which a business's activities are subject to corporation tax'* (CFM95120). MNEs may

Corporate Interest Restriction (CIR) **2.38**

use interest deductions to minimise tax liabilities. The interest deduction should not exceed a MNE's net third-party interest expense of 'real' interest expense (*'guiding policy objective'*). The rules operate on a WWG basis, based on IFRS consolidation rules for each period of account of the group's ultimate parent.

2.34 The aim is to make finance costs commensurate with activities of group that are subject to UK corporation tax. Both interest and payments economically equivalent to interest are taken into account. These restrictions are designed to prevent loading companies with debt in high-tax jurisdictions, thereby lowering taxable profits, to shift profits to lenders in low-tax jurisdictions. The aim is to ensure that financing costs are deductible in the jurisdiction in which the corresponding profits are earned.

2.35 The CIR increases taxable profits (or reduces allowable losses) in current years by disallowing an element of tax-interest expense, on the basis that, in national terms, a company is over-capitalised by debt. It does this by requiring the disallowed amount to be left out of account in the accounting period in which the expense is incurred: TIOPA 2010, ss 375(2), 376(6). The disallowed amount can be carried forward to subsequent accounting periods: TIOPA 2010, s 378(2). There it may be reactivated as an interest expense: F(No 2)A ss 379, 380. It is kept separate from trading losses and other losses otherwise carried forward, being subject to its own special regime.

2.36 While the financial position of the WWG (ie, companies resident in the UK + non-UK resident companies) has to be taken into account, a WWG is only within the CIR if it has one UK member. In turn, it is only the UK member or members ('the UK group') of the WWG whose corporation tax liability can be increased through the CIR.

2.37 The CIR adopts two basic methods of interest restriction:

(i) the fixed ratio rule, which allows a UK group to deduct loan relationship and similar debits (*Aggregate net tax-interest expense, ANTIE*) up to a specified proportion (30%) of the UK group's *aggregate tax-EBITDA* (TIOPA 2010, s 397); and

(ii) the group ratio rule, as an optional alternative, if the group ratio > fixed ratio. The group ratio allows the UK group to deduct loan relationship and similar costs at the ratio of the group's third-party interest expense (*qualifying net group-interest expense, QNGIE*) to the *group-EBITDA*, as opposed to using a fixed benchmark of 30% (TIOPA 2010, s 398).

2.38 In either case, the limitations are strengthened by the modified debt cap (MDF) which curbs the global net tax-interest expense. This is a fallback restriction which applies if lower than the applicable percentage of

2.39 *Corporate Interest Restriction (CIR)*

aggregate tax-EBITDA. This is the *fixed ratio debt cap* (if the fixed ratio rule applies) or *group ratio debt cap* (if the group ratio applies). The purpose of the MDF is to prevent the WWG from gearing up the UK sub-group by means of intra-group loans which are not matched by external borrowing.

2.39 Where the rules apply, in any accounting period the UK group's *basic interest allowance* for corporation tax purposes limited to the lower of:

- 30% of the *aggregate tax-EBITDA*, or
- the *fixed ratio debt cap*

or, on election, the lower of:

- the *group ratio percentage* of aggregate tax-EBITDA, or
- the *group ratio debt cap*

(TIOPA 2010, ss 396–398).

If a WWG consists solely of UK companies, in most cases the only interest allowance is 30% of the aggregate tax-EBITDA. This will necessarily be less than the fixed ratio debt cap or group ratio debt cat. Hence, many of the complexities of the CIR fall away.

Example

A WWG has ANTIE of £11m for an accounting period, and *aggregate tax-EBITDA* of £30m. It has the following limits:

(i) Fixed ratio basic allowance: 30% × 30m = £9m (= a)

(ii) Fixed ratio debt cap: £10m (= b)

Fixed ratio rule (FRR) tax allowance is the lower of a and b = c

(iii) Group ratio basic allowance: (say) 35% × 35m = £12.25 (=d)

(iv) Group ratio debt cap: £13m (=e)

Group ratio rule (GRR) tax allowance is the lower of d and e = f

So, interest allowance is c, unless f gives a higher allowance. Group ratio basis allowance produces a more favourable result and is lower than group ratio debt cap. So, the group elects to apply GRR.

Corporate Interest Restriction (CIR) **2.44**

2.40 The fixed ratio accordingly applies a predetermined benchmark to the earnings of an entity or local group to calculate the maximum deductible interest expense for an accounting period. This is intended to ensure that a proportion of the entity's profits remain subject to tax in the country of residence, so that – in the case of the UK – the UK tax deductible interest expense does not exceed the net third-party interest expense of the WWG.

2.41 The alternative and optional group ratio takes account of the actual third-party borrowing of the world-wide group. This is divided by the EBITDA of the WWG, to give a percentage (QNGIE/group-EBITDA × 100). If this percentage is higher than the fixed ratio of 30% of the UK group, UK entities may deduct interest expenses up to the level of the group ratio.

2.42 A CIR disallowance is allocated amongst the UK companies by the UK group reporting company. In deciding whether to allocate a CIR disallowance between group companies, the reporting company will, in turn, need to consider what the impact of such allocation would be on a company's loss carry-forward position.

2.43 Payments economically equivalent to interest, to which the CIR extends, include:

- payments under profit participating loans;
- imputed interest on instruments such as convertible bonds and zero coupon bonds;
- amounts under alternative finance arrangements, such as Islamic finance;
- the finance cost element of finance lease payments;
- capitalised interest included in the balance sheet value of an asset or the amortisation of capitalised interest;
- amounts measured by reference to a funding return under transfer pricing rules;
- notional interest amounts under derivative instruments or hedging arrangements;
- foreign exchange gains and losses on instruments and borrowings connected with the raising of finance;
- guarantee fees with respect to financing arrangements; and
- arrangement fees.

2.44 Unlike transfer pricing adjustments, which require consideration of an individual entity's circumstances and transactions, the legislation is

2.45 *Corporate Interest Restriction (CIR)*

intended to work in a mechanical fashion, without reference to 'purpose' tests or computation of transfer prices, and so produces different results. Like transfer pricing rules, the CIR rules do not re-characterise, for tax purposes, part of the group's debt finance as equity finance but instead disallow a finance cost in respect of interest payments, so increasing the tax borne by equity shareholders.

2.45 There are two gateways: (i) the WWG which contains at least one UK member, and (ii) the *de minimis* amount which is UK group ANTIE > £2m. The legislation only applies to (a) UK companies which are members of a WWG, and (b) to UK group companies whose aggregate finance costs in an accounting period exceed the *de minimis* amount. If either of these conditions is not satisfied, the CIR does not apply.

2.46 A 'UK group company' is a member of the WWG that is within the charge to UK corporation tax: TIOPA 2010, s 492. If a UK group's tax-interest expense for an accounting period is <£2m, it elects to file an abbreviated CIR return. Otherwise, it files a full CIR return. In either case this is a separate return from the CTSA return. Compliance is managed at group level by the UK reporting company. The rules operate on a WWG basis, based on IFRS consolidation rules for each period of account of the group's ultimate parent.

Section E: Steps in applying the legislation

2.47 In setting out the steps in applying the legislation, the following terminology is used:

- 'Derive' = obtain directly from the accounts.
- 'Calculate' = a step taken in a stage, having derived a figure from the accounts.
- 'Find' = find a determinate figure from another or related source.

Before going through the various steps, the gateways should be checked: (i) there is a WWG; (ii) the annual finance expense of the UK group is likely to exceed £2m.

A common verbal infelicity is to say 'the Group Ratio Percentage is (y)%'. While it is clear what this means, the second '%' is pleonastic. The legislation expresses the concept accurately by saying that the group ratio percentage is *'the following proportion expressed as a percentage ...'* (s 399(1)).

Corporate Interest Restriction (CIR) **2.48**

2.48 The steps in applying the legislation are as follows:

Stage 1: Find the basic interest allowance using the Fixed Ratio Rule

Stage 1(i)

- *Step 1*: Derive the *ANTIE* of the UK group for the accounting period.
- *Step 2*: Derive the *aggregate tax-EBITDA of the UK group*, which is based on the *adjusted corporation tax earnings*.
- *Step 3*: Find the fixed ratio basic interest allowance, being 30% of aggregate tax-EBITDA = a.

Stage 1(ii)

- *Step 1*: Derive the net group-interest expense (NGIE) of the WWG.
- *Step 2*: Using the NGIE, calculate the adjusted ANGIE.
- *Step 3*: Find the excess debt cap and add to ANGIE, to give the fixed rate debt cap = b.

Stage 1(iii)

Basic interest allowance = c = min (a, b)

Note: If the WWG comprises solely UK companies, ANTIE = ANGIE = QNGIE and Stage 2 is unnecessary unless there is related party debt.

Stage 2: Find the basic interest allowance using the Group Ratio Rule

Stage 2(i)

- *Step 1*: As Stage 1(i), Step 1. Derive the ANTIE of the UK group for the accounting period.

2.48 *Corporate Interest Restriction (CIR)*

- *Step 2*: As Stage 1(ii), calculate ANGIE.
- *Step 3*: Use ANGIE (Stage 1(ii), Step 2) to calculate *qualifying net-group interest expense (QNGIE)*.
- *Step 4*: Calculate from the WWG accounts *group-EBITDA* (TIOPA 2010, ss 396, 308, 414, 415, 416).
- *Step 5*: Divide QNGIE (numerator) by *group-EBITDA* (denominator) and multiply by 100 to obtain *group ratio percentage* = y%.
- *Step 6*: Basic interest allowance is y% × ANTIE (Stage 1(i), Step 1) = d.

Stage 2(ii)

- *Step 1:* Add QNGIE (Stage 2(i), Step 3) to *excess debt cap* (Stage 1(ii), Step 3) to give *group ratio debt cap* = e.

Basic interest allowance = f = (min d, e).

Stage 3: Find the interest capacity of the UK group and disallowance

- *Step 1: Basic interest allowance* is max (c, f) (ie, use c (default method) unless f>c).
- *Step 2*: Derive *aggregate net tax-interest income (ANTII)* from UK group accounts.
- *Step 3*: Add *basic interest allowance* (max c, f) to ANTII to give *interest allowance*.
- *Step 4*: Find unused interest capacity carried forward.
- *Step 5*: Add unused interest capacity carried forward to *interest allowance* to give *interest capacity*.
- *Step 6*: If *interest capacity* < ANTIE, the difference gives rise to interest disallowance. If interest capacity > ANTIE (see Stage 1(i), Step 1) the difference is the *interest reactivation cap*.
- *Step 7*: Allocate disallowance amongst UK members of WWG according to Interest Restriction Return (IRR).

Corporate Interest Restriction (CIR) **2.49**

Section F: Diagram

2.49 These steps can be represented diagrammatically:

Stage 1: Using the Fixed Ratio Rule

Stage 1(i)

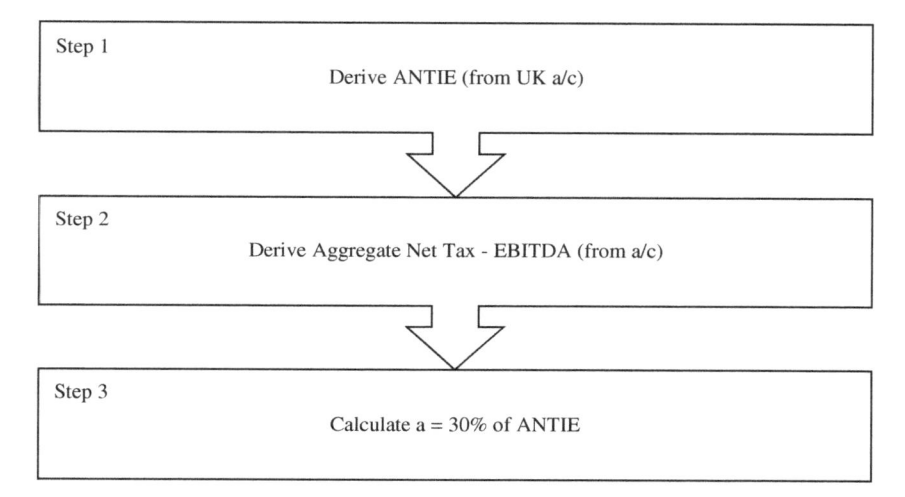

```
Step 1
        Derive ANTIE (from UK a/c)
```
⬇
```
Step 2
        Derive Aggregate Net Tax - EBITDA (from a/c)
```
⬇
```
Step 3
        Calculate a = 30% of ANTIE
```

Stage 1(ii)

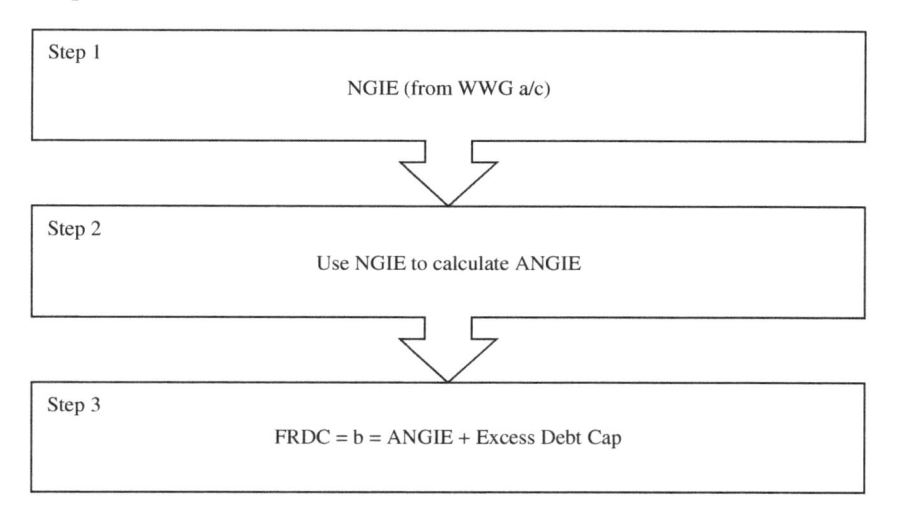

```
Step 1
        NGIE (from WWG a/c)
```
⬇
```
Step 2
        Use NGIE to calculate ANGIE
```
⬇
```
Step 3
        FRDC = b = ANGIE + Excess Debt Cap
```

2.49 *Corporate Interest Restriction (CIR)*

Stage 1(iii)

1st possibility for allowance = c = min (a, b)

Stage 2: Using the Group Ratio Rule (not necessary if group is UK only, unless related party debt)

Stage 2(i)

Step 1: As Stage 1 (i) to step 1 (ANTIE)

Step 2: As Stage 1(ii) Step 2 (NGIE)

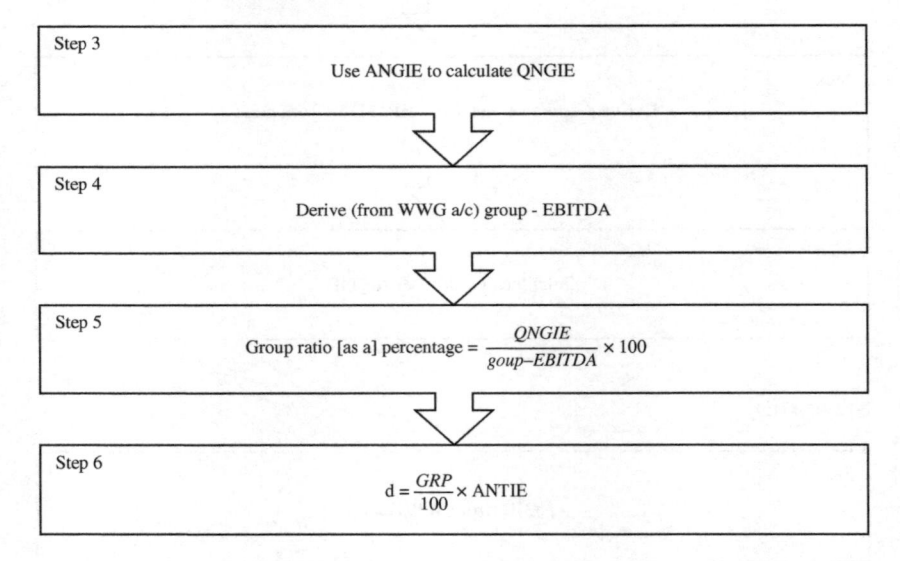

Step 3

Use ANGIE to calculate QNGIE

Step 4

Derive (from WWG a/c) group - EBITDA

Step 5

Group ratio [as a] percentage = $\dfrac{QNGIE}{goup-EBITDA} \times 100$

Step 6

$d = \dfrac{GRP}{100} \times ANTIE$

Stage 2(ii)

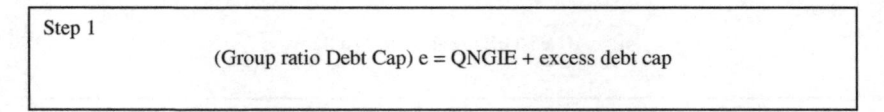

Step 1

(Group ratio Debt Cap) e = QNGIE + excess debt cap

Stage 2(iii)

Basic interest allowance – f = min (d, e)

Stage 3

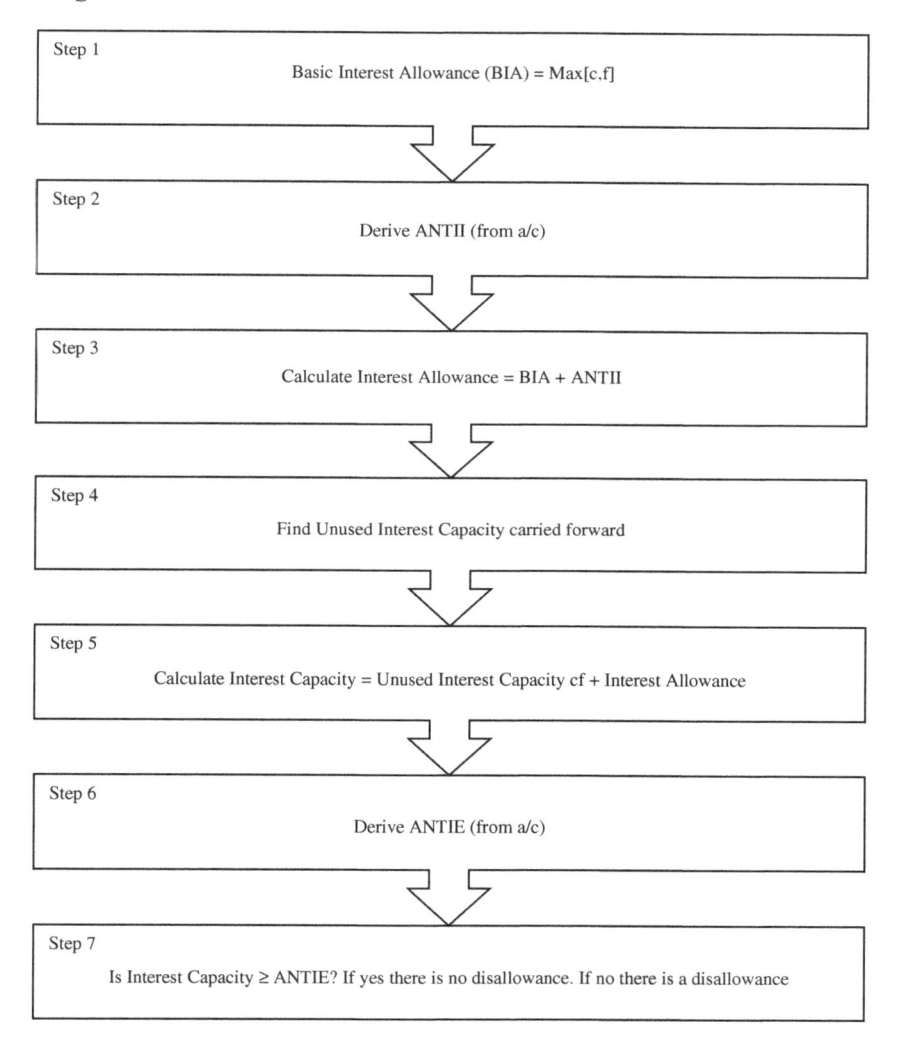

```
Step 1
    Basic Interest Allowance (BIA) = Max[c,f]
         ↓
Step 2
    Derive ANTII (from a/c)
         ↓
Step 3
    Calculate Interest Allowance = BIA + ANTII
         ↓
Step 4
    Find Unused Interest Capacity carried forward
         ↓
Step 5
    Calculate Interest Capacity = Unused Interest Capacity cf + Interest Allowance
         ↓
Step 6
    Derive ANTIE (from a/c)
         ↓
Step 7
    Is Interest Capacity ≥ ANTIE? If yes there is no disallowance. If no there is a disallowance
```

Section G: The key rules

2.50 From the foregoing it follows that the key rules are:

1. UK companies which belong to a WWG are subject to interest deduction restrictions in a period of account of the group if the *ANTIE exceeds the interest capacity of the group* for the period.

2.50 *Corporate Interest Restriction (CIR)*

2. The ANTIE is the total (aggregate) of *net tax-interest expense amounts* of each relevant company for the accounting period.

3. The ANTIE is compared with the *aggregate tax-EBITDA of the UK group*, which comprises the aggregate of the adjusted corporation tax earnings (as defined for UK corporation tax purposes) for each UK group company for the accounting period, to find the fixed rate allowance.

4. The *basic interest allowance* of the UK group is the amount of the *aggregate net tax-interest expense* of the UK group given by either the *fixed ratio rule* or (by election, where it gives a higher basic interest allowance) the *group ratio rule*.

5. Where the fixed rate rule applies, the basic interest allowance is the lower of (i) 30% of the *aggregate tax-EBITDA of the UK group*, and (ii) the *fixed ratio debt cap*.

6. The *fixed ratio debt cap* is (i) the adjusted net group-interest expense of the group (ANGIE) for the period, plus (ii) *the excess debt cap*. The excess debt cap is the excess of ANGIE for the previous accounting period over 30% of the aggregate tax-EBITDA for that period.

7. Where the group ratio rule is applied, the basic interest allowance is the lower of (i) the amount of the ANTIE of the UK group which is given by the *group ratio percentage*, and (ii) *the group ratio debt cap*.

8. The QNGIE is the ANGIE minus downward adjustments.

9. The *group ratio percentage* is derived from the ratio of the QNGIE to the *group-EBITDA* for the period.

10. The *group ratio debt cap* is (i) QNGIE, plus (ii) the *excess debt cap*.

11. The *interest allowance* is the *basic interest allowance* plus any *ANTII*. The *interest capacity* of the UK group is the interest allowance + unused and unexpired interest allowance carried forward to the period of account.

12. If interest capacity < ANTIE the difference gives rise to interest disallowance. If interest capacity > ANTIE the difference is the interest reactivation cap. Disallowed tax-interest expense, unused interest capacity and excess debt cap can be carried forward at the individual company or group level.

13. The allocation of disallowance is made within the UK group to group members either by an appointed reporting company's discretionary allocations or on a pro rata basis in the case of no reporting company.

14. There are special rules for particular businesses and business structures.

15. There are 15 different elections which a company can make to vary the application of the rules.

Corporate Interest Restriction (CIR) **2.52**

2.51 Each of these rules requires detailed explanation, which is set out below. The figures required to make the calculations may be derived from either (i) the consolidated accounts of the UK group, or (ii) in the case of an international group, the consolidated accounts of the WWG.

2.52 The various items, and their sources, are as follows:

Item	Accounts	Purpose	Legislation
ANTIE (aggregate net tax-interest expense)	UK group	Fixed ratio rule and group ratio rule	s 382
ANTII (aggregate net tax-interest income)	UK group	Interest allowance and interest capacity	s 393(3)(4)
Interest capacity	UK group	Fixed ratio rule and group ratio rule	s 392
Aggregate tax-EBITDA	UK group	Fixed ratio rule and group ratio rule	s 405
Basic interest allowance	UK group	Fixed ratio rule and group ratio rule and interest capacity	ss 396–398
NGIE (Net group-interest expense)	WWG	Group ratio rule	s 410
ANGIE (adjusted net-group interest expense)	WWG	Fixed ratio debt cap and group ratio rule	s 413
Excess debt cap	UK group	Fixed ratio debt cap and group ratio debt cap	s 400
QNGIE (qualifying net-group interest expense)	WWG	Group ratio rule and group ratio debt cap	s 414
Group-EBITDA	WWG	Group ratio rule	s 416
Fixed ratio debt cap	WWG	Fixed ratio rule	s 400(1)
Group ratio debt cap	WWG	Group ratio rule	s 400(2)

Example 1

The ABC Group comprises a UK HoldCo, with three wholly owned subsidiaries, A Ltd and B Ltd (UK resident) and C Corp (non-resident). All have an accounting period ending on 31 March. The structure is:

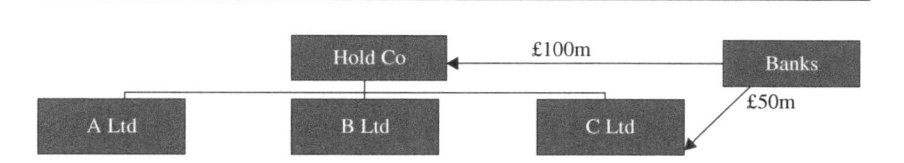

2.53 *Corporate Interest Restriction (CIR)*

Hold Co has lent money to A Ltd and B Ltd. A third-party bank has lent £100m to HoldCo at 5%. HoldCo has lent this sum to A Ltd and B Ltd at 4.5%. The interest payments between A Ltd and HoldCo, and B Ltd and HoldCo are eliminated on consolidation. A third-party bank has lent £50m at 5% to C Ltd.

2.53 The UK accounts (entity and consolidated) for the accounting period ending 31 March 2021 show:

Fixed ratio rule

Company	Aggregate tax-EBITDA	FRR 30%	ANTIE	Carried-forward allowance	Interest capacity (iii) + (v)	Fixed ratio debt cap	Interest disallowance (vi) – (lower of (iii) and (vii))
(i)	(ii)	(iii)	(iv)	(v)	(vi)	(vii)	(viii)
HoldCo	10	3	5	1	3 + 1 = 4	5.5	4 – 5 = (1)
A Ltd	7						
B Ltd	3			0			
C Corp	n/a	n/a	n/a	n/a			
Total	10	3	5	1	4		(1)

Group ratio rule

Group	Group-EBITDA in £m	ANGIE	QNGIE	Group ratio %	Group ratio allowance	Carried forward allowance	Interest capacity	Group ratio debt cap	Group Interest disallowance (vii) – (lower of (vi) and (viii))
(i)	(ii)	(iii)	(iv)	(v)	(vi)	(vii)	(viii)	(ix)	(x)
UK group	10	5.5	5.5			1	3.4 + 1 = 4.4		(0.5)
C Corp	6								
Total	16	5.5	5.5	34%	3.4	1	4.4	5.5	4.4 – 5 = (0.6)

So, using the FRR, the disallowance is £1m; using the GRR, the interest disallowance is £0.6m. If the rate of corporation tax is 19%, the UK group must pay additional corporation tax of 19% × 600,000 = £114,000. Its effective rate of corporation tax is increased from 19% to 20%.

Example 2

In the accounting period the ultimate parent (UP, non-UK) pays £65m of third-party interest, and the group-EBITDA is £200m. ANGIE of UP is £55m. QNGIE is also £55m.

The UK group has ANTIE of £20m, comprising interest paid to ultimate parent. The aggregate tax-EBITDA of the UK group is £50m. The UK group has no excess debt cap and no unused interest allowance.

The fixed rate interest allowance is 30% × 50m = 15m. The fixed rate debt cap is 55m.

The group ratio interest allowance is: 65/200 × 100 = 32.5%. 32.5% × 50 = 16.25m. The group ratio debt cap is £55m.

The interest capacity is £16.25m. The interest disallowance is (16.25 − 20) = (3.75m).

Example 3

The UP is UK resident as are all the subsidiaries. There is therefore no alternative Group Ratio Rule. Interest paid to it by UK subsidiaries is nil on consolidation. UP pays £30m interest to the third-party lender, so UK group ANTIE is £30m. Aggregate tax-EBITDA is £120m.

Fixed rate rule interest allowance is 30% × 120 = 36m. Disallowance is (30 − 36) = £6m.

Example 4

The WWG comprises two companies: the UK parent and the UK subsidiary

In accounting period 1:

- UK parent pays interest of £10m to third-party lender.
- UK sub pays interest of £10m to UK parent.
- ANTIE is 10 (10 + 10 − 10).
- Aggregate tax-EBITDA is £30m.

Fixed rate rule interest allowance = 30% × 30 = £9m.

Fixed rate debt cap = 10 (Note: where there are no non-UK members of the WWG, ANTIE = ANGIE).

2.54 *Corporate Interest Restriction (CIR)*

Basic interest allowance = £9m.

Interest disallowance (9 – 10) = £1m.

Excess debt cap carried forward is £1m.

In accounting period 2

- UK parent pays interest of £10m to third-party lender.
- UK sub pays interest of £10m to UK parent.
- ANTIE is 10 (10 + 10 – 10).
- Aggregate tax-EBITDA is £40m.

Fixed rate rule interest allowance = 30% × 40 = £12m.

Fixed rate debt cap = 10 + 1(excess debt cap) = £11m.

Basic interest allowance = £11m.

Interest disallowance (11 – 10) = £1m unused interest allowance which is carried forward.

Section H: Accounts adjustments

2.54 Both the commercial and the tax accounts entity and consolidated have to be significantly adjusted for the purposes of the CIR rules. See IF-BEPS, pp 161–163.

2.55 Although the CIR rules operate by reference to the consolidated accounts of the WWG, these have to be adapted to produce an approximation of the outcomes produced by the application of the UK tax rules. Further, a number of elections can be made to override a number of consolidation rules, either by expanding or restricting their scope. Moreover, the UK tax accounts have to be modified to produce the ANTIE. All this means that accounts for CIR purposes, whether drawn up applying UK-GAAP or IFRS, are *sui generis*. The detailed compliance burdens which this imposes are considerable.

2.56 The CIR rules allow fair value movements on derivatives which have a hedging function to be disregarded, and so treated as 'excluded derivative contract amounts', where a company has made no reg 6A election to achieve such a result, in cases where hedge accounting is not used. Where there is a hedging relationship between the relevant asset and a derivative contract,

Corporate Interest Restriction (CIR) **2.59**

which falls or would fall within reg 7 (fair value gains and losses on derivative currency contracts hedging foreign exchange risk, reg 7A (fair value gains and losses on derivative currency contracts hedging forecast transaction or firm commitment), reg 8 (commodity contracts) or reg 9 (interest rate contracts which hedge balance sheet items) fair value gains and losses on the derivative contracts are disregarded in calculating *group-EBITDA*, and replaced by a 'appropriate accruals basis', in accordance with the Disregard Regulations (SI 2004/3256). The WWG profit is required to recognise the profit which would have been recognised had these regulations applied for UK corporation tax purposes (TIOPA 2010, ss 420, 421).

2.57 Accordingly, TIOPA 2010, ss 420, 421 provide that, for the purposes of the CIR, a group can make an irrevocable election to apply the Disregard Regulations (see Chapter 16). If companies have not made a reg 6A election for the DR to apply in the case of undesignated hedges, a notional election into the DR can be made for the purpose of calculating 'tax interest' and 'tax-EBITDA' for CIR purposes. Where derivative contracts are in a hedging relationship, the accounting treatment will apply for general UK tax purposes unless the company makes an election under reg 6A of the Disregard Regulations for regulations 7, 8 and 9 to apply. These regulations apply to hedging transactions, such as currency, commodity and debt contracts used to hedge forecast transactions or firm commitment (regs 7 and 8), interest rate contracts hedging loan relationships (reg 9) and currency contracts used to hedge a net investment in a foreign operation (shares, ships or aircraft) (regs 3 and 4).

2.58 For a detailed treatment, see Chapter 16 of the 10th edition, 'Hedging and Deferral'. As explained in that chapter, the core area of application of the DR is: (i) the undesignated hedge (ie, hedging transactions which do not meet the prescriptive requirements of IFRS 9); and (ii) the ineffective proportion of undesignated hedges.

2.59 Regulation 9 applies to interest rate derivatives which hedge assets and liabilities accounted for on an amortised cost basis, and requires the derivative contract to be accounted for on an 'appropriate accruals basis' (rather than a fair value basis), so that only the overall transaction is reflected in the income statement (synthetic single instrument). These adjustments have to be applied where non-UK accounts are being adapted to match the UK treatment for the purposes of NTIE/ANGIE/QNGIE. Where group company A has entered into a derivative contract to hedge a risk carried by group company B, group company A is regarded as carrying both the derivative contract and the hedged item, in order to work out the amount to be recognised in respect of the derivative contract in the period of account: TIOPA 2010, s 421(1)(d). DR, reg 4 (matching to shares ships or aircraft, which takes precedence

2.60 *Corporate Interest Restriction (CIR)*

over currency contracts in reg 7) is disapplied: TIOPA 2010, s 421(1)(c). Accordingly, profits and losses on the hedging instrument are recognised for the purposes of CIR as on the hedged item.

2.60 Where derivative contracts are accounted for at fair value in group accounts (eg, hedge of an overseas operation) and are acting as a hedge on a group basis, the group accounts inputs must be adjusted to the amounts which would be recognised in the UK accounts for tax purposes, if the DR were to apply.

Example

Universal Electronics Inc draws up its consolidated accounts based on South Korean GAAP. In calculating NGIE and ANGIE amounts of fair value movements arising on derivative contracts which have a hedging function, albeit an undesignated hedge, are removed for the purposes of CIR. Instead, the amounts from those derivative contracts are recognised in line with the hedged item, applying an 'appropriate accruals basis', in accordance with DR, reg 9(2) which provides:

> '(2) Where paragraph 9(1), applies, credits and debts shall be brought into account for the purposes of s 598(1)(b) of CTA 2009 on the assumption that an appropriate accruals basis had been used in relation to the contract for that accounting period.'

'*Appropriate accruals basis*' is then defined in detail in reg 9(4).

Universal Electronics borrows US$100m @ 10% floating annual interest and enters into a floating-to-fixed interest rate swap for the same notional principal and term. The hedge is undesignated. When the floating rate is 6% the annual accounts show:

	US$m
Interest on loan	(10)
Net periodic payments received on swap	(4)
Fair value movements on swap	(20)

For CIR purposes, applying an appropriate accruals basis, the finance expense is taken to be US$ 14m.

2.61 Where before 1 April 2017 a company is party to a loan relationship accounted for on an amortised cost basis, but the accounts of the WWG account for it on a fair value basis or as part of a designated fair value hedge, it is assumed that the WWG also adopts an amortised cost basis for the loan: Corporate Interest Restriction (Financial Statements: Group Mismatches) Regulations (SI 2017/1224), regs 1, 2.

In computing ANGIE (and also *group-EBITDA*) it is necessary to exclude items such as dividends on preference shares and interest paid to *related parties*. In order to apply this rule, it may be necessary to amalgamate the rights of connected persons in ways which are not required in the preparation of consolidated accounts. So, for example, investors in an unlisted partnership holding vehicle may be 'related' to the WWG, even if they would not form part of the WWG. Capitalised interest may also need to be extracted for inclusion in group interest inputs.

2.62 IFRS 16 is effective for accounting periods beginning on or after 1 January 2019 but can be adopted earlier. It only applies to lessees and largely reclassifies most operating leases as finance leases. This brings such leases on balance sheet, and significantly increases the after-tax cost of leasing by leading to greater CIR disallowance. CTA 2009, ss 180–182, 261, 262 apply where a company carrying on a UK property business changes its accounting basis. The net result of the change of basis is taken into account in the accounting period in which the change takes effect. This amount is not taken into account as net-tax interest income or expense where the change in accounting treatment results from the fact that a finance lease ceases to be treated as a right-of-use lease under FRS 16 because of its short term or low value: FA 2019, Sch 14, para 19.

2.63 For lessees, the impact of CIR on lease payments is as follows:

(i) As long as existing leases can be accounted for as operating leases, CIR has no impact.

(ii) Companies using FRS 102 may continue to distinguish between operating and finance leases.

(iii) Companies using FRS 101 and IFRS 16 need to account for most leases as finance leases post-1 January 2019. The finance element of finance leases increases the tax-interest expense, thus aggravating the effect of CIR.

(iv) Any reclassification of operating leases as finance leases increases both EBITDA and ANTIE, but as only 30% of EBITDA enters into the CIR calculation, while 100% of ANTIE is used in calculating the interest disallowance, the after tax cost of financing leasing is increased.

2.64 *Corporate Interest Restriction (CIR)*

(v) Tax charges on lessors remain unchanged, thus leading to greater asymmetry between lessors and lessees.

Section I: The worldwide group (WWG)

2.64 The shareholders of a parent company have an indirect interest in the net assets and in the profits or losses of the company's subsidiaries. Accordingly, parent companies are required to prepare and present one set of accounts for the group as a whole in recognition of the fact that a parent company and its subsidiaries are, to the extent of consolidation, a single economic unit.

2.65 An entity is part of a group for accounting and company law purposes if it is directly or indirectly controlled by a company or is a company which has control of other companies. A group is a multinational group if it operates in more than one jurisdiction, including through a PE.

2.66 Accounting standards require consolidated accounts to be prepared for all entities forming part of a group. Consolidated accounts are prepared by the top-level company, so that the results of subsidiary companies are incorporated on a line-by-line basis (ie, intra-group sales and purchases, loans and debts, are eliminated). Assets held at fair value by investment companies and investment companies whose shares are held by the parent for disposal at fair value, may not be consolidated ('non-consolidated subsidiaries'). The key issue on consolidation is what is included and what is excluded. The definition of a group is based on the consolidated financial statements prepared by the ultimate parent (ie, the top-level company).

2.67 The main international standards which apply to the preparation of group accounts are IFRS 10 *Consolidated Financial Statements* (replacing IAS 27) and IFRS 3 *Business Combinations*. 'Control' requires three elements set out in IFRS 10, para 7, namely:

- power;
- exposure or right to variable return; and
- the ability to use that power to affect those returns.

These standards are concerned with groups in general, including those with unincorporated subsidiaries. In practice, however, most groups are made up of companies.

2.68 The consolidated statements of the ultimate parent and its subsidiaries must be drawn up in accordance with IFRS or on the basis of GAAP in the UK, Canada, China, India, Japan, South Korea or the USA.

2.69 Standalone companies are outside the CIR rules, unless they exceptionally constitute part of a WWG, because they are controlled by a partnership or trustees who also control other entities or because they have a PE outside the residence state. The point about a standalone company is that it cannot pay interest to an associated company. All its finance costs will be, by definition, third party, except in the case of loans by individual shareholder owners.

2.70 'Worldwide group' is defined in TIOPA 2010, ss 473–474. Under ss 473(1)(4)(d) and 475A a 'multi-company WWG consists of:

(i) the ultimate parent company of an International Accounting Standards (IAS) group;

(ii) its consolidated subsidiaries; and

(iii) an entity which is not a member of an IFRS group ('a single company worldwide group').

In order to be a parent company, a company cannot itself be a consolidated subsidiary ('the first non-consolidation condition' (s 473(2)); alternatively, it cannot itself be a member of an IAS group (the 'second non-consolidation condition' (s 473(3)).

2.71 'Group' and 'subsidiary' are defined by reference to IAS (TIOPA 2010, s 473(5)). Control over a subsidiary is usually achieved by holding 51% or more of its ordinary shares. It is important to appreciate that these group (consolidated) accounts are primarily intended for the shareholders of the parent company and investors in the group generally, such as banks and investment funds. Indeed, that was the whole reason for the introduction of the IAS Regulation (2002/1606/EC), which took effect from 1 January 2005. The UK accounts require extensive adjustments to be made before they can be used for tax purposes.

2.72 An entity (X) which would be a subsidiary of Y and so consolidated for the purposes of IAS, will be a 'non-consolidated subsidiary' and would thus be excluded from the WWG if Y measures the X shares at fair value as a 'non-consolidated subsidiary': TIOPA 2010, s 475. Such a subsidiary is regarded as an asset held for sale or distribution to the owners. Where an insurance entity is part of a WWG and holds a subsidiary as a portfolio investment (ie, it holds the shares at fair value) then the subsidiary does not form part of the WWG: TIOPA 2010, s 453.

2.73 Under TIOPA 2010, s 454A, investment management subsidiaries are excluded from the WWG if three conditions are satisfied:

(i) the investment management subsidiary (S) is part of the WWG because other group companies manage or hold interests in S;

2.74 *Corporate Interest Restriction (CIR)*

(ii) the entity managing S does not provide investment management services; and

(iii) management of S is not co-ordinated with the management of any other person or entity.

It follows that because S is excluded from the WWG, so are subsidiaries of S.

2.74 Where two entities which would otherwise be the ultimate parent of a WWG are stapled together (so that shares in entity A carry equivalent rights in shares in entity B and vice versa), both entities are deemed to be consolidated subsidiaries of a single deemed parent entity: TIOPA 2010, s 477. The same applies where two entities constitute a business combination under IFRS 3.

2.75 Parents and subsidiaries must be 'relevant entities' (ie, companies or entities whose shares or other interests are publicly traded and sufficiently widely held). Governmental bodies are not relevant entities: TIOPA 2010, s 474. An unlisted partnership would not qualify, so any subsidiary of that partnership would potentially form a WWG in its own right.

2.76 It might be thought that a group must, by definition, consist of at least two companies. However, a single company (the ultimate parent) can form a group with the PE, having regard to the 'distinct and separate entity' hypothesis (Model Tax Convention, arts 7, 9; CTA 2009, ss 21, 22). In that case it will be a 'single-country worldwide group': TIOPA 2010, s 473(4)(c).

Periods of account

2.77 A WWG has a period of account, which is the period of account for the consolidated accounts, provided that these are 'drawn up on acceptable principles' as defined in TIOPA 2010, s 481, ss 480–485. The ultimate parent's period of account is the period of account for the WWG: s 480. However, the accounts must not be drawn up for a period longer than 18 months: TIOPA 2010, s 487.

2.78 The CIR rules are applied with reference to the period of account of the WWG. Where the ultimate holding company does not prepare consolidated accounts, an election may be made to align the group's period of account with the individual UK companies' corporation tax accounting periods, so as to reduce the need for apportionments to be performed.

2.79 If the ultimate parent does not prepare consolidated accounts, but prepares entity accounts, the accounting period of the entity accounts is the accounting period of the WWG: TIOPA 2010, s 484.

Corporate Interest Restriction (CIR) **2.86**

2.80 If there are no group accounts, this is an 'accounts-free period' after 1 April 2017: TIOPA 2010, s 485(1). IAS accounts will be treated as being drawn up for the 'default period of account', so that a period is not an 'accounts-free period' if it forms part of an accounts free-period: TIOPA 2010, s 485(2). The ultimate parent can elect out of the default treatment under s 486.

2.81 TIOPA 2010, s 490 defines 'relevant accounting period' for subsidiaries. A relevant accounting period is a period which falls within or partly within the accounting period of the WWG. Only amounts which fall within the *relevant accounting period* (ie, the accounting period of the WWG) are included in the CIR calculations: TIOPA 2010, s 490. Amounts apportioned to or falling in 'disregarded periods' are ignored, ie,

- periods which fall outside the group accounting period (eg, non-coterminous accounts); or
- periods when the company was not a member of the WWG (eg, if a subsidiary leaves a group within the WWG accounting period).

2.82 Apportionment of receipts and expenses is made to take account of *'disregarded periods'*. These are parts of accounting periods which do not coincide with the accounting period of the WWG or during which the relevant company is not a member. Where amounts under an accounting period fall in a disregarded period, they must be allocated on a *just and reasonable basis* between the regarded and the disregarded period.

2.83 It is in the nature of large corporate organisations that they are continuously reorganised and restructured, in the endless and untiring search for return on capital employed (ROCE). A WWG will retain its continuity of identity as long as the ultimate parent does not change: TIOPA 2010, s 476.

2.84 The UK charges corporation tax on a single entity basis, not on a consolidated basis. The main reason for this policy is the problem of minority interests. So, the starting point for tax purposes is the entity accounts.

UK rules on consolidation

2.85 For CIR purposes the group is defined more widely than for group relief and loss carry-forward purposes and under capital gains tax rules. It also includes PEs located in the UK.

2.86 Under the CIR entities within the UK tax group are treated as a single entity for the purpose of applying the fixed ratio rule and group ratio rule. The benchmark fixed ratio will be applied to the UK group's *aggregate*

2.87 *Corporate Interest Restriction (CIR)*

tax-EBITDA. Calculations are carried out at the group level, by aggregating individual UK group company figures for finance expenses and income, and then allocating the available tax deduction at individual company level, according to the attribution made by the group reporting company. The consolidated accounts enable the group's net third-party interest expense and EBITDA to be established.

2.87 In the consolidated accounts intra-group debt and interest are eliminated. Where the group ratio method is used the consolidated accounts are used to calculate a limit for tax deductible finance costs, which is then applied to the UK group and then apportioned between the individual UK companies. Accordingly, entity taxation is overridden by reference to the consolidated or aggregate accounts position.

2.88 The CIR continues to charge tax on a company by company basis but decides the deductible interest expense of a company within a WWG by reference to its membership of a WWG. While, therefore, the interest cap is established at the UK group or WWG level, the actual implementation of the restriction is at single entity level, via an interest restriction calculated and allocated at group level.

2.89 'Worldwide' has no particular connotation, save that it indicates that the group can include both UK and non-UK companies. A 'multi-company worldwide group' can consist solely of UK companies, and a single UK company can be a 'single-company worldwide group'.

2.90 For the purposes of consolidated accounts, UK company law attaches importance to two main types of corporate group:

- holding (parent) companies and subsidiary companies; and
- parent undertakings and subsidiary undertakings.

The consolidated accounts used for the purposes of the CIR other than the application of the group ratio rule are the consolidated accounts of the UK group, compiled in accordance with UK corporate law.

2.91 Company law only recognises the economic interdependence of group companies to a limited extent:

- a company or one of its subsidiaries cannot give financial assistance for the purchase of its own shares (CA 2006, ss 678, 679);
- parent companies must produce group accounts (CA 2006, s 399); and
- a company cannot be a member of its holding company (CA 2006 s 136).

Corporate Interest Restriction (CIR) **2.96**

2.92 UK rules on the scope of the consolidation requirement are found in Companies Act 2006, which (a) gives domestic effect to the Seventh Company Law Directive (EEC/83/349), and (b) gives legal effect to FRS 102, Section 9, Consolidated and Separate Financial Statements. The crucial aspect in consolidated accounts is the definition of the entities which must be included within their scope. The narrower the definition, the greater the risk of excluding potential risks and gains.

2.93 Under CA 2006, ss 1159, 1160, Sch 7, S is a subsidiary of P if:

- P holds the majority of voting rights;
- P is a member of S and has the right to appoint the majority of the board; and
- P is a member of S and has control of the majority of voting rights.

2.94 Under CA 2006, ss 1160–1162 and Sch 7, S will be a subsidiary undertaking and P a parent undertaking if:

- P holds the majority of the voting rights in S;
- P is a member of S and has the right to appoint the majority of directors;
- P is a member and controls the majority of voting rights;
- P has dominant influence (Sch 10A, para 4(1)) over S by means of articles and control contract (Sch 10A, para 4(2)) (legal control); and
- P has a participating interest (s 260) in S and actively exercises dominant influence or P and S are managed on a unified basis (factual control).

2.95 CA 2006, s 399 states that a parent company must prepare consolidated accounts dealing with both parent and subsidiary undertakings. Under s 405 all subsidiary undertakings are to be included in the consolidation. 'Parent undertaking' and 'subsidiary undertaking' are defined in ss 1159, 1160 so as to encompass incorporated and unincorporated bodies. The UK consolidation model is based on the principle of control of economic benefits, not just control of a company. The tests based both on legal control and factual control only exist in the accounting context. The IAS approach is broadly similar.

2.96 Where a company has securities listed on a regulated exchange in the EEA, it is required to produce consolidated accounts based on IAS. As noted at para 2.71 the IAS standard for consolidation is IAS 27. The test of whether one company is a subsidiary of another is based on control, which may be voting rights or economic power (IAS 27, para 13), ie

- holding 51% of voting rights;
- control of 51% of voting rights through shareholder agreement;

2.97 *Corporate Interest Restriction (CIR)*

- power to govern the financial and other operating policies of the other enterprise by statute or agreement;
- power to appoint or remove the majority of directors; and
- power to cast the majority of votes at a meeting of the board of directors.

2.97 The preparation of consolidated accounts requires the elimination of all intragroup dealings and consolidation of all external assets and liabilities. So, if a UK company has a minority stake but a dominant influence in a partnership, the assets, liabilities, profits and losses of the non-controlling interest must be consolidated.

Examples of WWG

2.98

Examples of WWGs

(i)

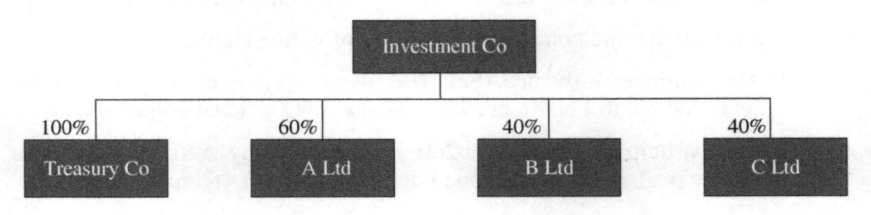

```
                    Investment Co
        ┌───────────┬──────┴──────┬───────────┐
      100%         60%           40%         40%
    Treasury Co   A Ltd         B Ltd       C Ltd
```

Investment Co, Treasury Co and A Ltd form a WWG

(ii)

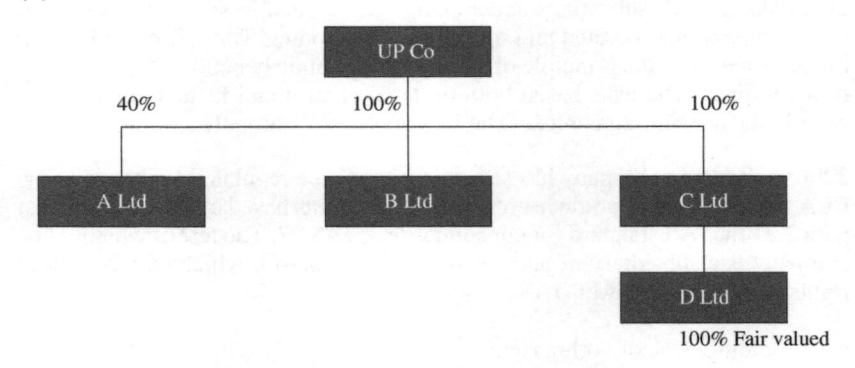

```
                      UP Co
        ┌─────────────┬─┴───────────┐
       40%          100%          100%
      A Ltd         B Ltd         C Ltd
                                    │
                                  100%
                                  D Ltd
                              100% Fair valued
```

UP Co, B Ltd and C Ltd form a WWG.

48

(iii)

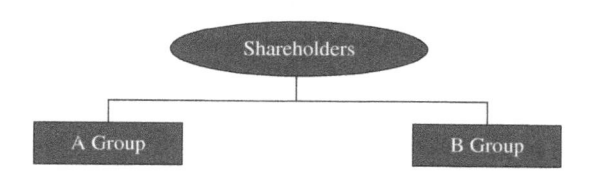

[Diagram: Shareholders at top, with A Group and B Group below]

A Group and B Group cannot together form a WWG because control is through shareholders who are individuals.

Section J: Rule 1

2.99 Rule 1 states:

1. UK companies which belong to a worldwide group are subject to interest deduction restrictions in a period of account of the group if the *aggregate net tax-interest expense of the group (ANTIE)* exceeds the *interest capacity* of the group for the period.

2.100 The legislation requires the accounts figures to be extensively adjusted, to give tax-interest expense and income and tax-EBITDA. Hence just as accounting profits differ from 'taxable total profits' for the purposes of CTA 2010, s 4(2), and taxable total profits different from 'relevant profits' under the loss-carry-forward rules, so tax-EBITDA is also quite different from taxable total profits.

2.101 All UK entities which belong to the WWG are regarded as a single entity for the purposes of the CIR. TIOPA 2010, s 373(1) states that the consequence of being a WWG is that the UK companies in the group are subject to interest deduction restriction in a period of account of the group if the ANTIE exceeds the *interest capacity* of the group for the period:

'(1) A worldwide group is "subject to interest restrictions" in a period of account of the group if –

  (a) the aggregate net tax-interest expense of the group for the period ... exceeds

  (b) the interest capacity of the group for the period.'

So, s 373(1) contains three concepts:

- WWG;
- ANTIE; and
- interest capacity

2.102 *Corporate Interest Restriction (CIR)*

2.102 The non-deduction arises from the allocation of the group non-deductible amount amongst UK group companies in accordance with the statement of allocated interest restrictions contained in interest restriction return (IRR) prepared by the group reporting company: TIOPA 2010, Sch 7A, para 22. The charging provision is in TIOPA 2010, s 375(2). This states:

> '(2) A company that is listed on the statement under paragraph 22 of Schedule 7A (statement of allocated interest restrictions) must in any accounting period for which the statement specifies an allocated disallowance, leave out of account tax-interest amounts that, in total, equal that allocated disallowance.'

Section K: Rule 2

2.103 Rule 2 states:

2. The *aggregate net tax-interest expense of the group* (ANTIE) is the total of *net tax-interest expense amounts* of each relevant company for the accounting period.

2.104 '*Aggregate net tax-interest expense of the group*' (TIOPA 2010, s 373(1)) itself contains the concepts of '*tax-interest*' and '*aggregate net tax-interest*'. The basic definition of ANTIE is contained in s 382. The '*aggregate net tax-interest expense*' of a WWG in an accounting period is the total of the net tax-interest expense of the UK members of the group, less the *aggregate net tax-interest income* (s 390(1)). Negative amounts are nil (s 390(2)). ANTIE is the aggregate net deductible expenses for UK tax purposes of the UK group in respect of loan relationships, derivative contracts, finance leases and guarantee fees, excluding foreign exchange movements, impairments and derivatives hedging trading transactions unrelated to capital structure (other than finance trades).

2.105 '*Tax-interest*' is '*tax-interest income amount*' or '*tax-interest expense amount*'. It is the notion of tax-interest which links the CIR to the loan relationships and derivative contracts legislation. However, there is no simple read-across from loan relationships and derivative contracts legislation because the amounts in question must be 'relevant', as defined in TIOPA 2010, ss 382–391A.

2.106 *Tax-interest expense*' constitutes debits of a UK member of the WWG ('*a relevant company*' – s 390(5)) under (i) the loan relationships rules, plus (ii) the derivative contracts rules, plus (iii) implicit finance charges in finance leases (TIOPA 2010, s 382(1)–(5)), other than *excluded debits*. Guarantee fees are also tax-interest expenses: TIOPA 2010, s 385(6). A *tax-interest*

Corporate Interest Restriction (CIR) 2.108

expense amount of a UK company must be an amount brought into account for corporation tax purposes which satisfies conditions A, B or C: TIOPA 2010, s 382(1)–(5):

- Condition A – relevant loan relationship debit (s 383);
- Condition B – relevant derivative contract debit (s 384); and
- Condition C – finance cost implicit under relevant arrangement or transaction, as defined in s 382(5) (mainly finance leases).

Example

A company enters into a finance lease for the lease of an asset for five years which costs £300,000 and has nil value at the end of the lease. The monthly lease payments are £6,000 (total £6,000 × £60 = £360,000). Of the monthly payments, 60/360 × 6,000 = £1,000 is a tax-interest expense.

'Relevant loan relationship debits' are defined in s 383. Loan relationship debits are 'excluded debits' if they are in respect of foreign exchange and impairment losses: TIOPA 2010, s 383.

2.107 Relevant derivative contract debits are defined in TIOPA 2010, s 384. Derivative contract debits are 'excluded debits' if they are in respect of foreign exchange and impairment losses, or losses unrelated to the capital structure of the company or WWG. Moreover, the underlying subject matter of the derivative contract must be a financial index, currency or a loan relationship, to give rise to relevant debits and credits (TIOPA 2010, s 384(4)).

2.108 Credits and debits relating to a derivative contract will be left out of account where the derivative contract is:

- a hedge of a risk arising in the normal course of a trade (other than a financial trade); and
- is entered into for reasons wholly unrelated to the capital structure of the company or WWG.

Example

An investment company holds a portfolio of shares. The directors are concerned that the shares may fall in value. They purchase put options on the

2.109 *Corporate Interest Restriction (CIR)*

shares (or enter into a total return swap on the shares). Debits and credits on the put options are excluded from CIR because the underlying subject matter does not qualify.

2.109 Capitalised interest is a loan relationship debit in accordance with CTA 2009, s 320. The priority which the intangible fixed assets legislation ordinarily has over the loan relationships legislation (CTA 2009, s 906(1)) does not apply for the purposes of the CIR with effect from 1 January 2019 (TIOPA 2010, s 391A). This means that finance costs capitalised in the carrying value of intangible fixed assets are taken into account in calculating tax-interest expenses. 'Impairment loss' is defined in s 391 and does not include fair value debits, in the rare cases in which liabilities can be fair valued.

2.110 There are a number of special rules.

(i) CTA 2009, s 499 allows distributions of co-operative associations and community benefit associations to be treated as interest payments.

(ii) Under TIOPA 2010, s 459 if the creditor is a charity, and interest is paid by a trading subsidiary, which could have qualified as a gift aid donation, this is not tax-interest expense, or a tax-interest credit of the charity.

(iii) In the case of authorised investment funds (OEICs and AUTs), investment trust funds and approved investment trusts (AITs), interest distributions are not treated as tax-interest expense amounts: Authorised Investment Funds (Tax) Regulations, SI 2006/964, rr 18(2A), 19, 23, 69Z16(2A), 69Z17.

(iv) Securitisation companies are taxed in accordance with the Taxation of Securitised Companies Regulations (SI 2006/3296), reg 22 in accordance with a 'permanent' or 'interim' regime. The tax-interest income is the 'retained profit'.

2.111 *'Tax-interest income'* comprises relevant credits under the loan relationships and derivative contracts legislation and is the mirror image of tax-interest expense (ss 385–387). It includes guarantee fees. A *tax-interest income amount* of a company is an amount brought into account for corporation tax purposes which satisfies conditions A, B, C or D (s 385(1)–(6)):

- Condition A – relevant loan relationship credit (s 386);

- Condition B – relevant derivative contract credit (s 387);

- Condition C – finance income implicit under relevant arrangement or transaction, as defined in s 385(5) (mainly finance leases); and

- Condition D – guarantee fees.

2.112 If an investment company holds assets which are fair valued, an election can be made to account for interest-income and expenses on amortised cost basis for the purposes of CIR: ss 456, 457. If an insurance company holds an interest in a collective investment scheme, it is deemed to be a loan relationship under the bond fund rules.

2.113 A company's *'net tax-interest expense'* is the excess of its tax-interest expenses over tax-interest income in an accounting period, and *'net tax-interest income'* is the opposite (s 389). Again, *'aggregate net tax-income amount'* means the reverse of *aggregate net tax-income expense* (s 390(3)).

2.114 Where a credit carries double taxation relief, the receipt is reduced to take account of the foreign tax credit in order to give the notional untaxed income in accordance with TIOPA 2010, s 18 (s 388).

Example

X Ltd receives foreign interest of £100,000, subject to withholding tax of £10,000. It is subject to corporation tax at 19%. The notional untaxed income is $(100{,}000 - (10{,}000 \times 100/19)) = 100{,}000 - 52{,}631 = £47{,}369$.

2.115 A group has *ANTII* where it has aggregate net taxable income rather than net deductible expense (s 390(3)(4)). ANTII is added to the basic interest allowance to give the *interest allowance* of the WWG (s 396).

Section L: Rule 3

2.116 Rule 3 states:

3. The *aggregate net tax-interest expense of the group* (ANTIE) is compared with the *aggregate tax-EBITDA of the UK group*, which comprises the aggregate of the adjusted corporation tax earnings (as defined for UK corporation tax purposes) for each UK group company for the accounting period, to find the fixed rate allowance.

The next concept introduced by the legislation is *aggregate tax-EBITDA*, which is the UK group's net taxable earnings, before taking into account tax interest, tax depreciation (capital allowances and relief for capital expenditure on intangible fixed assets) and qualifying tax reliefs.

2.117 Most other tax rules, including the transfer pricing rules, need to be applied to determine taxable profits before the CIR calculation

2.118 *Corporate Interest Restriction (CIR)*

can begin. The taxable total for corporation tax profits are adjusted to give '*adjusted corporation tax earnings*' for the purposes of CIR. This is defined in TIOPA 2010, s 406 and is done to remove the risk that figures for tax-interest expense may be understated and figures for tax-interest income may be overstated. Losses are treated as nil because otherwise the tax-EBITDA of the UK group would be reduced, thus permitting a higher level of interest deduction.

2.118 Section 372(7)(i) introduces the '*tax-EBITDA of a company for a period of account of a worldwide group*':

> 'the tax-EBITDA of a company for a period of account of a worldwide group (which is an amount derived from amounts brought into account for the purposes of corporation tax)'.

It follows that the concept is only concerned with the earnings of UK members of the WWG.

Where only one accounting period of a company falls within the period of account of the WWG, that is the applicable period of account. Where the company has more than one accounting period which falls within the period of account of the WWG, the tax-EBITDA of the company is the aggregate of adjusted corporation tax profits for each of those accounting periods, allocated to the accounting period of the WWG on a just and reasonable basis: TIOPA 2010, ss 406(7), 490. Adjustments are also made where the company is not a member of the WWG for the whole of the accounting period.

2.119 Section 372(7)(ii) brings in '*aggregate tax-EBITDA*':

> 'the "aggregate tax-EBITDA" of a worldwide group for period of account of the group (which is an amount derived from the tax-EBITDA of members of the group)'.

2.120 Section 406 then defines the tax-EBITDA of a company for the purposes of s 405(a) as the company's *adjusted corporation tax earnings for the period of account.*

2.121 The '*tax-EBITDA of a company*' is calculated in accordance with s 406 as the '*adjusted corporation tax earnings*': TIOPA 2010, s 406(1)(2). That is derived from '*total taxable profits*' as defined by CTA 2010, s 4(2) (TIOPA 2010, s 406(3)(a)). Tax-EBITDA is the earnings of a company before interest, tax, depreciation and amortisation computed according to corporation tax rules.

2.122 The included items must satisfy conditions A or B. Condition A is that the amount is brought into account in determining the company's 'total taxable profits' (CTA 2010, s 4(2), TIOPA 2010, s 406(3)(a)) and is not an 'excluded amount' within s 407. Condition B is that the amount would have been brought into account if the company had profits and is not an excluded item.

2.123 'Excluded amounts' (ie, excluded in calculating *adjusted corporation tax earnings*) are defined in TIOPA 2010, s 407(1)(2). These include:

- tax-interest income and tax-interest expense amounts;
- allowances or charges under CAA;
- brought forward or carried back deficits on loan relationships;
- brought forward management expenses of investment companies;
- losses arising in another group company or from another accounting period (CTA 2010, s 188CK); and
- qualifying tax reliefs.

2.124 Sections 407(3) and 408 then define 'qualifying tax reliefs'. These include:

- R&D expenditure credits;
- pre-trading expenditure of SMEs;
- film reliefs;
- qualifying charitable donations;
- intangible fixed assets debits; and
- group relief for carried-forward losses.

Net intra-group inter-expense does not include capitalised interest, because tax-EBITDA is based on amounts which go through the income statement, in accordance with CTA 2009, s 306A.

2.125 Where income qualifies for double tax relief, the taxable amount is reduced by deducting the amount of the foreign tax credit divided by the rate of corporation tax, the deductible amount being 'notional untaxed income' (s 409).

2.126 Non-taxable income such as branch profits or dividend income that benefits from the participation exemption are not included in tax-EBITDA.

2.127 *Corporate Interest Restriction (CIR)*

2.127 Section 405 states that the aggregate tax-EBITDA of a WWG is the sum of the tax-EBITDAs for each company in the UK group, but if a company has negative EBITDA, its tax-EBITDA is nil.

Section 405 states:

'… "the aggregate tax-EBITDA" of a worldwide group for a period of account of the group is –

(a) the total of the tax-EBITDAs for the period of each company that was a member of the group at any time during that period or

(b) where the amount specified in paragraph (a) is negative, nil.'

Section M: Rule 4

2.128 Rule 4 states:

4. The *basic interest allowance* of the UK group is the amount of the *aggregate net tax-interest expense* of the UK group given by either the *fixed ratio rule* or (by election, where it gives a higher basic interest allowance) by the *group ratio rule*.

2.129 Section 396 states:

'(1) … "the interest allowance" of a worldwide group for a period of account of the group is A + B where –

- A is the basic interest allowance of the group for the period

- B is the amount (if any) of the aggregate net interest income of the group for the period (see section 393(3) and (4)).

(2) In subsection (1) "the basic interest allowance" means –

(a) where no group ratio election is in force in relation to the period, the basic interest allowance calculated using the fixed ratio method (see section 397);

(b) where such an election is in force in relation to the period, the basic interest allowance calculated using the group ratio method (see section 398).'

2.130 The *basic interest allowance* is (s 396(2)) the allowance given by the fixed ratio rule (s 396(2)(a)) or the group ratio rule (s 396(2)(b)). The *interest* *allowance* is the basic interest allowance + aggregate net tax-interest income (ANTII) for the period (s 396(1)).

2.131 Each UK group of companies has a basic interest allowance determined by one of two methods. Fractions of the allowance are then allocated by the reporting company (ie, the UK group company which administers the scheme) to individual UK companies in the UK group, who make their CTSAs on that basis. The interest restriction will take the form of confining the group's deductible interest expense to the amount given by fixed ratio or group ratio rule. Finance costs in excess of the UK group companies' interest allowance are a group attribute which are carried forward at the group level.

2.132 The two methods are:

(i) The fixed ratio rule

This is 30% of the tax-EBITDA of UK group companies or the *fixed ratio debt cap* if lower.

This is the standard method, unless the reporting company opts to use the alternative. The level of net tax-interest expense in an entity is limited with reference to a fixed percentage of tax-EBITDA of the UK group companies. The fixed ratio method prescribes a normative basis to determine how much of a company's operations 'should' be financed by debt rather than equity, limiting such deductions to a fixed proportion of the company's pre-tax earnings (TIOPA 2010, s 397). In this method account is taken of the actual net finance costs of a company. This limits net interest expense for UK corporation tax purposes where the UK entities' net interest deductions, including payments to related non-UK entities, is higher than that of the WWG to which they belong.

(ii) The group ratio rule

The optional group ratio method allows a higher rate of financing expense as a proportion of group-EBITDA where groups are highly leveraged with third-party debt for non-tax reasons. The measure of deductible finance expense is the WWG's net external interest and economically similar expense (TIOPA 2010, s 398). Where an option is made to use this method, this displaces the fixed ratio method. This allows an entity with net interest expense above a country's fixed ratio to deduct interest up to the level of the net interest/EBITDA ratio of its WWG.

2.133 Both the fixed ratio rule and the group ratio rule provide a fall back which would give a lower rate of interest restriction.

2.134 *Corporate Interest Restriction (CIR)*

2.134 The *interest capacity* is defined in TIOPA 2010, s 392(1) as the *interest allowance + available and unexpired interest capacity* brought forward from earlier accounting period.

2.135 Section 393 determines the amount of the interest allowance for an '*original period*' which can be carried forward so as to be '*available for a later period of account of the group ('the receiving period')*. The amount in question is any unused interest allowance for the originating period which is unexpired in the receiving period. The carried forward amount expires at the end of five years following the end of the originating period: TIOPA 2010, ss 394–395.

2.136 The *interest capacity* measures the ability of a UK group to deduct ANTIE in an accounting period. In any accounting period of the WWG, the deductibility of finance costs of the UK group is restricted to the group's *interest capacity* for that year. The *interest capacity* is a group attribute, not an attribute of an individual company. It is the amount of deductible finance cost which the UK group companies incur in an accounting period.

2.137 A UK company belonging to a WWG suffers a disallowance where its ANTIE for a period of account exceeds its *interest capacity*. If the tax-interest expense is < £2m the CIR does not apply because if the group's interest capacity is < £2m (the *de minimis* amount), its interest capacity is the *de minimis* amount. The *de minimis* amount for the UK companies who are members of the WWG is £2m: TIOPA 2010, s 392(2)(3).

2.138 TIOPA 2010, s 392(2)(3) provides:

'(2) When the amount determined under subsection (1) is less than the de minimis amount for the current period, the interest capacity of the worldwide group for the period is the de minimis amount.

(3) ... "the de minimis amount" for a period of account is

(a) £2 million, or

(b) where the period is more than or less than a year, the amount mentioned in paragraph (a) proportionately increased or reduced.'

2.139 There is, then, a threshold of group net annual financing costs of £2m before the legislation is triggered. This will exclude many SMEs. The *de minimis* allowance carves out groups which have a low level of net interest expense. When a group has more than one entity in a jurisdiction, the threshold is applied to the total net interest expense of the UK group. The £2m must be allocated among group companies. If a UK group has less than £2m interest capacity in a given accounting period, the excess up to £2m cannot be carried forward. It is only the net tax-interest expense which exceeds both the benchmark fixed ratio and the group ratio which is disallowed.

2.140 Where on or after 29 October 2018 a company ceases to be the ultimate parent of a WWG and is replaced by another ultimate parent as a result of a 'qualifying takeover', the new ultimate parent takes over the interest allowance of the predecessor (CTA 2010, 724A; TIOPA 2010, s 395A). A 'qualifying takeover' is the acquisition of all the issued shares in the acquired company within CTA 2010, s 724A (disregard of change of ownership of parent company, so allowing losses to be carried forward).

Section N: Rule 5

2.141 Rule 5 states:

5. Where the fixed rate rule applies, the basic interest allowance is the lower of (i) 30% of the *aggregate tax-EBITDA of the UK group*, and (ii) the *fixed ratio debt cap*.

2.142 The fixed ratio rule is defined in ITEPA 2010, s 397. Section 397 states:

'(1) For the purposes of section 396, the basic interest allowance of a worldwide group for a period of account of the group, calculated using the fixed ratio method, is the lower of the following amounts:

(a) 30% of the aggregate tax-EBITDA of the group for the period;

(b) the fixed ratio debt cap of the group for the period.'

Section O: Rule 6

2.143 Rule 6 states:

6. The *fixed ratio debt cap* is (i) the adjusted net group-interest expense of the group (ANGIE) for the period, plus (ii) the *excess debt cap*. The *excess debt cap* is the excess of ANGIE for the previous accounting period over 30% of the aggregate tax-EBITDA for that period.

This is designed to apply in cases where the net group interest expense (NGIE) in the preceding period is below the 30% limit, but in the current accounting

2.144 *Corporate Interest Restriction (CIR)*

period exceeds the debt cap. The fall back fixed ratio debt cap (or group ratio debt cap where the group elects for the group ratio rule to apply for an accounting period) is directed at situations where a non-UK members of a WWG finance the UK group, which applies the fixed ratio rule, but the WWG as a whole has little external debt: HM Treasury and HMRC, *Tax Deductibility of Corporate Interest Expense* (2016), para 2.39.

The fixed ratio debt cap is [X + (A − B)], where:

X = ANGIE for accounting period

A = ANGIE for previous accounting period

B = 30% of aggregate tax-EBITDA for previous accounting period.

Example

(i) Accounting period	(ii) ANGIE	(iii) 30% aggregate tax-EBITDA	(iv) Excess debt cap	(v) Fixed ratio debt cap [(ii) + (iv)]
1	10	8		
2	7	10	2	7 + 2 = 9

2.144 The *NGIE* is the finance cost recognised in the income statement of the consolidated accounts of the WWG in respect of loans and financial transactions (TIOPA 2010, s 410). The starting point (prior to adjustment) is the *net group-interest expense*. Section 410(1) states that the *net group-interest expense of the group* is (A − B), where A = *relevant expense amounts* and B = *relevant income amounts*.

2.145 Both amount A and amount B are derived from the consolidated accounts of the WWG. Those accounts may be drawn up in accordance with the GAAP of another state. Accordingly, at this point the UK tax authority delivers itself into the hands of non-UK accounting rules and non-UK tax authorities. That is why the BEPS project as a whole has placed such emphasis on international compliance and conformity. Moreover, the UK authorities, having decided to adopt BEPS Action 4 hook, line and sinker, may not have realised the extent to which they were transferring power to pesky foreigners.

2.146 *Relevant expense amounts* are defined in TIOPA 2010, s 411(1) as interest and payments economically equivalent to interest. The amounts in question are:

(a) debits taken into account under the loan relationship and derivative contracts rules, excluding exchange losses, impairment relief and losses on hedging contracts unrelated to capital structure;

(b) dividends on preference shares treated under IAS 32 as liabilities;

(c) alternative finance returns payable under alternative finance arrangements;

(d) payments related to stock lending and repos;

(e) amounts recognised in the income statement; and

(f) capitalised interest, where the amount recognised in the income statement arises as the result of the write down of the carrying value of a relevant asset.

2.147 Accordingly, if finance costs attributable to non-relevant assets have been capitalised, such amounts are written back to income (if costs) or expenses (if income) (TIOPA 2010, s 410(2)–(6)). Non-relevant assets are items which are not financial assets and not shares (s 417(5)(6)).

2.148 Dividends payable on preference shares treated as a liability under IAS 32 are included: s 411(1)(d). Exchange losses and impairment losses on loan relationships are excluded: s 411(1)(e), as are losses arising on derivative contracts in the ordinary course of the trade other than a financial trade: s 411(1)(e)(iii). Derivative contracts are *'relevant derivative contracts'* if the USM is interest, currency, a financial index or an asset or liability representing a loan relationship: s 412.

2.149 *Relevant income amounts* are defined in s 411(2) as the mirror image of *relevant expense amounts.*

2.150 The *adjusted net group-interest expense* (ANGIE) is defined in s 413. ANGIE is (A + B – C), where

A = net group-interest expense (NGIE)

B = upward adjustments and

C = downward adjustments (s 413(1)).

NGIE is adjusted to align with UK tax rules (eg, excluding dividends on preference shares treated as a liability, which for UK purposes are distributions, not loan relationship debits). ANGIE seeks to make NGIE track

2.151 *Corporate Interest Restriction (CIR)*

UK corporation tax rules. In computing ANGIE (and also *group-EBITDA*) it is necessary to exclude items such as dividends on preference shares

2.151 ANGIE enters into the calculation of both the *fixed rate debt cap* and the *group ratio percentage*. It is the fallback limit for the interest restriction applying the fixed ratio rule, and the starting point for calculating the group ratio percentage.

2.152 Under TIOPA 2010, s 413(3), *upward adjustments* are:

- depreciation: s 413(3)(a);
- debt releases falling within CTA 2009, s 322(2) (debt-equity swaps etc, debt restructurings falling within s 323A): (s 413(3)(d));
- capitalised interest; and
- expenses recognised in equity in accordance with CTA 2009, s 320B (hybrid capital instruments).

2.153 Under TIOPA 2010, s 413(4), *downward adjustments* include:

- the release of liabilities in an insolvency situation or where the creditor is connected with the borrower (s 413(4)(d));
- credits not brought into account following insolvency or impairment of connected company loan relationships (s 413(4)(d));
- income recognised in equity in accordance with CTA 2009, s 320B; and
- dividends on mandatorily redeemable preference shares (s 413(4)(e)).

2.154 Payments related to pension schemes are excluded from both expense and income amounts: TIOPA 2010, s 411(3)(4).

2.155 The excess debt cap for the immediately preceding period of account depends upon whether the fixed ratio or the group ratio rule applied for that period. Where the fixed ratio rule applied in the immediately preceding period, s 400(3) defines *excess debt cap* as the excess of *fixed rate debt cap* for the preceding period over *30% of the aggregate tax-EBITDA of the group for the preceding period:*

> '(3) Where no group ratio election is in force in relation to a period of account of a worldwide group ("the generating period") "the excess debt cap" of the group that is generated in the period is (subject to subsections (5) and (6) is
>
> A – B

Where –

A is the fixed ratio debt cap of the group for the accounting period; and

B is 30% of the aggregate tax-EBITDA of the group for the generating period.'

2.156 Accordingly, where the group ratio rule applied in the immediately preceding period of account (but the fixed ratio rule applies in the current period of account) the *excess debt cap* generated in the preceding period of account is the excess of the *group ratio debt cap* for that period over the *basic interest allowance* for that period (ie, 30% of *aggregate tax-EBITDA* is less than ANTIE). The amount of the excess debt cap is the difference between the two amounts. If 30% of *aggregate tax-EBITDA* is greater than ANTIE, the excess debt cap is nil.

2.157 Excess debt cap carried forward increases the fixed rate debt cap or group ratio debt cap in subsequent periods. However, the amount of the increase is limited to the excess debt cap in the immediately preceding accounting period, plus the interest disallowance for the generating period. These provisions mean that the practical importance of the fall-back limit is limited because, save in unusual circumstances, the basic interest allowance will be less than the fixed rate debt cap or group ratio debt, and the basic interest allowance will therefore be the limiting factor for tax deduction purposes.

Section P: Rule 7

2.158 Rule 7 states:

7. If the group ratio rule is applied, the basic interest allowance is the lower of (i) the amount of the aggregate net tax-interest expense (ANTIE) of the UK group which is given by the *group ratio percentage*, and (ii) *the group ratio debt cap*.

2.159 The '*basic interest allowance calculated using the group ratio method*' (s 396(2)(b)) is defined in s 398 as the '*group ratio percentage of the aggregate tax-EBITDA of the group*':

'(1) For the purposes of section 396, the basic interest allowance of a worldwide group for a period of account of the group, using the group ratio method, is the lower of the following amounts –

(a) the group ratio percentage of the aggregate tax-EBITDA of the group for the period;

(b) the group ratio debt cap for the period.'

2.160 *Corporate Interest Restriction (CIR)*

2.160 Section 398 accordingly introduces a new concept, namely, the '*group ratio percentage*'. This is explained in s 399, which introduces two further concepts, namely:

- qualifying net-group interest expense of the group; and
- group-EBITDA of the group.

2.161 Section 399 defines the *group ratio percentage:*

'(1) ... "the group ratio percentage" of a worldwide group for a period of account of the group is ... the following proportion expressed as a percentage –

A/B

Where –

A is the qualifying net-group interest expense of the group for the period;

B is the group-EBITDA of the group for the period.'

2.162 Accordingly, both the fixed ratio and the group ratio deduction percentages are applied to the same amount, namely, the ANTIE of the UK group for the period. The group ratio percentage for an accounting period is:

$$\frac{QNGIE}{Group\text{-}EBITDA} \times 100$$

The group ratio percentage is 100% if the result is negative or above 100%, or if group-EBITDA is zero (TIOPA, s 398(1))

2.163 The OECD suggested a corridor of 10%–30% for the fixed ratio rule. The UK chose to come in at the maximum level. On the face of it this looks generous to groups. The effect, if not the purpose, is that the group ratio will rarely give a more beneficial result than the fixed rate ratio. One suspects that an additional policy reason was to push the pesky foreigners out by the back door, having admitted them through the front door (§2.114).

2.164 Though in many cases the group ratio rule will be of academic rather than practical interest, groups will still have to make the comparison between the application of the two different rules, so adding to the already considerable additional compliance burdens.

2.165 Accordingly,

- the *net group-interest expense* (NGIE) is derived from the consolidated accounts of the WWG by taking *relevant expense amounts* and deducting *relevant income amounts*;

- the NGIE is adjusted to give the *net group-interest expense* (ANGIE) (ss 410–414): see above at 2.150. The adjustment takes the form of adding *upward adjustments* and subtracting *downward adjustments*; and
- the *adjusted net group-interest expense* is then further adjusted to give the *qualifying net group-interest expense of the group* (QNGIE). The adjustment takes the form of subtracting *downward adjustments*.

Section Q: Rule 8

2.166 Rule 8 states:

8. The qualifying net group-interest expense (QNGIE) is the adjusted net group-interest expense (ANGIE) minus downward adjustments.

QNGIE is the numerator in calculating the *group ratio percentage*. It is also used to calculate the *group ratio debt cap*. QNGIE is largely concerned with the related party rules. The purpose of the related party rules is to limit the ability of a party which is related to members of the WWG but not itself a member to use loans and other instruments in place of equity to increase the interest capacity of the group through the group ratio method or public infrastructure rules. It does this by excluding from QNGIE finance expenses paid to related parties.

2.167 ANGIE is converted into QNGIE. QNGIE differs from ANGIE in excluding related party debt costs, even if they are at arm's length. Accordingly, related party debt costs cannot increase the group ratio or the group ratio debt cap. In many cases, this will make the group ratio election of no benefit, as is intended. This may, in turn, mean that a UK group will not obtain a tax deduction for the full cost of external third-party interest expense.

2.168 This is effected by TIOPA 2010, ss 414, 415. Section 414(1) states that QNGIE is A – B, where

A = ANGIE

B = downward adjustments.

2.169 As compared with ANGIE, QNGIE deducts as '*downward adjustments*' related company finance costs paid to 'related parties' (which will include interest paid by a UK company to non-UK related companies) and income payments made on equity-type securities. Expenditure is only disregarded if it passes through the income statement.

2.170 The most important downward adjustment is the payment of interest to *related parties*. Accordingly, under TIOPA 2010, s 414(3), QNGIE is based

2.171 *Corporate Interest Restriction (CIR)*

on ANGIE but excludes some expense amounts that are taken into account in computing ANGIE, mainly amounts payable in respect of:

- financial liabilities owed to a person who, at any time during the period, is a related party of a member of the group;
- results-based financial instruments (special securities) (ss 414(3)(b), 415(4)–(6), (8)); and
- perpetuals and long-dated financial instruments (equity notes).

2.171 QNGIE is ANGIE *minus* expenses relating to transactions with related parties, result-dependent securities and equity notes. This gives rise to three possibilities:

(i) The WWG has no related party funding: ANGIE = QNGIE.

(ii) The WWG has related party funding: ANGIE > QNGIE.

(iii) The WWG is wholly equity funded: ANGIE = QNGIE = 0.

2.172 Thus, leverage based on third-party, lending as opposed to related party lending will give a higher group ratio percentage, whereas related party lending gives a lower group ratio percentage. This is central to the working of the group ratio percentage.

2.173 So s 414(3)(4) states:

'(3) In this section "downward adjustment" means a relevant expense amount that meets the condition in subsection (4), so far as it relates to –

(a) a transaction with, or a financial liability owed to, a person who at any time during the period, is a related party or a member of the group,

(b) results-dependent securities, or

(c) equity notes.

(4) The condition mentioned in subsection (3) is that the amount –

(a) is recognised in the financial statements of the group for the period, as an item of profit and loss, and is not (and is not comprised in) a downward adjustment for the purposes of section 413 (adjusted net-group interest expense), or

(b) is (or is comprised in) an upward adjustment for the purposes of that section.'

2.174 The question is, therefore, what is a *'related party'*? Related parties are defined in TIOPA 2010, ss 462–465. Related parties are:

(1) consolidated entities applying Companies Act test in CA 2006, s 399 ('consolidation condition') (§§2.96–100);

(2) an entity participating in management, control or capital of the other, as defined by the transfer pricing rules on any day ('participation condition'); or

(3) an entity which has a 25% investment in the other on any day; or

(4) a third party which has a 25% investment in both entities on any day ('investment condition').

2.175 The 25% shareholding test is met if P holds (i) 25% of voting shares in C, or (ii) is entitled to 25% of the profits of C, or (iii) is entitled to 25% of the assets of C (s 464). Section 465 provides that in each case to which s 464 applies (25% investment) it is necessary to amalgamate the interests of connected persons and partners to apply the 25% test. 'Connected persons' are defined using the definition in CTA 2010, s 1122. The participation test is defined in the same terms as parties are related for transfer pricing: TIOPA 2010, ss 157–160. There is a special rule for securitisation companies.

Accordingly, P is credited with all the rights and interests of (s 465(1)):

- any person connected with P; and

- any person who is a member of a partnership or is connected with a member of a partnership to which P belongs or of which a person connected with P is a member.

So, if C is related to D, and C lends money to D, interest paid by D to C is disregarded in the computation of QNGIE and thus reduces the group ratio percentage.

2.176 Sections 466 and 467 go on to deem three categories of liabilities to be related party loans where they would not otherwise be related party loans, namely:

(i) a third-party loan guaranteed by a related party;

(ii) where a third party is indirectly a creditor (eg, C deposits funds with P who lends them to D, and C and D are related); and

(iii) shareholders make loans pro rata related to their shareholdings.

2.177 *Corporate Interest Restriction (CIR)*

2.177 There are also five categories of liabilities deemed not to be related party loans where they would otherwise be related party loans, namely (s 468):

(i) loans where more than 50% are held by unrelated parties;

(ii) loans arising on a corporate rescue (eg, a debt-equity swap);

(iii) ordinary independent financing arrangements by banks and others (eg, shareholders who are related parties take up part of a syndicated debt issue on the same terms as third-party lenders);

(iv) loans by relevant public bodies; and

(v) finance leases granted before 1 April 2017.

2.178 A debt will not be related party debt if it was

- entered into before 1 April 2017;
- provided by another member of the group;
- simply pledges share or loans in a group; and
- is a performance guarantee.

2.179 There are extensive attribution rules and deeming rules which extend and vary the scope of the related party rules, and have the effect of disregarding interest on shareholder debt in calculating QNGIE, thus decreasing the group ratio percentage (QNGIE being the numerator of the fraction). P is taken to have all the rights and interests of a third person (T) if P and T act together in relation to a third person (U) for the purpose of influencing the conduct of U's affairs (s 465(3)–(5)).

Example

The structure is:

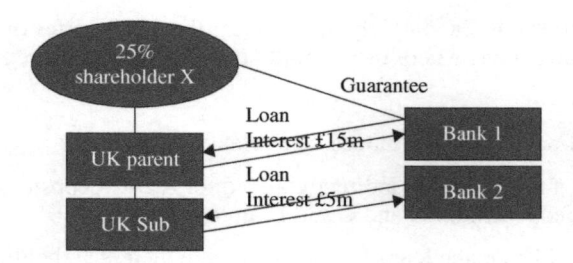

Shareholder X is a related party of UK parent (s 463(1)(c), 464(1)). The effect of the shareholder guarantee of Bank Loan 1 is to make the GRR inapplicable.

		No shareholder guarantee of Bank 1 loan	Shareholder guarantee of Bank 1 loan
		£m	£m
FRR	ANTIE	**20**	20
	Aggregate net-tax EBITDA	50	50
	FRR 30%	15	15
	Excess debt cap	0	0
	Fixed rate debt cap, 20+0 (ANTIE = ANGIE)	20	20
	Disallowance 15 – 20 =	(5)	(5)
GRR	QNGIE	20	20 – 15 = 5
	Group EBITDA	50	50
	Group ratio % QNGIE/Group-EBITDA	40%	10%
	Group ratio percentage	20	5
	Excess debt cap	0	0
	Group ratio debt cap	20	15
	Disallowance	0	15

Section R: Rule 9

2.180 Rule 9 states:

9. The group ratio percentage is derived from the ratio of the qualifying net group-interest expense (QNGIE) to the group-EBITDA of the group for the period.

2.181 Having fixed QNGIE, it only remains to find the *group-EBITDA of the group for the period*. This is defined in s 416 as the group's pre-tax profit for the period, without allowing for finance costs or depreciation. The group's pre-tax profit is increased by net group-interest expense and adjustments for depreciation and amortisation.

2.182 The *group ratio percentage* is calculated by dividing the group's *'qualifying net group-interest expense'* (QNGIE) by its *'group-EBITDA'* for the period. This percentage is capped at 100%.

2.183 *Group-EBITDA* is calculated by reference to amounts recognised in the group's consolidated finance statements, in accordance with s 416. It is the overall profit of the WWG before tax as reported in its financial statements,

2.184 *Corporate Interest Restriction (CIR)*

before taking account of interest and interest-like amounts and relief for capital expenditure.

2.184 *Group-EBITDA* is defined as PBT + I + DA (TIOPA ss 415–43) where:

PBT = pre-tax profit

I = *net group-interest expense* (NGIE)

DA = depreciation and amortisation adjustment

2.185 Under s 416(5), for tax purposes, detailed adjustments must be made to the pre-tax profit. The *depreciation and amortisation adjustment* is the sum of

- the capital (expenditure) adjustment;
- the capital (fair value movement) adjustment; and
- the capital (disposals) adjustment).

2.186 The capital (expenditure) adjustment adds back to profits amounts which have passed through the income statement in respect of *relevant assets* (s 417). If an asset is a relevant asset within s 417(5), no amount is included in NGIE for write off. Relevant assets comprise

- plant, property and equipment (PPE);
- investment property;
- intangible assets;
- goodwill;
- shares; and
- equity-return investments.

2.187 The capital (fair value movement) adjustment eliminates from profit fair value movements on capital assets which have passed through the income statement (s 418).

2.188 The capital (disposals) adjustment eliminates capital gains on the disposal of assets and instead brings into profits gains (but not losses) to the extent that the disposal proceeds exceed the costs (s 419).

2.189 Under TIOPA 2010, s 422 (Group-EBITDA (chargeable gains) election) the reporting company can make an irrevocable election for the capital gain to be determined in accordance with TCGA 1992, s 422(7) but subject to a number of modifications (Sch 7A, para 15). HMRC have the power to substitute a different attribution: Sch 7A, para 54.

2.190 A UK member of the WWG can make an irrevocable election that for the purpose of computing its tax-EBITDA for the purposes of TIOPA 2010, s 406 these regulations should be taken to apply (so that the profits of the company on its derivative contracts would not be included in profits for the purposes of CTA 2009, s 597(1)).

Example

	£m
Pre-tax profits	50
NGIE	15
Depreciation	10
Profit on sale of fixed asset	(5)
Revaluation loss	3
Fair value gains on DCs	4
Group-EBITDA	77

Section S: Rule 10

2.191 Rule 10 states:

> The *group ratio debt cap* is (i) *qualifying net group-interest expense* (QNGIE) plus (ii) the *excess debt cap*.

This is set out in ss 398(2) and 400(2)(4). As in the case of the FRR, this is a simple arithmetic calculation. The underlying concepts have been explained in relation to Rules 6 and 8. Where a group ratio election was in force in the preceding accounting period (generating period), the group ratio debt cap for that period, less the group ratio percentage of the aggregate tax-EBITDA for that period, gives the excess debt cap.

Section T: Rule 11

2.192 Rule 11 states:

> The *interest allowance* is the *basic interest allowance* plus any aggregate net tax-interest income (ANTII). The *interest capacity*

2.193 *Corporate Interest Restriction (CIR)*

of the UK group is the *interest allowance* + unused and unexpired interest allowance carried forward to the period of account.

2.193 The FRR or GRR gives the *basic interest allowance* for an accounting period. To this is added any *aggregate net tax-interest income (ANTII)*, to give the *interest allowance*. This can then be increased by the addition of any unused interest allowance carried forward from earlier accounting periods.

Section U: Rule 12

2.194 Rule 12 states:

If interest capacity < ANTIE the difference gives rise to interest disallowance. If interest capacity > ANTIE the difference is the interest reactivation cap. Disallowed tax-interest expense, unused interest capacity and excess debt cap can be carried forward at the individual company or group level.

2.195 There are three kinds of carry forward. *First*, the carry forward and reactivation of disallowed interest. The disallowed interest can only be carried forward and reactivated within a UK company indefinitely to be available for reactivation as a deduction in a later period in which there is sufficient interest capacity to accommodate the reactivation claim. Since it is a company attribute, it is retained if the company changes groups.

2.196 Under ss 380 and 381, reactivation applies where:

(i) for an accounting period a group's interest allowance exceeds the ANTIE;

(ii) at least one company in the group is UK resident;

(iii) at least one UK resident company has carried-forward disallowed interest which is available for reactivation;

(iv) a full interest restriction return (IRR) under TIOPA 2010, Sch 7A, para 20(3) is submitted for that period;

(v) that return includes the statement that the group is subject to a reactivation claim and allocates part of the reactivation claim to company making the claim;

(vi) in the subsequent accounting period the trade of the company (if trading) is not 'uncommercial and non-statutory'; and

(vii) in the subsequent accounting the investment business of the company (if carrying on investment business) company has not become small or negligible.

2.197 The reactivation of carried forward interest expense is forbidden in the absence of a reporting company.

2.198 The *second* is carry forward of unused interest allowance. If interest capacity > ANTIE the difference is the *interest reactivation cap* (TIOPA 2010, s 373(3)). The excess capacity can be carried forward at company level for up to five years. Unused interest capacity cannot be carried forward if an abbreviated allocation interest return is submitted. Where amounts are carried forward, amounts for earlier periods are used before those from later periods. This is a group attribute and is lost if the ultimate parent changes.

2.199 The *third* is carry forward of excess debt cap (s 400(3)(4)). Excess debt cap arises where:

- ANGIE > basic interest allowance (FRR).
- QNGIE > basic interest allowance (GRR).

It is carried forward into the next accounting period and increases the fixed ratio debt cap or group ratio debt cap applicable in that period. It is not possible to carry forward excess debt cap for the preceding period where there is a change of ownership of the ultimate holding company, except where a new holding company is inserted between ultimate holding company and its shareholders (TIOPA, s 400A).

2.200 Since disallowed interest, unused interest allowance and excess debt cap are each carried forward, and used to calculate any interest disallowance, groups and group members need to monitor and record these figures to make sure that they are available when the interest restriction has to be calculated and allocated.

2.201 Where a disallowed interest-expense amounts is reactivated, the normal order of allocation is against:

- NTLRDs;
- non-trading debits on derivative contracts;
- trading loan relationship debits;
- trading derivative contracts debits; and
- implicit finance costs in finance leases, debt factoring and service concession arrangements.

2.202 *Corporate Interest Restriction (CIR)*

Section V: Rule 13

2.202 Rule 13 states:

The allocation of disallowance is made within the UK group to group members whether by an appointed reporting company's discretionary allocation or on a pro rata basis in the cost of no reporting company.

2.203 A group is required to appoint a UK member to be group reporting company for the purposes of CIR: TIOPA 2010, Sch 7A, para 1. In practice this is likely to be the same company which acts as reporting company for the notification and allocation for relief within the group of carried-forward losses. A UK company which is a member of a WWG must file an interest restriction return (IRR). In accordance with the scheme of corporation tax self-assessment (CTSA), the CIR is a self-reporting system, which requires companies to give notice of chargeability to CIR. The relevant legislation is in TIOPA 2010, ss 373–377 and Sch 7A. The general obligation is in FA 1998, Sch 18, para 2(1). The amount disallowed is the disallowed tax-interest expense amount (TIEA). The amount of the disallowance is either the allocated disallowance (where a reporting company files a valid IRR in respect of a consenting company)(s 375) or in other cases a *'pro-rata share' of the total disallowed amount* (TIOPA 2010, s 376, Sch 7A, para 24).

2.204 Companies in a group will be managed as a single economic unit, while allowing a measure of autonomy to entities within the group. The CIR differs fundamentally from general company taxation in being based on the UK group rather than individual companies. In this respect it has important commonalities with carried-forward loss relief (Chapter 3). The expectation is that in most cases UK members of a WWG will appoint one of their number as a 'reporting company', which will be responsible for the operation of the CIR. Such companies are 'consenting companies': 50% of the members of the UK group need to consent to the appointment, and must inform HMRC of their consent (TIOPA 2010, Sch 7A, paras 1, 10(1)–(3)).

2.205 A company is a 'consenting company' if, before the IRR is submitted, it notifies the reporting company and HMRC that it agrees to apply the interest disallowance in accordance with the allocation of the reporting company (TIOPA 2010, Sch 7A, paras 10 and 11).

2.206 The reporting company should normally be appointed within six months of the group's year end. If a group fails to appoint a reporting company, HMRC may appoint one, other than a dormant company: TIOPA 2010, Sch 7A, para 4. Groups with a first CIR period of account ending on or before 30 September 2017 were required to appoint a reporting company by 31 March 2018 and 50% of non-dormant group companies within the charge to UK corporation tax must agree to the appointment. Group companies who do not consent to the appointment are 'non-consenting companies'.

2.207 Instead of adapting the existing CTSA system set out in TMA 1970 and FA 1998, Sch 18, the CIR establishes a parallel, separate system of administration and compliance, which shadows the standard system. A separate system is instituted on the grounds that:

(i) the CIR is concerned with UK groups, not with companies as separate entities, and involves a group reporting system quite distinct from the ordinary CTSA system; and

(ii) the great majority of companies will be unaffected by the CIR.

However, the logic behind this is not overwhelming:

(i) groups invariably operate through a group tax and finance department, as that is the economic reality of a group and achieves self-evident efficiencies. Groups will move in and out of the CIR from accounting period to accounting period;

(ii) many more groups will have to investigate whether they fall within the CIR than actually do so;

(iii) the standard reporting system in any case already has important group aspects, e.g. group relief, carried-forward loss relief; and

(iv) groups will also have to take into account the CIR in calculating their quarterly corporation tax payments.

2.208 The primary responsibility of the reporting company system is to prepare and submit the Interest Restriction Returns (IRR) prepared by the reporting company (TIOPA 2010, s 374, Sch 7A, para 7(2)). This must be filed within 12 months of the end of the accounting period to which it relates, but an amended return can be filed within 36 months of the end of the accounting period (para 8). This acknowledges the potential scope and complexity of the IRR.

2.209 There are three main components of the IRR:

(i) it is the only means of exercising a series of important elections;

(ii) it contains detailed calculations of the interest disallowance; and

(iii) it allocates the total interest disallowance for the accounting period amongst the consenting companies.

2.210 *Corporate Interest Restriction (CIR)*

2.210 A series of important elections must be made in and through the IRR. The details of these elections are set out in Sch 7A, paras 12–19. Other elections have to be made in the company's CTSA return (para 68). See Rule 15.

2.211 The IRR must include 'the detailed statement of calculation, and an explanation of how this restriction has been allocated between the UK companies and how any carry forward interest or capacity is allocated (paras 20–26). The IRR must include:

- a statement of calculations (para 21);
- a statement of allocated interest restrictions (para 22); and
- a statement of allocated interest reactivations (para 26).

The IRR must contain a detailed calculation of interest restrictions (paras 20, 21). The return must then allocate the total disallowance amongst the consenting companies ('allocated disallowances') and provide details of unused allowances and interest reactivations. The IRR will both show the aggregate income restriction and then allocate it amongst the members of the WWG. The reporting company must allocate both the £2m *de minimis* amount and the deductions amongst group companies. The IRR quantifies the group CIR and allocates it amongst the members to which the IRR relates.

2.212 The reporting company has complete discretion as to:

(i) how to allocate the restriction amongst the consenting UK companies; and

(ii) against what tax interest expenses the disallowance should be allocated.

As regards (i), disallowance will be allocated to non-consenting companies included in the return on a pro rata basis ('pro-rata share', para 23(2)). This will correspondingly reduce the disallowance allocated to the consenting companies. As regards (ii), this needs to be done so as to maximise carry-forward loss reliefs which operate outside the CIR. For example, it may be beneficial to allocate the restriction to a company which would otherwise generate a loss, because the loss-carry forward may itself be subject to restrictions.

2.213 Under s 375(2), if the reporting company of a WWG submits an IRR under TIOPA 2010, Sch 7A, companies mentioned in the return must disallow the tax-interest expense allocated to them in the return:

> '(2) A company that is listed on the statement under paragraph 22 of Schedule 7A (statement of allocated interest restrictions) must, in any accounting period for which the statement specified an allocated disallowance, leave out of account tax-interest expense amounts that, in total, equal that allocated disallowance.'

Corporate Interest Restriction (CIR) **2.218**

2.214 IRRs may be full IRRs or abbreviated IRRs. A group which will exceed the £2m limit appoints a reporting company which files a full IRR. Otherwise an abbreviated IRR may be submitted. If a company can conclude that that a restriction is highly unlikely based on reasonable estimates of 'aggregate tax-interest expense', 'aggregate tax-EBITDA' and 'adjusted net group-interest expense, it does not have to perform a full CIR calculation.

2.215 Special provision has to be made for 'non-consenting companies' or cases where the reporting company is regarded by HMRC as unsuitable. In such cases HMRC may appoint a reporting company (Sch 7A, para 4(2)). That company then comes under a duty to file and IRR. Paragraph 24 allocates the disallowance amongst the relevant companies on a pro rata basis. Where a company has to disallow, but no reporting company has been appointed or the reporting company has not filed a return, the order of disallowance is in respect of:

(i)   non-trading loan relationship debits;

(ii) non-trading derivative contract debits;

(iii) debits on trading loan relationships;

(iv) debits on trading derivative contracts; and

(v)   debits on finance leases.

2.216 HMRC has power to make determinations of liability to CIR where no reporting company has been appointed or no IRR has been filed or a non-compliant return has been submitted (para 56). HMRC has extensive information powers in relation to the CIR (paras 60–65). The provisions of FA 2008, Sch 36 (information powers) are imported into TIOPA 2010, Sch 7A (para 66).

2.217 Penalties are imposed for non-submission of an IRR or for inaccuracies (paras 29–37). These parallel but are separate from the general penalty provisions and procedures in FA 2007, Sch 24. A notice of enquiry may be given in relation to an IRR, the general time limit being 39 months from the end of the accounting period to which the return relates (paras 40–44). An enquiry is brought to an end by a closure notice (para 49). If the closure notice requires the company to take steps to give effect to the conclusions stated in the notice (para 49(2)(b)), the company may appeal against the notice within 30 days from date of the receipt of the notice (para 52).

2.218 The CIR adds a significant dimension to group restructurings, where any of the following changes are under consideration:

- replacing equity with debt;

2.219 *Corporate Interest Restriction (CIR)*

- replacing debt with equity;
- transferring UK debt abroad;
- refinancing shareholder debt with third-party debt; and
- establishing and reviewing transfer pricing methodology.

Section W: Rule 14

2.219 Rule 14 states:

There are special rules for particular businesses and business structures.

2.220 There are special rules for a number of sectors, mostly businesses that naturally have high levels of debt as part of their business. These comprise, in the main, joint venture companies and public infrastructure companies.

Joint ventures

2.221 The CIR is constructed round consolidation. The problem with consolidation is always, what to bring in and what to leave outside the consolidation. Interests in joint ventures and associates will not be consolidated on a line-by-line basis in the group's financial statements. Interest and other finance costs incurred by non-group entities will not be included in group interest or in EBITDA.

2.222 In the case of highly leveraged joint ventures, the absence of consolidation is likely to depress the group percentage ratio. The *interest allowance (non-consolidated investment) election* (TIOPA 2010, ss 427–429) enables a group to include non-consolidated entities in its financial results for CIR, to boost QNGIE and group-EBITDA. The 'principal worldwide group' is treated as consolidated with the 'associated worldwide group' for CIR purposes. An associated WWG is a WWG of which a non-consolidated associate is the ultimate parent.

2.223 Where the election is made line by line consolidation will for CIR purposes be substituted for the equity method, so

- disregarding income and expense amounts payable between the principal WWG and the associated WWG;
- including in ANTIE the interest amounts relating to financial liabilities of the associated WWG;

- increasing QNGIE by reference to obligations to the associated WWG; and

- increasing group-EBITDA by including the results of the associated WWG.

By contrast, the *interest (consolidated partnerships) election* (s 430) allows deconsolidation of investments in partnerships. The reporting company of a WWG can make an irrevocable election to exclude income and expenses of a specified partnership from the group results, so that the partnership is not consolidated on a line-by-line basis. Instead, the partnership will be accounted for using the equity method (ie, recognise at acquisition cost and adjust carrying value to reflect participation in profits and losses). This election is not possible if the partnership has a subsidiary which is a company: s 430(6).

2.224 The *group ratio (blended) election* (ss 401–404) enables a JV group to combine the group ratios of its related party investors to establish its own group ratio for CIR purposes (Blended Group Ratio). The group ratio percentage is then calculated on the basis of a weighted average of the applicable percentages. An entity will be regarded as an investor if it has an interest in the ultimate entitling it to a share of profits and losses of the group.

Qualifying infrastructure companies (QIC)

2.225 The public infrastructure regime is designed to cater for situations where a public authority does not itself acquire the assets it requires for its functions, but procures them from private providers, whose business consists in providing such facilities on a long-term basis. Such providers will obtain long-term finance. The recourse of the lenders will be limited to the income and assets of the provider, other than the assets used for public functions. This model was developed in detail through the private finance initiative (PFI): 10th edition, paras 8.71–8.76.

Example

2.226 *Corporate Interest Restriction (CIR)*

If the bank is not repaid its lending, the hospital is not at risk of any disruption of its activities, and the recourse of the connected lender is limited to the assets of the provider other than its public infrastructure assets.

2.226 The *public infrastructure election* allows companies which provide qualifying public infrastructure or short-term letting of property to elect into the special public infrastructure regime. This applies for real-estate business which is a qualifying infrastructure company (QIC). If most of the company's assets and activities arise from qualifying activities and these are specified in the group's balance sheet, have a minimum 10-year economic span and are wholly taxable in the UK, a company may make a public infrastructure election (PIE): ss 432–449.

2.227 Under TIOPA 2010, s 433, a company must meet four conditions to be a Qualifying Infrastructure Company (QIS):

(i) the bulk of its profits must derive from qualifying infrastructure activity (public infrastructure income test);

(ii) its assets must substantially comprise public infrastructure assets;

(iii) it must be fully taxed in the UK; and

(iv) it must have made a valid PIE election before the end of the accounting period in which it is to take effect.

Under TIOPA 2010, s 433(5), public infrastructure assets include:

- tangible assets (buildings, land, structures) which meet the public benefit test, have an expected economic life of at least 10 years and meet the group balance sheet test;
- a service concession arrangement in respect of such assets;
- shares in or loans to QICs or loans financing public infrastructure activities; and
- pension scheme assets for the benefit of individuals carrying on public infrastructure activities.

To meet the public benefit test, an asset must be procured by a relevant public body or used for a regulated activity. To meet the group balance sheet test, the asset must be recognised in the balance sheet of a group company. Where a company is a member of a partnership, the asset must be recognised as a partnership asset and the company must have a significant interest in the partnership.

2.228 *Qualifying infrastructure* (TIOPA 2010, s 436) means the provision of a public infrastructure asset, and the carrying on of an activity which is ancillary to or facilitates the provision of the asset. The asset must meet the 'public benefit test', which requires that the asset should be procured by a relevant public body and be used in a regulated activity. The asset must have a useful economic life of ten years. Examples are:

- hospitals;
- offshore wind farms;
- waste-processing facilities;
- buildings occupied by relevant public bodies; and
- court or prison buildings.

Infrastructure authorities are listed in TIOPA 2010, s 437(2)

2.229 Under TIOPA 2010, s 436(5), a building or part of a building may be a public infrastructure asset of a company if the company or another company in the WWG carries on a UK property business which

- is let on a short-term basis to unrelated parties;
- has, or is likely to have, an expected economic life of at least 10 years; and
- the building meets the group balance sheet test.

2.230 Where a QIC so elects, interest and other expense amounts payable to unrelated parties are not treated as interest expense amounts, provided that lending is limited recourse. This status allows debt expenses on limited recourse loans (and grandfathered related party debt) to be excluded from the ANTIE, as well as ANGIE/QNGIE, and to be excluded from the disallowance under the CIR rules (TIOPA 2010, s 438). In that case, the tax-interest income and tax-EBITDA of the QIC will be nil in the accounting period in which the QIC is eligible: TIOPA 2010, ss 440–442. The group-EBITDA is calculated as if the group did not include the PIC: TIOPA 2010, s 442(3). The WWG comprising the QIC cannot benefit from the £2m *de minimis* (s 443). The public infrastructure election only applies to non-related party debt (other than grandfathered debt).

2.231 Under TIOPA 2010, s 438(4), the recourse of a creditor in the event of non-performance by the QIC of its obligations must be restricted to:

- income of the QIC;
- assets of the QIC; and
- shares in or debt issued by a QIC.

2.232 *Corporate Interest Restriction (CIR)*

Guarantees are ignored if they are provided before 1 April 2017, provided at a later time by an unrelated party or a relevant public body, or before 29 October 2018 by a non-UK company within the charge to corporation tax on its property business profits: s 438(5),(5A),(6).

Example

A WWG contains a UK QIC.

		No public infrastructure election	Public infrastructure election
		£m	£m
FRR	ANTIE	100	60
	EBITDA	300	200
	30% EBITDA/Basic interest allowance	90	60
	Disallowance	(10)	(0)
GRR	QNGIE	120	80
	Group-EBITDA	350	250
	Group ratio %	34	32
	Basic interest allowance: EBITDA x Group ratio %	102	64
	Interest reactivation	2	4

Banks and insurance

2.232 Third-party interest is the main source of income of a banking and insurance business. The definition of tax-interest is modified (TIOPA 2010, ss 382, 384, 450). Impairment losses and reversals are excluded in the calculation of NTII and ANTIE. Banks and insurance companies are unlikely to be affected by CIR and will normally file an abbreviated return. For banking companies there is an extended definition of 'tax-interest expense amount'. Insurance companies can elect to account for investments on an amortised cost basis, rather than a fair value basis. Further, certain consolidated investments held as portfolio investments are deconsolidated (TIOPA 2010, ss 453, 456). Companies that are members of Lloyd's are subject to the CIR.

Real Estate Investment Trusts

2.233 Real Estate Investment Trusts (REITS) within CTA 2010, s 534 are exempt from corporation tax, so their profits are ring-fenced from the other activities of the group: CTA 2010, ss 534, 541. The exempt business is classified as a 'property rental business', as distinct from the other activities of the group, 'the residual business company'. TIOPA 2010, s 452 provides that, for the purposes of the public infrastructure election, the two activities can be regarded as a single business.

RAAR

2.234 There is a regime known as the anti-avoidance rule (s 461). This is in the familiar form that any tax advantage that arises from the adoption of 'relevant avoidance arrangements' is to be counteracted. However, as the whole scheme and intent of the CIR is that it should be applied in an objective, mechanical fashion without reference to subjective intention, circumstances in which this rule will fall to be applied will be limited.

Section X: Rule 15

2.235 Rule 15 states:

> There are 15 different elections which a company can make to vary the application of the tax rules.

2.236 There are a wide range of significant elections which a group is able or required to make. All have their own detailed conditions. Some operate accounting period by accounting period, others are irrevocable. Several options can be exercised in conjunction with each other, or with other tax elections, to produce a combined effect. Most are made in the full or abbreviated interest restriction return.

2.237 The elections are set out below (A–O):

	Election	*Effect*	*TIOPA 2010*
A	Group ratio election	To opt for GRR in place of FRR	Sch 7A, paras 12(3)(a), 13. Election in IRR
B	Joint ventures: Group ratio (blended) election	To allow a WWG (JV group') to have as group ratio weighted average of investors' group rate profiles	ss 401–404; Sch 7A, paras 12(3)(b), 14 Election in IRR

2.237 *Corporate Interest Restriction (CIR)*

	Election	Effect	TIOPA 2010
C	Group-EBITDA (chargeable gains) election	Capital gains are calculated for group-EBITDA as if all the members of the group were within the charge to corporation tax on capital gains, the SSE did not apply and double taxation relief was not available	s 422; Sch 7A, paras 12(3)(c), 15. Irrevocable
D	Interest allowance (alternative calculation) election	Allows the group to align the calculations of amounts recognised in group accounts in respect of capitalised interest, employer pension contributions, employee share schemes and changes in accounting policy to the UK tax treatment. Capitalised interest become deductible as part of ANTIE	ss 423–426; Sch 7A, paras 12(3)(d), 16. Irrevocable
E	Interest allowance (non-consolidated investments) election	Allows proportionate consolidation of interests in non-consolidated entities, to avoid dilution of group-EBITDA	ss 427–429; Sch 7A, paras 12(3)(e), 17
F	Interest (consolidated partnerships) election	Allows deconsolidation of interests in consolidated partnerships to avoid dilution of QNGIE	s 430; Sch 7A, paras 12(3)(f), 17. Irrevocable
G	Abbreviated return election	To file abbreviated return rather than full IRR	Sch 7A, paras 12(3)(g), 19. Election in IRR.
H	Public infrastructure election	Allows a WWG which meets the 'public infrastructure test' (a QIC) to elect into the special public infrastructure regime. and have a minimum of 10 years economic span and is wholly taxable in the UK, a company may make a PIE election	ss 433, 434. Election must be made before the start of the relevant accounting period. Election may only be revoked after five years. May be made with CTA 2009, s 18A election (to exclude foreign permanent establishments)

84

Corporate Interest Restriction (CIR) **2.238**

	Election	*Effect*	*TIOPA 2010*
I	JV public infrastructure election	Allows a JV co which is a QICs to be treated as a single QIC with a JV Co which is not a QIC	ss 435, 444
J	Non-consenting company		s 375
K	Tax-interest expense amounts	Tax-interest expense amounts to be left out of account	s 377
L	Tax-interest expense amounts	Tax-interest expense amounts to be brought into account	s 380
M	Fair value creditor relationships	Interest-income and expenses on fair valued creditor relationships to be recognised on amortised cost basis.	ss 456, 457
N	Abbreviated return election	A reporting company may make an abbreviated return election. This is made in the IRR	Sch 7A, para 18
O	Derivative contracts election	Notional DR reg 6A election made	ss 420, 421

2.238 Under TIOPA 2010, s 422 (Group-EBITDA (chargeable gains) election) the reporting company can make an irrevocable election for the capital gain to be determined in accordance with TCGA 1992, but subject to a number of modifications: TIOPA 2010, Sch 7A, para 15. For the purposes of this election, all members of the WWG are assumed to be UK resident; the substantial shareholdings exemption does not apply; and there is a deemed disposal if a member of the group leaves. If the member leaves the group through a sale of shares, the reporting company must make a just and reasonable attribution of the gain between the shares and the relevant asset TIOPA 2010, s 422(7). HMRC have the power to substitute a different attribution: TIOPA 2010, Sch 7A, para 54.

Chapter 3

Loss Relief

Chapter Contents

Section	Topic	Paragraphs
A	History of the UK rules	3.1–3.17
B	Compliance costs	3.18–3.19
C	The legislation	3.20
D	Outline of the system	3.21–3.36
E	Carried on on a commercial basis	3.37–3.44
F	In-year and carry back loss relief	3.45–3.48
G	Current year group and consortium relief	3.49–3.67
H	Transitional accounting periods	3.68–3.75
I	Interaction with CIR	3.76–3.78
J	Current year losses	3.79–3.85
K	Flexible relief	3.86–3.89
L	Banks and insurance companies	3.90–3.96
M	Carried-forward losses, post-1 April 2017	3.97–3.99
N	Carried-forward losses post-1 April 2017 (single company/within RM)	3.100–3.114
O	Group relief for carried-forward losses	3.115–3.123
P	Definition of group	3.124–3.130
Q	Carried-forward losses available to be group relieved	3.131–3.144
R	The loss cap	3.145–3.150
S	The key concepts in the loss cap	3.151–3.172
T	Relevant profits	3.173–3.188
U	Relevant maximum	3.189–3.208
V	The cap on relievable carried-forward losses	3.209–3.210
W	Corporate capital loss restriction	3.211–3.222
X	Corporate acquisitions followed by transfer of trades and assets	3.223–3.242

Section A: History of the UK rules

3.1 All businesses make losses from time to time. If it were easy or guaranteed to make profits all the time, everyone would do it. Corporate tax systems seek to tax the profits of equity shareholders over the life of the business. This means relieving losses as well as taxing profits.

3.2 In this vein in *R v IRC, ex p Unilever plc* [1996] STC 681 at 690 Bingham MR observed:

> 'The taxpayer's entitlement to deduct trading losses from other profits in the same year ... gives effect to a very basic principle. A tax regime which did not give effect to such an entitlement could scarcely be regarded as equitable. A right of set-off against earlier or later accounting periods is less fundamental. But a tax on a corporation's profit which did not permit account to be taken of trading loss would be offensive to ordinary notions of fiscal fairness.'

The cautionary words here are *'a right of set-off against earlier or later accounting periods is less fundamental'*. However, if there are no other profits in the loss-making period, which will be the normal case, loss relief can only be given against the profits of earlier or later accounting periods. The UK introduced a significant restriction on carry-forward loss relief for larger companies and groups with effect from 1 April 2017, combined with a more limited extension of such loss relief. These restrictions are extended to capital losses with effect from accounting periods beginning on or after 1 April 2020.

3.3 In the UK there is no general tax on income. It is only charged in respect of particular types of income because the UK largely retains a schedular system of income taxation: CTA 2009, s 2. A schedular (analytic) system of income tax distinguishes different types of income (eg, interest, dividends, trading profits or rents). It also distinguishes between income and capital gains. The corollary of a schedular system of income tax is that losses are in general streamed (ie, a loss on a particular head of income can only be offset against income from the same source).

3.4 The schedular system introduced in 1806 had two purposes: (a) to prevent the Surveyor of Taxes from knowing what the total income of a taxpayer was; and (b) to ensure that the bulk of tax was collected by deduction at source by the payer. Only Schedule D Case I (trading profits and emoluments of private employments) was not collected by deduction at source because profits are a net figure (ie, income minus expenses). All other sources of income were taxable on a gross basis, without allowing for deductions.

3.5 Loss Relief

3.5 In the UK, each type of income was classified in a different schedule to the income tax legislation. A pure schedular system identifies separate types of income and applies different computational rules and rates of tax to each and allows no set off between different schedules.

3.6 The schedular system was abolished by the Tax Law Rewrite. However, different types of income are still distinguished and separate rules applied to each. The different types of business income are:

- trading profits;
- property income;
- loan relationships;
- derivative contracts;
- intangible fixed assets;
- company distributions;
- furnished lettings income; and
- miscellaneous income.

3.7 The most important category in the context of companies is trading income. However, the loss relief rules allow trading losses to be set against other types of income, departing from the schedular boundaries. This facility was significantly extended by changes to the carried-forward loss rules in 2017 by the introduction of flexible loss relief for all companies.

3.8 By contrast, a global (pure income or synthetic) system brings into charge both income of all types and unrealised capital accretions. Changes in the valuation of assets as income and expenditure are recorded as income and expenditure. In fair value accounting this is regarded as a profit or loss. Losses will be recognised on a current-year basis. That goes against the realisation principle (ie, that an action is needed before the financial position of a business is affected). A transaction requires a transaction with a third party. A transaction is not simply a valuation change.

3.9 In many cases current year trading losses will not be relievable in full against other profits or gains for the loss-making year or the accounting year preceding it, or by means of current year group relief. The surplus of unrelieved losses can only then be carried forward for set off against the profits of later accounting periods.

3.10 The ability to monetise losses is central to financial management. Losses available for immediate tax relief are more valuable than losses

Loss Relief **3.12**

available for future relief. Current year losses are available for relief in full, to the extent that there are profits or gains from which they may be deducted. Current year losses must be claimed before any question of loss carry forward arises. Losses not relievable in the current year, but which may be relieved in the future, become a deferred tax asset (DTA). If the rate of corporation tax is reduced in the future, or the likelihood of tax relief becomes remote, such assets must be written down.

3.11 Prior to 1 April 2017, trading losses could be carried forward without limit as to amount or time to set against future profits from the same trade (ie, streamed). The same principle applied to other types of loss, which were streamed and so could only be set against current year profits of the same description, with unrelieved losses carried forward to be set against future profits of the same income type: CTA 2009, s 458(1).

3.12 From 1 April 2017 three fundamental changes were introduced:

(i) Carry forward relief was made flexible, in that post-1 April 2017 losses which cannot be set against in-year reliefs can be carried-forward to be deducted from total profits for a subsequent accounting period, rather than income from a particular source ('flexible relief'). All companies great and small benefit from flexible relief. However, the advantages of flexible relief are significantly reduced with effect from 1 April 2020, after which carried forward income losses cannot be set against capital profits (ie, 'total profits' after that date no longer include capital gains for the purposes of carry-forward relief). It remains possible to set past losses of a particular type (usually trading) against income generally.

(ii) Carried-forward losses which qualify for flexible relief can be surrendered intra-group, so that group or consortium relief is available not only in respect of current year losses but also in respect of carried-forward losses ('group carried-forward relief').

(iii) A general restriction on the amount of all carried-forward income losses which can be set against current year profits was introduced, with the same numerical restriction applied to single companies and groups. This is the 'loss cap' or corporate income loss restriction (CILR). Like the corporate interest restriction (CIR), this is targeted at larger groups, partly for reasons of administrative practicality and convenience.

To these are added from 1 April 2020:

(iv) A general restriction on the amount of carried-forward capital losses which can be set against current year capital gains: the corporate capital loss restriction (CCLR).

3.13 Loss Relief

Thus, the same groups are likely to find themselves subject to CIR, CILR and CCLR. Apart from the significant additional tax cost, the compliance tasks for corporate tax departments are greatly increased.

3.13 The CILR applies alike to flexible relief losses (which can be set against total profits) and restricted relief losses (which can only be set against income from the same source). Each standalone company and group has an annual loss allowance of £5m (the 'deductions allowance' (DA)), and it is only when losses exceed this figure that the restriction applies. The restriction applies to 50% of 'relevant profits' (not, it must be emphasised, 'total profits'). This gives rise to each company of a 'relevant maximum' (RM). The RM is 50% of relevant profits plus the DA.

3.14 Because of the annual allowance of carry forward of losses without restriction up to £5m, the great majority of companies can benefit from flexible relief without suffering the restriction. This is both a simplification measure and a realistic recognition that losses on this scale will usually be fatal for smaller companies and groups. However, it is precisely in such a situation that a financially stronger corporation will acquire the loss-making company or group. Hence the legislation has also included a substantial revision of the rules on the use of acquired losses following change of ownership.

3.15 For larger enterprises, a £5m loss allowance goes nowhere. Larger groups can suffer losses running into billions (10^8) of pounds. It is also larger enterprises which are subject to the CIR. Thus, they suffer a double blow. Their taxable profits are increased and their tax losses are reduced by adding back part of their finance costs.

3.16 The increase in tax arising from the loss cap exceeds the decrease in tax arising from flexible relief. The Treasury prediction of increased tax revenues arising from the measure was £395m in 2017/2018, £415min 2018/2019 £295m in 2019/2020 and £255m in 2020/2021. These are lower than the additional revenues anticipated from the CIR. Additional tax revenue come from restricting pre-2015 bank losses to 25%. However, the net tax yield from the changes depends also on the rate of corporation tax. The higher the rate, the more valuable are losses in tax relief terms.

3.17 Moreover, these figures do not take into account the introduction of the corporate capital loss restriction (CCLR). The impact of the carried forward loss restriction is increased, and benefit of flexible relief reduced, by the introduction from 1 April 2020 of a CCLR. The CILR applies only to income losses. Flexible loss relief means that carried forward income losses can be set against in-year capital gains. However, the corporate income loss restriction is combined with the CCLR, with the £5m annual loss allowance being applied to both. Thus, the benefits of flexible relief, and the benefit of the DA will be significantly curtailed.

Loss Relief **3.19**

Section B: Compliance costs

3.18 Increased corporation tax revenues, and flexible loss relief, are only part of the story. Compliance costs are significantly increased for all companies because of the complexity of allowing carry forward relief in groups, and the need to determine whether the £5m loss cap is triggered both at a single company and at a group level. All companies which might be within the restriction have to establish whether or not the restriction applies to them each year, and what is their RM. In all cases the optimum use of losses requires careful calculation and forward planning, and consideration of the impact of the CIR. Moreover, losses have to be claimed or otherwise become unavailable, and all companies must specify their DA in their corporation tax self-assessment (CTSA) returns. At the same time, penalties for inaccuracies in returns have been sharply increased.

3.19 CTM04835 gives broad guidance on compliance requirements and indicates some of the complexities involved, noting that 'most carried-forward losses are within the scope' of the restriction:

(i) The restriction at Part 7ZA (ie, CTA 2010, ss 269ZA–269ZZB) only limits the amount of carried-forward losses a company can use where the company's profits are above the amount of its DA. The DA is what prevents smaller companies and groups from having their use of losses affected by the restriction.

This means that the requirements set out below, concerning the DA itself, can affect any company that wishes to deduct carried-forward losses from its profits, as long as those losses are within the scope of the restriction. Most carried-forward losses are within the scope.

As a result, although most smaller companies and groups are unlikely to have their use of carried-forward losses affected by the restriction, they may still have to fulfil administrative requirements.

(ii) The following applies for a company that

- has losses carried-forward from an earlier accounting period,
- wishes to deduct some or all of those carried-forward losses from its profits of the current period, and
- is not in a group, as defined at CTA10/S269ZZB (CTM05160).

The company will need to specify the amount of its DA in its return (CTA10/S269ZZ). It can do this, for example, in its tax computations submitted as part of its return.

3.20 Loss Relief

The amount of the company's DA will generally be £5m per 12-month accounting period beginning on or after 1 April 2017 (CTM05130, CTA10/S269ZW).

Section C: The legislation

3.20 CTA 2010 has become a treasure house of insertional curiosities. The corporate losses legislation is distributed as follows:

(NTLRD = non-trading loan relationship deficit)

Act	Sections	Coverage	Effect
CTA 2009	456–463	NTLRDs pre-1 April 2017	Carried forward for relief against non-trading profits
CTA 2009	463A–463I	NTLRDs post-1 April 2017	Relief for losses of deficit period must be given before relief for trading losses. If the company carries on investment business, NTLRDs can be carried forward and set against total profits
CTA 2010	37–45	Current year and carry-back relief for trading losses	Unchanged post-1 April 2017
CTA 2010	45A–45H	Carry forward of trading losses	Flexible relief for carried-forward single company trading losses
CTA 2010	188AA–188FD	Group relief for carried-forward losses	Allows group relief for carried-forward losses
CTA 2010	269ZA–269ZZA	Loss cap for carried-forward losses	Carried-forward losses relievable up to RM
CTA 2010	269ZR–269ZZB	DA for companies in a group	Nominated company must provide group allowance allocation statement
CTA 2010	269D–269DO	Banking companies	Imposes banking surcharge and restricts carried-forward relief
FA 2012	123–127	Carry forward of BLAGAB losses	Ring-fences BLAGAB losses

Loss Relief **3.23**

Act	Sections	Coverage	Effect
CTA 2010	303A–327; 356NE–356NJ	Carry forward of losses – oil activities	Ring-fences losses on oil and gas activities
CTA 2010	940A–943	Transfer of trade without change of ownership	Allows successor to claim losses of acquired trade
CTA 2010	672–691	Transfer of trade without change of ownership	Imposes periods of restriction where change in ownership and change in nature or conduct of business

Section D: Outline of the system

3.21 The carried-forward loss rules apply to five types of losses ('relevant deductions'): CTA 2010, s 269ZD(3). Carried-forward losses which qualify for flexible relief fall into the following categories:

- Trading losses (CTA 2010, s 45A).

- Non-trading loan relationships deficits (NTLRD, CTA 2009, s 463G).

- Non-trading losses on intangible fixed assets (NTLIFA, CTA 2009, s 753).

- Excess management expenses of investment companies (CTA 2009, ss 1219, 1223).

- UK property business losses (CTA 2010, ss 62, 63).

3.22 Trading losses arise from trading activities. Non-trading losses (ie, all losses other than trading losses) arise from non-trading activities. The distinction between trading activities and non-trading activities is important for a number of reasons. Trading losses will, in general, only qualify for various forms of loss relief firstly, if the activity constitutes a trade and secondly, if that trade is carried out on a commercial basis and with a view to profit: see paras 3.37–3.42 below).

3.23 The trading/non-trading distinction is also important in relation to working out Qualifying Trading Profits' (QTP) and Qualifying Non-trading Profits (QNTP) as part of the process of computing the RM (ie, the total amount of profits against which carried-forward losses can be set). The reason for this is that post-1 April 2017 trading profits qualify for flexible relief (ie, against total profits) whereas other forms of carried-forward losses may

3.24 Loss Relief

only qualify for relief on a restricted basis (ie, against profits of the same type) and so must be excluded from the profits which are available for flexible loss relief in respect of carried-forward losses.

3.24 Trading profits, other types of income and capital gains and losses are computed and recorded separately. Income and capital losses are carried forward separately, and trading profits are distinguished from non-trading income.

3.25 Current year trading losses can be relieved flexibly by being set against current year profits and gains or carried back to the previous accounting period for similar set off. The same treatment applies to NTLRDs and three other specified types of income.

3.26 Post-1 April 2017 trading losses, NTLRDs and other forms of income are carried forward and can be set against total profits (ie, current year income from other sources and capital gains, but subject to the loss cap).

3.27 Pre-1 April 2017 losses (trading losses and NTLRDs) continue to be streamed and can only be set against current year income from the same source.

3.28 The introduction of flexible relief has the consequence that carried-forward losses can also be used for group relief and consortium relief, but subject to prior use within the company whose losses are carried forward to a later profit-making year. The definition of group is broadly but not exactly the same as for current year group relief.

3.29 There is a DA of £5m. Up to £5m of losses can be carried forward without restriction, save for streamed pre-1 April 2017 losses. For carried-forward losses above that limit, the loss cap applies, restricting the amount of carried-forward losses which can be set against current year profits, whether at single company or group level, to 50% of losses which exceed the DA.

3.30 The key formula defines the carried-forward losses which are available for carry forward relief as the 'relevant maximum'. The key formula is:

$$RM = \frac{(QP - DA)}{2} + DA$$

Where:

RM = Relevant maximum

QP = Qualifying profits

DA = Deductions allowance

Loss Relief **3.34**

Relevant profits are qualifying profits less the DA: s CTA 2010, 269ZF(1). Qualifying profits are defined in ss 269ZF and 269ZFA in terms of 'relevant profits'.

3.31 It follows that there are four key concepts in the loss cap:

- deductions allowance (DA) (CTA 2010, s 269ZW);
- relevant deductions (RD) (CTA 2010, ss 269ZB(3)(4), 269ZC(2), 269ZD(3));
- relevant profits (RP) (CTA 2010, ss 269ZD(5), 269ZF, 269ZFA); and
- relevant maximum (RM) (CTA 2010, ss 269ZB–269ZD).

3.32 As regards the definition of relevant profits (CTA 2010, s 269ZF(3)):

- where carried-forward losses include pre-1 April 2017 losses it is necessary to calculate relevant trading profits and relevant non-trading profits separately; and
- where carried-forward losses are all flexible, it is only necessary to compute relevant total profits (prior to 1 April 2020).

Hence, the calculation of 'relevant profits' is simplified where CTA 2010, s 269ZFA (introduced with effect from 6 July 2018) applies, because only flexible losses are concerned.

3.33 A company is liable to corporation tax on its 'profits'. Profits are income plus capital gains: CTA 2009, s 2(1). Income profits include income from shares, though distributions are in most cases exempt for corporation tax purposes. The method of computation is set out in CTA 2010, s 4. The profits of a company which are charged to corporation tax are the 'taxable total profits' of the company. If current year relief for losses from trade sources equals or exceeds current year profits from other sources, a company has no taxable profits. Losses in excess of what can be relieved in the current year may be carried forward to set against future profits. Capital gains are added to 'total profits' after allowing for brought-forward capital losses: CTA 2010, s 4(3), Step 2.

3.34 'Income' means the amount on which a company is chargeable to tax after the deduction of current year reliefs. 'Chargeable gains' means gains realised in the accounting period after the deduction of all reliefs. Such reliefs will be source specific. Other reliefs may be deductible from 'total profits'. 'Total profits' are therefore profits net of reliefs deductible in computing income or gains from a particular source, but before deducting amounts only deductible from total profits, such as gift aid: CTA 2010, ss 4(3), 1119.

3.35 *Loss Relief*

3.35 Taxable total profits are the profits of the company on which corporation tax is chargeable net of current year reliefs: CTA 2010, s 4(2). 'Taxable total profits' are for loss relief carry-forward purposes determined in accordance with CTA 2010, ss 269ZB–269ZD. The CIR (see Chapter 2) take priority over any other such restrictions, in particular the restrictions on relief for carried-forward losses. Accordingly, taxable total profits means the profits of the company on which corporation tax is chargeable, net of all reliefs against total profits, taking account of all restrictions on such reliefs.

3.36 Non-trading profits are defined as '*so much of the company's profits as does not consist of trading income for the purposes of Section 37 of CTA 2010*': CTA 2009, ss 457(5); 463H(10).

Section E: Carried on on a commercial basis

3.37 As noted at para 3.22 it is a condition of sideways relief, carry-back relief and flexible carried-forward relief for trading losses (trade loss relief) that in both the loss-making period and the claim period the trade is carried on '*on a commercial basis with a view to profit or reasonable expectation thereof*'. CTA 2010, s 44(1) states:

'(1) Relief under section 37 (sideways relief) is not available for a loss made in a trade unless for the loss-making period (see section 37(3)(a)) the trade is carried on –

(a) on a commercial basis, and

(b) with a view to the making of a profit in the trade or so as to afford a reasonable expectation of making such a profit.'

This condition does not apply where the trade is carried on in the exercise of statutory functions.

3.38 The concept goes back at least to s 1(1) of the Partnership Act 1890 ('*carrying on a business ... with a view to profit*'). In *Wannall v Rothwell* [1996] STC 450 at 461, Walker J said that the purpose of the test was to distinguish 'serious' trades from 'hobby' trades. The tax legislation uses the test in a variety of places in a variety of forms. The Income Tax (Trading and Other Income) Act 2005, s 863(1) says that if an LLP carries on '*a trade, profession or business with a view to profit*', it is regarded as transparent for tax purposes, so that actions of the LLP are regarded as actions of the members. Income Tax Act (ITA 2007), s 66 says with regard to trade losses:

'(1) Trade loss relief against general income for a loss made in a trade in a tax year is not available unless the trade is commercial.

Loss Relief **3.42**

(2) The trade is commercial it is carried on throughout the basis period for the tax year –

(a) on a commercial basis, and

(b) with a view to the realisation of profits of the trade.'

3.39 The intention to make a profit may be subsidiary to or pursued in combination with some other purpose and does not need to be the sole or dominant purpose. A barrister who could earn £50,000 a year, but chooses to earn £25,000 because he is working for professional satisfaction rather than money, could be said to be carrying on his profession as a 'hobby' rather than on a 'serious' basis. Winston Churchill when Prime Minister, preferred to make farming losses on a farm managed by his son-in-law instead of paying income tax at penal levels. A person may open his historic home to the public for 30 days a year on a paying basis to help with maintenance expenses or to avoid an annual tax on enveloped dwellings (ATED).

3.40 Henderson LJ has stated that the test carries two tests, a test of commerciality and a profits test:

'The conditions therefore embody two tests: a text of commerciality, and a profits test ... broadly speaking it (the profits test) requires the trade to have been carried on with a view to making profits.'

Samarkand Film Partnership Nos 3 v R & C Comrs [2017] STC 926 at [84].

3.41 This does not tell us what time period is to be used for the purposes of applying the test. A new supermarket or restaurant is carried on on an uncommercial basis, notwithstanding that it is anticipated that it will make losses for the first five years of operation. Many businesses are carried on without ever making a profit. The losses, far from showing that the business was 'uncommercial', may show the seriousness of the trader's purpose, in that he was prepared to lose his money in the hope – unfulfilled – of future profits. Unlike communism, capitalism often operates on very long time scales, sacrificing immediate enjoyment in the hope, in most cases disappointed, of long-term gain. Against that, there will be a point at which future income becomes too remote to be taken into account, or the prospect of tax relief outweighs commercial considerations.

3.42 The law was reviewed in *Beacon v R & C Comrs* [2018] SFTD 846, where the Tribunal concluded that, in a case where the taxpayer had incurred large losses in purchasing and renovating an Italian monastery with a view to carrying on a holiday business at the premises, but only obtained modest income, the trade was carried on on a commercial basis with a view to profit.

3.43 Loss Relief

3.43 This condition was analysed in detail in *Ingenious Games LLP v R & C Comrs* (2019) UKUT 0226 (TCC) at [297]–[432]. The Upper Tribunal concluded that the test was *'a purely subjective one'* [333]; *'The question is whether there is a real and serious intention to make a profit'* [140]. If the subjective test is satisfied, then it does not matter how, objectively, likely it is that a profit will be realised. The intention must be supported by evidence [341]–[377]. Otherwise, the test will be satisfied by a project for making moonbeams out of cucumbers. Moreover, this formulation tells us nothing about how much profit, or over what time span or whether the possibility of finding a crock of gold at the end of the rainbow can be accorded any weight.

3.44 The test and its application to detailed facts was considered extensively in *R (on the application of Cobalt Data Centre No 2 and Others) v R & C Comrs* (2019) UKUT 342 (TCC). LLPs entered into contracts with a developer and contractor for the construction of data centres in Enterprise Zones, the expenditure on which would (it was planned) qualify for 100% capital allowances. The expenditure was financed 30% in cash, 70% in limited recourse loans. Having regard to the anticipated tax subsidies, the development expenditure was in excess of the market value of the sites, and the anticipated rentals were in excess of those likely to be obtainable. After exhaustive consideration of the law and the facts, the Upper Tribunal concluded at [121]–[189] that the commercial basis test was satisfied.

Section F: In-year and carry back loss relief

3.45 Current year reliefs are unaffected by the 2017 changes. For current trading losses (including losses on trading loan relationships and derivative contracts) the following year reliefs are provided (CTA 2010, ss 37, 39, 45, 46, 99):

- surrender for group relief on a current year basis;
- set-off against *total profits* of the *same* accounting period;
- set-off against *total profits* of the *previous* accounting period; and
- *carried back* for three years to claim terminal loss relief.

3.46 Accordingly, the following were not altered by the 2017 rules:

- sideways (current year/in-year) loss relief (CTA 2010, s 37(3)(a));
- in-year group relief (sideways/current year) (CTA 2010, s 99);
- carry-back (previous year) loss relief (CTA 2010, ss 37(3)(b), 38, 39); and

- ring-fence losses incurred by oil and gas companies (being subject to their own special regime).

3.47 For accounting periods beginning before 1 January 2016, where a company had profits or losses on a loan relationship after it had ceased to be party to that obligation ('a post-cessation period') the character of the loan relationship (trading or non-trading) was determined by its status before the company ceased to be party to it: CTA 2009, ss 331(3)–(4). For post-cessation period beginning on or after 1 January 2016, what matters is the character of the debt in that accounting period: CTA 2009, s 330A(7).

3.48 For deficits on non-trading loan relationships the following current year and carry back reliefs are provided (CTA 2009, ss 456–463; CTA 2010, s 99):

- treated as trading losses and surrendered by way of group relief on a current year basis;
- set-off against *any profits* for the deficit period; and
- set-off against *loan relationship and derivative contract profits* of the *previous* accounting period.

Section G: Current year group and consortium relief

3.49 Rules for current year group and consortium relief are unchanged by the 2017 reforms. The rules for group relief for carried-forward losses use many of the same concepts and definitions.

3.50 For current year group relief, two companies are members of a group if one is a '75% subsidiary' of the other or both are 75% subsidiaries of a third company. CTA 2010, s 1154 applies to determine the meaning of '75% subsidiary' by reference to the holding of 75% of ordinary share capital, directly or indirectly. The group relief rules in CTA 2010, ss 157–182 apply for defining equity holders and profits available for distribution. An 'equity holder' is an ordinary shareholder or a loan creditor who holds a loan of the company other than an ordinary commercial loan: CTA 2010, s 158. 'Ordinary commercial loan' is, in turn, defined in CTA 2010, ss 162 and 163 as a loan issued for new consideration, which is non-convertible, not a non-commercial security (CTA 2010, ss 1000(1), 1005, ie, which gives a rate of return in excess of an ordinary commercial return for the principal and is not a 'special security' (CTA 2010, s 1000(1)F, 1015, ie, a security the return on which is related to the profits of the business or a part of the business. CTA 2010, ss 169–182 cut down on the scope of the definition of group for current year group relief purposes by excluding arrangements where the parent may not have economic ownership of the subsidiary or there are option arrangements in existence by

3.51 *Loss Relief*

virtue of which the subsidiary company could cease to be a subsidiary of the parent.

3.51 The 75% test requires voting, income and assets entitlement. Under the definition for current year group relief, the parent company must beneficially own 75% of the ordinary share capital of the subsidiary, and be entitled to 75% of the votes in the subsidiary, 75% of the profits available for distribution and 75% of the assets available to equity holders on a winding up: CTA 2010, ss 151, 152, 1154. 'Ordinary share capital' means all shares other than fixed rate preference shares (CTA 2010, s 1119). Fixed rate preference shares:

- are issued for consideration which is or includes new consideration;
- do not carry any right to conversion into shares or securities or to the acquisition of any additional shares or securities;
- do not carry any right to dividends other than dividends which are of a fixed amount or fixed rate per cent of nominal value, and represent no more than a reasonable commercial return on the new consideration received in respect of the issue of shares; and
- do not carry, on repayment, any rights to an amount exceeding the new consideration received.

Group relief will be denied where there are option arrangements in force which, if implemented, would deprive a member of the parent of the requisite level of beneficial ownership of shares in the subsidiary: CTA 2010, ss 154–155B.

3.52 Trading losses and non-trading deficits on loan relationship, may be surrendered by way of group relief on a current year basis. Unlike other cases of surrender of losses by way of group relief, such as management expenses and property business losses, the loss is not restricted to the excess over profits of the company for the accounting period.

3.53 A consortium company is a company in which at least 75% of the ordinary shares are owned by companies, each of which has at least a 5% shareholding (ie, a consortium has a maximum membership of 20).

3.54 In the case of consortium relief, CTA 2010, ss 132, 133 state that consortium relief is only available where one company is a member of a consortium and the other is:

(a) a trading company owned by the consortium and which is not a 75% subsidiary of any company;

(b) a trading company which is a 90% subsidiary of a holding company owned by the consortium and is not a 75% subsidiary of a company other than the holding company; or

Loss Relief **3.57**

(c) a holding company owned by the consortium and which is not a 75% subsidiary of any company.

3.55 For these purposes, a holding company is defined in CTA 2010, s 185(2). In broad terms, a holding company means a company which holds shares or securities in trading subsidiaries which are its 90% subsidiaries. Thus, in the case of direct ownership by the consortium, the consortium-owned company must be a trading company; whereas, in the case of a holding company owned by a consortium, the holding company must own a 90% interest in trading companies in the relevant period.

3.56 Consortium relief is a by-product of and supplementary to group relief, available in circumstances where group relief is inapplicable because the 75% common ownership test is not achieved. Consortium relief revolves around a number of definitions. The key definition is 'company owned by a consortium', which implies a definition of 'consortium' and 'member of a consortium'. To be 'a company owned by a consortium', a company must first be either a 'trading company' or 'holding company' of 90% subsidiaries which are all trading companies. The 90% test must satisfy the 'voting rights', 'profits' and 'assets' tests (see below). A company will be owned by a consortium if 75% or more of its ordinary share capital is owned by other companies, each of which holds at least 5% of the shares. The members of the consortium must be 'equity holders', and an equity holder is a person who holds ordinary share capital in a company or loan creditor in respect of a loan which is not a normal commercial loan.

Link companies and group/consortium companies

3.57 A link company is a member of a group and a consortium. For example, S2 is a link company. Consortium companies can surrender losses to S2, and S2 in turn can group relieve losses.

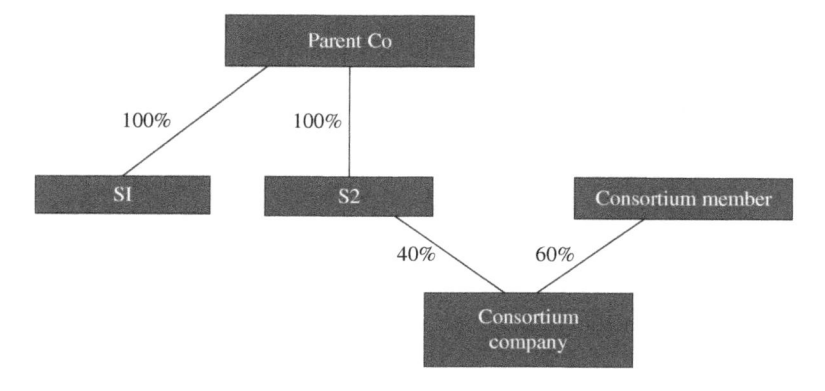

3.58 *Loss Relief*

The link company can transmit losses of the consortium company to other group companies. Equally, losses of the link company's group can be surrendered to the consortium company. If S1 has losses of 100, and S2 and X each have profits of 200, S1 can surrender 100 of its losses to S2, which in turn can surrender 60 of those losses down to X. The link company must either be UK resident or have a UK trade.

3.58 For consortium relief to be available, consortium condition 1, 2 or 3 must be met.

Under CTA 2010, s 132, consortium condition 1 is satisfied:

- where a company owned by a consortium is a trading company or holding company, it surrenders losses upwards to a claimant company which is a member of a consortium; or

- where a member of a consortium is a trading company or holding company, it surrenders losses downwards to a company owned by a consortium, and both companies are 'UK related'.

3.59 Under CTA 2010, s 133(1), consortium condition 2 is satisfied if:

- where a company owned by a consortium is a trading company or holding company, it surrenders losses upwards to a claimant company which is not a member of a consortium;

- the claimant company belongs to the same group as a link company which is a member of a consortium; and

- the surrendering company, claimant company and link company are all 'UK related'.

3.60 Under CTA 2010, s 133(2), consortium condition 3 is satisfied if:

- the surrendering company is not a company owned by a consortium but is a member of the same group as a link company;

- the link company is a member of a consortium;

- the claimant company is a company owned by a consortium and is a trading company or holding company; and

- the surrendering company, claimant company and link company are all 'UK related'.

3.61 'UK related' means a UK resident company or the UK permanent establishment of a non-resident company: CTA 2010, s 134. The members of the consortium can be resident anywhere in the world, and so may comprise

Loss Relief 3.65

resident and non-resident companies. A UK resident company can be treated as a consortium company as long as it is at least 75% owned by two or more companies, wherever those companies are resident. If a consortium company is a holding company of a trading group, it need not be UK resident, nor need the majority of its trading subsidiaries be UK or EU resident.

3.62 Where one of the conditions for relief is fulfilled, both the consortium and the company owned by the consortium are treated as tax transparent. The consortium company can surrender up losses to a consortium member proportionate to that member's shareholding in the consortium company, while the consortium member can surrender down to the consortium company a similar amount of its own losses. In either case, the claim is a 'consortium claim'.

3.63 If the claimant company and surrendering company do not have co-terminous accounting periods ('overlapping period'), relief will be restricted accordingly: CTA 2010, ss 139, 142. A member's share in a consortium is determined by reference to his accounting period.

3.64 A consortium member's share of a consortium, in relation to the accounting period of the surrendering company, is limited to 'the ownership proportion of the surrenderable amount': CTA 2010, s 143(2). This is the lowest of

- the percentage of ordinary share capital beneficially owned by that member ('voting test');

- the percentage of profits available for distribution to equity holders to which it is entitled ('profits test'); and

- the percentage of assets available for distribution to equity holders on a notional winding up ('assets test').

(CTA 2010, s 143(3).)

3.65 *R & C Comrs v South Eastern Power Networks plc* [2020] STC 298 concerned the application of consortium condition 3 (para 3.60 above) (surrendering company member of same group as link company; link company member of consortium; claimant companies consortium-owned companies). The issue was whether the losses which the surrendering companies (consortium conditions 1–3) were restricted to 74.6% or 50% of the profits of the claimant consortium-owned companies, having regard to CTA 2010, s 146B: see [16]. This applied if there were arrangements in place whereby a person could prevent the link company from having control of the consortium-owned companies, and these arrangements had the purpose of securing a tax advantage for the claimant companies. If such arrangements

3.66 *Loss Relief*

were in place, the profits of the claimant companies which could be group relieved were limited to 50% of those profits.

3.66 The structure was:

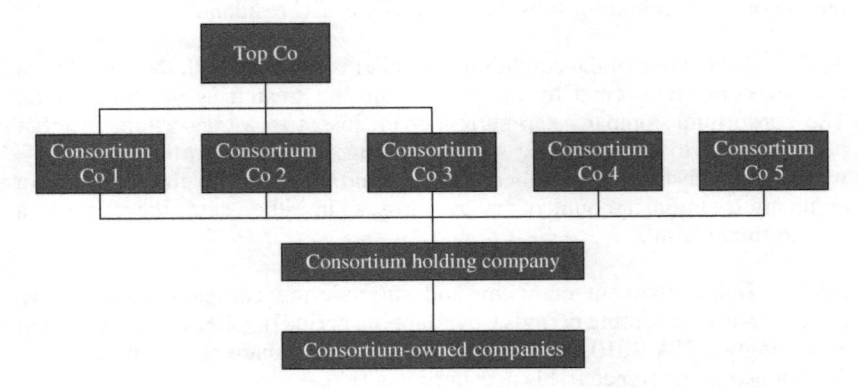

```
                        Top Co
    ┌──────────┬──────────┬──────────┬──────────┐
 Consortium Consortium Consortium Consortium Consortium
   Co 1      Co 2      Co 3      Co 4      Co 5
                        │
              Consortium holding company
                        │
              Consortium-owned companies
```

3.67 Consortium companies 1, 2 and 3 were the link companies. Companies 1–3 owned 74.6% of the shares in the consortium-owned companies. However, they had entered into a voting agreement, whereby the articles of association of the consortium holding company provided that a shareholders' resolution would require a 75% majority. The question was whether this was an arrangement which allowed someone (Consortium cos 4 and 5) to prevent the link companies (Consortium cos 1–3) from having control of the consortium-owned companies. The Upper Tribunal did not decide this question either way but held that it was a question into which HMRC could continue to enquire.

Section H: Transitional accounting periods

3.68 For accounting periods which span 1 April 2017, losses are crystallised at that point, and the accounting periods which straddle 1 April 2017 are divided into two periods, one from the commencement of the period to 31 March 2017, the other from 1 April 2017 to the end of the period. Where accounting periods straddle 1 April 2017, profits and losses should be apportioned on a time basis so as to calculate the pre- and post-1 April 2017 split, as long as this produces a fair and reasonable result. After deduction of in-year reliefs, pre-1 April 2017 losses should be relieved before post-1 April 2017 losses.

3.69 The basic position, subject to adjustment if the CIR applies, is set out in Finance (No 2) Act (F(No 2)A) 2017, Sch 4, para 190(1), and says that the

Loss Relief **3.72**

new system for loss relief has effect in relation to accounting periods beginning on or after 1 April 2017. Paragraph 190(2) says that where an accounting period begins before and ends after 1 April 2017 ('a straddling period'), it is to be divided into two notional accounting periods, one running from the previous accounting year end to 31 March 2017 and the other running from 1 April 2017 to the normal year end. Profits and losses for the first notional accounting period crystallise at 31 March 2017.

Example

A company has a 31 December year end. The straddling accounting period is split into notional AP1 (1 January–31 March 2017) and AP2 (1 April–31 December 2017). The new rules apply to AP2 for all purposes.

3.70 The apportionment of profits between AP1 and AP2 is on a time-apportionment basis under CTA 2010, s 1172, unless the time basis produces a result which is 'unjust and unreasonable': F(No 2)A 2010, Sch 4, para 190(2)(b).

3.71 In *R & C Comrs v Total E & P North Sea UK Ltd* [2019] STC 1110, the Upper Tribunal considered similar apportionment provisions in FA 2011, s 7. This increased the corporation tax surcharge (CTS) which applied to oil- and gas-related ring fence profits from 20% to 32% with effect from 24 March 2011. For a straddling period, profits were to be apportioned on a time basis, unless the company elected for an alternative basis 'that is just and reasonable': FA 2011, s 7(5). Maersk had a 31 December 2011 accounting reference date. It elected to apportion the profits for the year ended 31 December 2011 between AP1 and AP2 on the basis that after 24 March 2011 it had incurred substantial expenditure qualifying for 100% capital allowances, and profits should be allocated on an actual basis rather than on statutory time apportionment. The First-tier Tribunal upheld Maersk's alternative basis, observing at [113]:

> 'It is intended to provide relief for companies whose profits are not smoothly spread throughout the year, but whose profits differ greatly from one part of the year to the other, and who could be disadvantaged by such a change of tax rate part way through an accounting period.'

3.72 The Upper Tribunal overturned this decision, on the basis that there was a presumption in favour of time apportionment, and the company's suggested basis amounted to re-computation rather than apportionment. This is to make time apportionment the rule and to deprive the legislation of its

3.73 *Loss Relief*

full effect. Moreover, any attribution on a basis other than time apportionment will, by its nature, involve a degree of re-computation. The only requirement of the legislation is that the apportioned profits for the two notional accounting periods should equal to profits for the actual accounting period.

3.73 Carry forward of unused pre-1 April 2017 trading losses remains automatic, but a company can opt for the relief not to be carried forward: CTA 2010, s 45(4)(b). Pre-1 April 2017 trading losses are carried forward post-1 April 2017 (CTA 2010, s 45(4)), unless the company opts out of the carry forward (CTA 2010, s 45(4A)–(4C)). Unlike trading losses arising in accounting periods beginning on or after 1 April 2017, carried forward pre-1 April 2017 trading losses can only be set against profits of the same trade: CTA 2010, s 45B (ie, pre-1 April 2017 carried-forward losses are always subject to the pre-1 April 2017 streaming rules). The cap on the use of carried-forward losses which applies to post-1 April 2017 trading losses also applies to losses carried forward from accounting periods beginning prior to 1 April 2017: CTA 2010, s 269ZB(3)(a).

3.74 CTA 2010, s 45(4)(a) allows pre-1 April 2017 trading losses to be carried forward to set against profits of the same trade, subject to the loss cap, indefinitely.

3.75 It may be advantageous to postpone pre-1 April 2017 trading losses to post-1 April 2017 trading losses where there are both non-trading profits and trading losses in the later accounting period. This is because post-1 April 2017 can be set against non-trading income, so releasing pre-1 April 2017 to set against trading profits.

Example

A company's accounting reference date is 31 December. It is a standalone company. Its profits are as follows, time apportioned for the transitional period.

	To 31.12.16	To 31.03.17	To 31.12.17	To 31.12.18
Trading	500,000	(1,000,000)	(3,000,000)	1,000,000
Loss relief	(500,000)			(1,000,000)
Non-trading	250,000	250,000	750,000	500,000
Loss relief	(250,000)	(250,000)	(750,000)	(500,000)
Available loss relief	750,000	1,000,000	3,000,000	2,250,000
Utilised loss relief	(750,000)	(1,000,000)	(750,000)	(1,500,000)
Carried-forward	0	0	2,250,000	750,000

Loss Relief **3.78**

Section I: Interaction with the CIR

3.76 The CIR potentially limits relief for all forms of carried-forward losses. The effect of the CIR rules is to increase taxable profits (or reduce losses or turn a profit into a loss) by disallowing for tax purposes finance costs which are deductible for accounting purposes. CIR adjustments take precedence over the loss carry-forward rules: F(No 2)A 2017, Sch 4, para 191. So taxable profits are profits increased (or potentially allowable losses are reduced) by any add back of disallowed interest expense.

3.77 The notional accounting period from 1 April 2017 to the end of the accounting period has to take into account the impact of the CIR as well as the carried-forward loss rules introduced from 1 April 2017. Where (i) an accounting period straddles 1 April 2017, and (ii) CIR applies for the notional period beginning on 1 April 2017, the standard apportionment provisions must be varied: CTA 2010, s 1172.

3.78 Where there is a profit for commercial and tax purposes, notwithstanding the CIR, in the accounting period ending after 1 April 2017:

(i) the financial result for the accounting period as a whole which would have been achieved but for the CIR is the 'notional amount';

(ii) profits adjusted for CIR are the 'amount concerned';

(iii) the first notional apportionment amount is the amount apportioned to the first notional accounting period, and is calculated by reference to the notional amount;

(iv) if the first notional apportionment amount is less than the amount concerned, the second notional amount apportioned to the second notional accounting period is (notional amount − first notional apportionment amount); and

(v) the second notional apportionment is then increased by the amount of the CIR attributable to the second notional accounting period.

Example

A company's accounting period ends on 31 December 2017. In that period it has profits of £10m, after deducting finance costs of £5m. The CIR (if applied to the whole year) restricts the allowable interest deduction to £2m.

The 'notional amount' is £10m.

3.79 *Loss Relief*

The 'amount concerned' is £13m.

The first notional apportionment amount is 90/365 x 10m = 2,465,753. This is not subject to the CIR.

The second notional apportionment amount is (10,000,000 − 2,465,753) = 7,534,247.

This is increased by the part of the amount concerned attributable to the second notional accounting period (ie, 13,000,000 x 275/365 = 9,794,520).

If the effect of the CIR for the actual accounting period is to negate in whole or in part the tax loss which would have otherwise arisen, then the entire profit of the actual accounting period ending beginning before and ending after 1 April 2017 is treated for loss relief purposes as arising in the notional period beginning on 1 April 2017.

Section J: Current year losses

Trading losses (CTA 2010, ss 45A–45F)

3.79 This includes losses on trading loan relationships and derivative contracts, and on intangible fixed assets held as part of a trade.

The structure of the loan relationship rules is to exclude (if otherwise applicable) the general rules on computing trading profits, impose instead a special loan relationships tax treatment and then put the result back into trading income (if the loan relationships are applicable) or subject it to a separate head of tax, namely, profits (deficits) from non-trading loan relationships.

3.80 Losses on loan relationships and derivative contracts entered into 'for the purposes of a trade it carries on' are pooled with trading income, and so loss relief is obtained either by reducing taxable profits or by increasing relievable losses: CTA 2009, s 297. In the case of a creditor loan relationship, a company is party to a loan relationship for the purposes of a trade it carries on only if it is party to the relationship 'in the course of activities forming an integral part of the trade': CTA 2009, s 298. This is only likely to apply in the case of banks and insurance companies.

3.81 Tax relief for the debits in respect of loan relationships held for the purposes of a trade result from the inclusion of such items in the computation of trading profits or losses.

NTLRDs (CTA 2009, ss 463A–463I)

3.82 Non-trading profits from loan relationships are separately charged to corporation tax: CTA 2009, s 299. Derivative contracts are also divided into trading and non-trading: CTA 2009, ss 573, 574. Profits and losses from non-trading loan relationships and non-trading derivative contracts are pooled. NTLRDs (other than those derivative contracts which come within the capital gains rules) are the subject of separate statutory provisions, which largely follow the rules on the utilisation of trading losses.

NTLIFAs (CTA 2009, s 753)

3.83 Non-trading losses on intangible fixed assets (NTLIFA) cannot be carried forward if the company ceases to have investment business in the accounting period following the deficit period: CTA 2009, s 753.

Expenses of investment companies (CTA 2009, ss 1218, 1223(3B))

3.84 Investment income is classified separately to trading income. Investment income is calculated on a gross basis and therefore does not give rise to losses. As regards investment companies, management expenses can be deducted from income for tax and accounting purposes. Excess management expenses can be carried forward for set off against income of future accounting periods so as to qualify for flexible or group relief, subject to the general post-1 April 2017 restrictions: CTA 2009, s 1223.

UK property business (CTA 2010, ss 62–67)

3.85 The profits of a UK property business are calculated on a notional trade basis (ie, as if a trade were being carried on: CTA 2010, ss 99(1)(e), 102, 246, 247). In that case there can be losses, but such losses, not being trading losses, can only be carried forward against future profits of the notional trade. In the case of a property business loan relationships come under the loan relationship rules, not the deemed trading rules, and are therefore non-trading loan relationships.

Section K: Flexible relief

3.86 Losses of these five types arising after 1 April 2017 which cannot be relieved in the current year or carried back may be carried forward for offset against 'total profits', but only to the extent of the RM. The ability to set

3.87 *Loss Relief*

such losses against 'total profits' means that carried-forward losses can be set against taxable profits from different activities and capital gains (flexible relief) or surrendered to other group members by making a group relief election for offset. As a general rule the carried forward trading loss is deducted from 'total profits' for the next accounting period, not just profits of the same trade (unlike the pre-1 April 2017 position). Capital gains are excluded from total profits from 1 April 2020, and instead are subject to the CCLR.

3.87 Flexible loss relief (non-source specific) was prior to 1 April 2017 only available on a current year (sideways) and carry back basis. Hence group relief for trading losses was only available on a current year basis. The extension of flexible relief to carried forward trading losses means that flexible relief is also available in the form of carried-forward group relief (ie, carried forward trading losses in one group company which can be surrendered to another group company, provided that the surrendering company is not able to set the carried-forward losses against its own current year profits). The rules for groups follow the single company rules, but the various amounts must be apportioned between the members of the group.

3.88 Special rules apply to losses arising from ring fence activities and oil contractor activities: CTA 2010, s 45A(2); Part 8, ss 270–356JNB; Part 8ZA ss 356K–356NJ. Ring-fenced profits cannot be relieved under CTA 2009, s 463G(11).

3.89 The creative industry tax reliefs (CTA 2009, ss 15–15E) are given special treatment, in that they are ignored for the purpose of the restriction on deductions from trading profits in CTA 2010, s 269ZB. Losses from overseas property businesses and furnished holiday lettings are not affected by the post-1 April 2017 rules.

Section L: Banks and insurance companies

3.90 Special provisions apply to banks under CTA 2010, ss 269A–269DO. In the case of banks and insurance companies all income of the company is trading income because the assets from which the income arises are held for the purposes of the trade, and not for the purpose of realising income outside the trade: *Liverpool and London and Globe Insurance Co v Bennett* 6 TC 327. For banks, pre-1 April 2015 losses are restricted to 50% of eligible profits: CTA 2010, s 269CA (FA 2015, Sch 2). From 1 April 2016 this was reduced to 25%.

3.91 For banks and building societies relief is restricted to 25% of taxable profits for carried-forward trading losses, NTLRDs and management expenses arising before 1 April 2015 to 25% (50% before 1 April 2016) of taxable profits: CTA 2010, ss 269CA–269CN. The general restrictions introduced for all

Loss Relief **3.96**

companies post-1 April 2017 are imposed on top of these specific restrictions for the financial sector.

3.92 A general insurance company is defined in s 269ZG(6). A 'contract of general insurance' is defined in the Financial Services and Markets Act 2000 (Regulated Activities) Order, SI 2001/544, Sch 1, Part 1. General insurance companies may be taxed on an I–E basis under FA 2012, s 68. The general rules in CTA 2010, ss 269ZB–269ZD are modified in the case of general insurance companies: s 269ZE. There are numerous special rules in the revised legislation for insurance companies. The stress test to measure the capital adequacy of insurance companies is net of tax relief. Hence, the restriction of tax relief for losses results in higher regulatory capital costs.

3.93 Where a company carries on business as a general insurance company, and is taxed on an I–E basis under FA 2012, s 68; CTA 2010, s 269ZD would otherwise apply (restrictions on deductions from total profits, as opposed to source specific deductions) so the sum of any relevant deductions may not exceed the 'modified loss cap': CTA 2010, s 269ZE(2)(7).

3.94 CTA 2010, ss 269ZB to 269ZE are ignored in determining the taxable total profits of a general insurance company for an excluded accounting period: CTA 2010, s 269ZG. An excluded accounting period is a period in which the company is in insolvency proceedings (as defined by s 269ZH) due to the non-viability condition (ie, where there is no realistic possibility that the company will be able to write future insurance business, as a result of 'qualifying latent claims'). These are defined in s 269ZI (non-forseeable potential claims arising from an employer's liability policy or public or products liability policy which goes back more than 10 years).

3.95 A 'shock loss' is one which is so catastrophic in nature that the insurance company will suffer a significant underwriting loss: CTA 2010, s 269ZK. Protection against shock losses is generally obtained through reinsurance. Where a 'shock loss' is carried forward and deducted under CTA 2010, s 45B, it is ignored for the purposes of s 269ZB(3). There is a special loss cap for insurance companies in certain cases: ss 269ZD(5), 269ZJ–269ZN. If the company is a Solvency 2 insurance company, no claim for relief can be made in respect of shock losses, except for current year relief. In the case of a Solvency 2 insurance company, where a NTLRD is partly (but not wholly) a shock loss; only that part which is not a shock loss can be relieved: CTA 2009, s 463G(13).

3.96 For Basic Life Assurance and General Annuity Businesses (BLAGABs), the policyholders' share of the profits are not subject to the loss cap in the first accounting period following the loss-making period. The loss cap rules do, however, apply in subsequent periods, to losses not relieved in the

3.97 *Loss Relief*

accounting period immediately following the loss-making period. BLAGAB losses may also be carried forward for surrender intra-group: CTA 2010, s 188BB(3)–(6). Losses of general insurance companies when the surrender period is an excluded accounting period, or where the insurance company is a Solvency 2 insurance company, may not be utilised for carry forward group relief, where the loss is NTIFA, excess management expenses or a UK property business loss: s 188BG.

Section M: Carried-forward losses, post-1 April 2017

3.97 Post-1 April 2017 carried-forward losses comprise:

(i) streamed trading losses, which may be only be set against current year profits of the same trade, and cannot be group relieved;

(ii) streamed NTLRD, which may only be set against current year non-trading loan relationship profits, and cannot be group relieved; and

(iii) flexible losses, which can be set against current year total profits and can be group relieved.

Hence (i) and (ii) are 'restricted relief losses' (RRLs), while (iii) constitute 'flexible relief losses (FRLs). RRLs and FRLs are not statutory terms. Trading losses and NTLRDs arising before 1 April 2017 are RRLs. Trading losses and NTLRDs arising after 1 April 2017 are FRLs, but subject to a number of exceptions (eg, where the CTA 2010, s 45A(3) conditions are not satisfied). Management expenses, UK property business losses and non-trading losses on intangible fixed assets (NTLIFAs) are always FLRs, whenever they arise. FRLs require a claim. RRLs are carried forward automatically.

3.98 Given that there are three types of carried-forward losses post-1 April 2017, it follows that there are three types of restriction on the use of such losses, in all cases being subject to the general restriction of the loss cap (the RM):

(i) streamed trading profits can be set off only against 'qualifying trading profits': CTA 2010, s 269ZB;

(ii) streamed NTLRD can be set off only against 'qualifying non-trading profits': CTA 2009, ss 457(3), 463H(5), CTA 2010, s 269ZC; and

(iii) flexible losses can be set off against 'qualifying profits': CTA 2009, s 269ZD.

These distinctions are important when it comes to calculating 'relevant profits' of the year to which the losses are carried forward for the purposes of

Loss Relief **3.100**

calculating the RM. As pre-1 April 2017 losses are used up, the importance of ss 269ZB, 269ZC will diminish.

3.99 In summary:

Type of loss	Legislation	FRL/RRL
Carried-forward post-1 April 2017 trading loss where trade continues and s 45A(3) conditions are met	CTA 2010, ss 45A, 45C, 269ZD	FRL
Carried-forward post-1 April 2017 NTLDR	CTA 2009, s 463G; CTA 2010, s 269ZD	FRL
Carried-forward post-1 April 2017 NTLIFA	CTA 2009, s 753	FRL
Carried-forward post-1 April 2017 excess management expenses	CTA 2009, ss 1219, 1223	FRL
Carried-forward post-1 April 2017 UK property business losses	CTA 2010, ss 62, 63	FRL
Terminal loss where no loss claimed for accounting period beginning before 1 April 2017	CTA 2010, s 45F	FRL
Carried-forward post-1 April 2017 trading loss where s 45A(3) not met	CTA 2010, ss 45B, 45D, 45E, 269ZB	RRL
Carried-forward pre-1 April 2017 trading loss	CTA 2010, s 45; 269ZB	RRL
Carried-forward pre-1 April 2017 NTLRD	CTA 2010, s 269ZC	RRL
NTLRD – company ceases to have investment business	CTA 2009, s 463H	RRL

Section N: Carried-forward losses post-1 April 2017 (single company/within relevant maximum)

3.100 In the case of trading losses where the trade has become small or negligible in a later accounting period, the trade has ceased or the s 45A(3) conditions have not been met for other reasons, relief is available on a restricted (ie, non-flexible) basis under CTA 2010, s 45B.

The general rule is that carried-forward loss relief is available on a flexible basis (ie, for offset against total profits and for surrender intra-group). Loss carry-forward is thus not restricted to carry forward against losses from the

3.101 *Loss Relief*

same source or restricted to the loss-making company. The legislation allows trading and other losses to be carried forward to future accounting periods for offset against all taxable profits both on a single company and on a group basis.

Flexible relief (unstreamed) – s 45A

3.101 For losses arising after 1 April 2017 the previous restrictions on offsetting different types of losses within both single companies and groups (including consortiums) against income of the same type are replaced by the concept of offsetting carried forward trading losses and NTLRDs carried forward against 'total profits'. Current year losses on income of one type can be set against current year profits of another type or carried back to the previous accounting period. Losses arising from 1 April 2017 can be carried forward and set against profits from other income streams or of other companies in the group. Trading loss carry forward is no longer confined to set off against profits of the same trade.

3.102 The general rule is in CTA 2010, s 45A(4)(5)(6) which say that trading losses arising in an accounting period beginning on or after 1 April 2017 can on a claim being made be carried forward to set against total profits (ie, including capital gains, until 1 April 2020) for the following accounting period ('the later period'). Thus, the loss is relievable against profits generally rather than profits of the same trade. However, relief under the section is subject to restrictions or modifications in the Corporation Tax Acts (ie, any such relief is capped in accordance with the new rules).

3.103 Accordingly, the unrelieved amount of trading losses arising after 1 April 2017 (ie, not relieved by sideways or carry back relief) can be carried forward under CTA 2010, s 45A and used against 'total profits' in a future accounting period provided that the company continues to carry on the trade in the later period, the trade did not become small or negligible in the loss-making period.

3.104 The conditions for s 45A(4) relief are set out in s 45A(3).

(i) In general:

- the loss must arise in a post-1 April 2017 accounting period;
- the trade must not be an oil or gas ring fenced trade;
- the loss is not a shock loss of a Solvency 2 insurance company; and
- a claim is needed (s 45A(5)(7), 45C(3)).

Loss Relief **3.106**

(ii) In the loss-making period:

- the loss would qualify for carry back or sideways loss relief under CTA 2010, s 37 (s 45A(3)(a));
- the trade must not have become small or negligible (s 45A(3)(a)); and
- losses must not be from a trade carried on wholly outside the UK (s 375)).

(iii) In the carry forward period:

- the company must continue to trade (ss 45A(1)(c), 45C(1)(d));
- the trade must be carried on on a commercial basis (ss 45A(3)(c), 45C(2)(b));
- the trade must not become small or negligible (s 45C(2)(a)); and
- the company is not an excluded accounting period of a general insurance company, as defined in s 269ZG.

The operative conditions of s 45A are reapplied for each subsequent 'later' or 'further' period.

Extended s 45A carry forward (reapplication): 'Later periods' and 'further periods' – s 45C

3.105 The accounting period in which the loss is incurred is the 'loss-making period' (Year 1). The accounting period immediately following the loss-making period is the 'later period' (Year 2). The accounting period immediately following the later period is the 'further period' (Year 3). If any part of the Year 1 loss remains unrelieved at the end of Year 3, Year 4 becomes the later period in relation to Year 3, Year 5 the further period, and so on indefinitely: ss 45C(3), 45D(2).

3.106 Where losses which are carried forward for relief under s 45A but cannot be used in the later period or group are relieved, they may be carried forward to the accounting period following the later period ('the further period') under s 45C. Under s 45C(2), relief is subject to three conditions:

(a) the trade did not become small or negligible in the later period;

(b) the trade is carried on on a commercial basis in the in the further period; and

(c) the further period is an 'excluded accounting period' of a 'general insurance company': s 269ZG.

3.107 *Loss Relief*

Restricted relief losses (streamed) – s 45B

3.107 The fall-back rule is that the carry forward loss relief is available on a restricted basis (ie, source-specific, where the conditions for flexible relief are not satisfied ('the s 45A(3) conditions'). No claim for default carry forward is necessary, unless an election is made not to claim to carry forward. The fallback rule applies where in the claim period the trade of the claimant company has become small or minimal, so that the operative conditions for s 45A relief are not satisfied. In such cases CTA 2010, s 45B provides a fallback where a s 45A claim is not possible, and allows a trading loss which is not otherwise relieved under sideways relief, group relief or s 45A to be set against the profits of the same trade for the following accounting period (the 'later period'). Where relief is not available under s 45A by reason of s 45A(3), the loss can be carried forward to set against profits of the same trade in the accounting period following the loss-making period (s 45B).

Extended restricted relief – ss 45D, 45E

3.108 If relief is not available under ss 45B or 45C in the later period, a section 45B claim can be made under s 45D in the accounting period next following the later period or the further period.

Terminal loss relief – s 45F

3.109 When carried-forward losses cannot be wholly relieved in the period in which trading ceases ('terminal period'), they can be set off against 'relevant profits' for the terminal period plus the three preceding years. CTA 2010, s 45F allows terminal loss relief in relation to unrelieved ss 45, 45A and 45B losses. The unrelieved amount of the loss can be carried back for three years prior to the terminal period so set against total profits (in the case of s 45A losses) and trading losses (in the case of s 45B losses). Section 45G provides for apportionment of losses where an accounting period preceding the terminal period falls partly within and partly outside the three-year period. Section 45H excludes terminal loss relief where there is a tax avoidance purpose for the cessation of trade.

3.110 When a company ceases trading, any unused carried-forward trade losses can be carried back without restriction for 36 months: CTA 2010, ss 45F, 43G.

3.111 Under the pre-1 April 2017 rules, the carry forward of unused trading losses for relief from future profits of the same trade, of unrelieved NTLRDs and of other types of loss against the same source in the future, was automatic.

This was because no other possibilities of utilising the loss existed, so this was simply the default position.

3.112 Under the post-1 April 2017 system, all forms of carry forward loss relief must be claimed (ie, there is no automatic carry forward except for restricted pre-1 April 2017 losses. A claim is needed before carried-forward losses can be set against total profits. The company can specify the type of loss which it wants to relieve and the amount of the relief. Any loss unused is carried forward to the next accounting period.

- relief for carried-forward trading losses is claimed under CTA 2010, s 45A(5);
- relief for carried forward NTLRDs is claimed under CTA 2009, s 463G(7);
- relief for carried forward NTLIFAs is claimed under CTA 2009, s 753;
- relief for carried forward excess management expenses is claimed under CTA 2009, s 1223(3B); and
- relief for carried-forward losses on a UK property business if claimed under CTA 2009, s 62(5A), CTA 2010, s 63(4).

3.113 Except in relation to CTA 2010, s 45B, the claim for carried-forward losses has to be made in the company's CTSA within two years of the end of the later accounting period, to which the loss is carried forward and in respect of which the relief is claimed: CTM04860/90630; CTA 2010, ss 45A(7), 62(5C), 63(6); CTA 2009, ss 463G(10), 753(2), 1223(3D). HMRC may allow a longer period and a claim can be made separately. It is not necessary for the loss to be used to the full extent possible. No claim need be made in the case of residual loss relief under s 45B. Section 45B carry forward is automatic, but the company can make an opt-out election for s 45B not to apply: CTA 2010, ss 45B(4), 45D(2)(5), 45E(2).

Non-trading loan relationship deficits

3.114 If a company has and continues to have investment business (as defined by CTA 2009, s 1218B) NTLRDs incurred in accounting periods beginning on or after 1 April 2017, can be claimed either on a flexible basis (CTA 2009, s 463G) or a restricted basis (s 463H). Accordingly, NTLRDs can be:

(i) set against profits of the deficit period: CTA 2009, s 463B(1)(a);

(ii) carried back against profits from the previous accounting period: CTA 2009, s 463B(1)(b);

3.115 *Loss Relief*

(iii) surrendered as group relief in the loss-making year: CTA 2010, s 99(1)(c);

(iv) carried forward against total profits for the first accounting period following the deficit period: CTA 2009, s 463G;

(v) surrendered as group relief in the later period: CTA 2010, s 188BB(a)(i);

(vi) carried forward to set against non-trading profits in that accounting period if a company's investment business has become small or negligible in the accounting period following the deficit period: CTA 2009, s 463H;

(vii) reinstated under s 463G if not relieved in the accounting period following the deficit period: CTA 2009, s 463I.

Example

Manufacturing Ltd is a trading company with a 31 December year-end.

Accounting period	31.12 18	31.12.19	31.12.20
Trading	10,000	(50,000)	28,000
Loss relief	(10,000)		(28,000)
NTLR	4,000	4,000	4,000
Loss relief	(4,000)	(4,000)	(4,000)
Available loss relief	0	50,000	32,000
Utilised loss relief		(18,000)	(32,000)
Carried forward		(32,000)	0

Section O: Group relief for carried-forward losses

3.115 The ability to set carried forward trading losses against profits generally (ie, total profits (CTA 2010, s 45A) necessitated a major change in the legislation, namely, to allow carried-forward losses to be group relieved. Otherwise a single company would be able to obtain relief for losses not available in a group context. Losses which qualify for flexible carry forward relief (ie, the five types of post-1 April 2017 loss which can be carried forward for relief against the 'total profits' of the company in the claim period), can alternatively be used to make a group relief or consortium relief carry forward claim, and surrendered to other members of the group. The corporation tax relief dealt with in CTA 2010, ss 188AA–188FD is called '*group relief for carried-forward losses*'. Accordingly, group relief is both a current year relief and a carried-forward relief.

3.116 Group relief for carried-forward losses has four essential aspects:

(i) quantifying the group losses available for carry-forward relief;

(ii) maximising reliefs in the loss-making companies;

(iii) allocating the available carried-forward losses amongst other profit-making group companies, having regard to CIR allocations; and

(iv) determining the RM (ie, the overall cap on total carried-forward losses which can be offset against current year profits). Standalone companies and groups alike have a RM calculated on the same basis.

3.117 Broadly speaking, available losses can be allocated amongst group companies on any basis chosen by the group, as long as the overall restrictions on carried-forward losses, as they apply to standalone companies and groups of companies alike, are observed.

3.118 Group relief for carried forward loses is available for losses incurred after 1 April 2017, if the loss to be carried forward is one of the five types which qualify for carry forward against total profits (FRLs): CTA 2010, ss 188, 188BC. A company can only group relieve losses which it is unable to set against its own profits for the loss-making year and the period to which losses are carried forward. By the same token, the claimant company can only benefit from losses carried forward for group relief after utilising its own current year and carried-forward losses: CTA 2010, s 188CD.

3.119 In summary:

(i) A company within a group or consortium must have carried-forward losses which qualify for relief on a flexible basis, which it cannot set against its own profits for the carry forward year on a flexible basis.

(ii) The surrendering company must give notice of consent to surrender those losses to the claimant company: CTA 2010, s 188BB; FA 1998, Sch 18, paras 70–71A.

(iii) The claimant company must claim the relief in its CTSA for the affected period: CTA 2010, ss 188CB, 188CC; FA 1998, Sch 18, paras 67–68.

3.120 Like single company claims, group claims are also subject to the same overall limit of the RM: CTA 2010, s 188BE. A company cannot use group relief and set carried-forward losses against profit in excess of the RM: CTA 2010, s 269ZD(3)(j). Each group company has as share of the RM allocated to it by the nominated group company.

3.121 The carried-forward loss claim remains that of an individual group company. There is no such thing as a 'group claim'. What is allowed is for

3.122 *Loss Relief*

a company with carried-forward losses to surrender them to another group company with relievable profits for the same or overlapping accounting period.

3.122 The rules are modelled on those for current year group and consortium relief in CTA 2010, ss 97–156. In the case of all surrenderable amounts, the '*group relief condition*', must be met, namely that the surrendering company and claimant company are members of the same group, and that both companies are 'UK related' (ie, UK resident or carrying on a trade in the UK through a PE: ss 188CE, 188CJ). Both conditions are also to be found in CTA 2010, s 131 (for current year group relief). Like current year relief, carried-forward group relief is available as a deduction from 'total profits', provided that the conditions for flexible relief are fulfilled.

3.123 In addition to the five types of general loss relief, group relief is also available for (i) excess carried forward non-decommissioning losses on ringfence trades (CTA 2010, s 303C); (ii) BLAGAB trade losses carried forward under FA 2012, s 124A(2), 124C(3); and (iii) qualifying charitable donations carried forward under CTA 2009, s 1223.

Section P: Definition of group

3.124 The definition of 'group' and 'consortium' for the purposes of carry forward relief largely follows (but is distinct from) the definition of 'group' for current year loss relief, as defined in CTA 2010, ss 150–152 (group) and s 153 (consortium): CTA 2010, s 269ZZB(3)(6). However, the carry-forward definition in CTA 2010, s 279ZZB is wider, because it brings in links other than through companies. The reason for the extension is to prevent companies in the same economic ownership from obtaining a separate DA, instead of a fraction of that of the group.

3.125 CTA 2010, s 1154 applies to determine the meaning of '75% subsidiary' by reference to the holding of 75% of ordinary share capital, directly or indirectly. The group relief rules in CTA 2010, ss 157–182 apply for defining equity holders and profits available for distribution: CTA 2010, s 269ZZB(5).

3.126 'Group' for carried forward loss relief purposes is defined separately but in broadly the same terms: CTA 2010, s 269ZZB. 'Group' means two or more companies, and one company is the 'ultimate parent' of the other company or companies, provided that no other company is the 'ultimate parent'. The 'ultimate parent' must be a 'parent' and, to be a parent, a company must hold 75% of the voting rights in the subsidiary, be entitled to 75% of the profits available for distribution to equity holders and be entitled to 75% of the assets available for distribution to equity holders on a winding up: CTA 2010, s 269ZZB(1)–(4).

3.127 For the purposes of this definition, the group relief provisions about equity holders, profits and assets available for distribution and meaning of '75% subsidiary' apply but CTA 2010, ss 169–182 are excluded for this purpose: CTA 2010, s 269ZZB(5).

3.128 The effect of these modifications to the current year relief definition of group and consortium is to make the carry forward definition somewhat wider:

(i) tests for grouping can be applied to economic rights: CTA 2010, s 269ZZB(7)(c);

(ii) shares with limited or temporary rights are classified without regard to these rights;

(iii) option arrangements relating to shares are disregarded;

(iv) where a non-UK resident is involved no assumptions need be made as regards (ii) and (iii);

(v) the rules for attribution of assets to a UK trade are not engaged; and

(vi) companies limited by guarantee and unincorporated associations can be group members, even though they do not have share capital: CTA 2010, s 269ZZB(7)(a)(b).

3.129 Section 269ZB(7) states that where a company does not have ordinary share capital, the tests for grouping are to be applied to economic rights. Group extends to companies without share capital, unincorporated associations and to ownership through entities other than company, trusts, or other arrangements.

3.130 The policy behind these differences reflects these considerations: (a) once a company's entitlement to current year relief has crystallised, it should not subsequently be lost by changes in the group relationship of secondary importance; (b) companies which join the group in the carry forward period should not automatically be able to benefit from the surrender of losses carried forward from earlier accounting periods; and (c) a company which does not qualify for current year group relief but is in the same economic ownership as companies who do should not be entitled to its own separate DA.

Section Q: Carried-forward losses available to be group relieved

3.131 The basic rule is in CTA 2010, s 188BB(1). This says that a loss capable of surrender within a group may be carried forward if it is a carried-forward:

(i) NTLRD under CTA 2009, s 463G;

3.132 *Loss Relief*

(ii)   NTLITF under CTA 2009, s 753(3);

(iii) excess management expense under CTA 2009, s 1223;

(iv)   post-1 April 2017 trade loss under CTA 2009, s 45A; and

(v)   loss in a UK property business under CTA 2010, ss 62, 63.

3.132 Losses may be surrendered (the 'surrenderable amount') in accordance with FA 1998, Sch 18, para 70; CTA 2010, s 188BB(6). Pre-1 April 2017 losses are not capable of carried-forward group relief: s 188BC. There must be an overlapping period common to the claim period of the claimant company and the surrender period of the surrendering company. Excess management expenses, NTDIFAs and UK property business losses cannot be surrendered intra-group if the business has become small or negligible before the claim period: CTA 2010, s 188BD.

3.133 A payment by the claimant company in respect of the surrender of losses by a surrendering company is not taken into account in determining the profits of either company for corporation tax purposes: CTA 2010, s 188FA.

Conditions for carried-forward loss claims

3.134 Under CTA 2010, s 188CB, the conditions for making a claim in relation to a surrendering company's surrenderable amounts are:

(1)   the surrendering company consents;

(2)   there is an overlap period between the surrendering company and the claimant company; and

(3)   during the overlap period, either the group condition is met (s 188CE) or consortium condition 1 is met (s 188CF) or consortium condition 2 is met (s 188CG).

Example

HoldCo has a 31 December accounting reference date. Its 100% subsidiary X Co has a 31 March accounting reference date. 9/12 of HoldCo carried forward relievable losses for the accounting period to 31 March 2020 are available for surrender to HoldCo for HoldCo's accounting period ending 31 December 2019.

3.135 The 'group condition' is that both companies are UK-related (CTA 2010, s 188CE). 'UK-related' means UK resident or non-UK resident but

Loss Relief **3.141**

carrying on a trade in the UK through a permanent establishment (PE). Where the group condition is not met, either consortium condition 1 or consortium condition 2 must be satisfied. Consortium relief is determined pro rata to the member's holding at the time the loss arises and is forfeited if the member of the consortium disposes of his shares.

3.136 Consortium condition 1 is that the claimant company is a trading company or holding company owned by a consortium, the surrendering company is a member of a consortium and both are UK-related: CTA 2010, s 188CF (see paras 3.34–3.45 above).

3.137 Consortium condition 2 applies where the surrendering company is not a member of the consortium but belongs to the same group as a link company which is a member of the consortium: CTA 2010, s 188CG.

3.138 Under CTA 2010, s 188CC, a claimant company can also make a claim for carried-forward loss relief if:

(i) the surrendering company consents;

(ii) there is an overlap period between the surrendering company and the claimant company; and

(iii) during the overlap period consortium condition 1 is met (s 188CF), consortium condition 3 is met (s 188CH) or consortium condition 4 is met (s 188CI).

3.139 A claim under this provision can only be made for consortium relief. Consortium condition 3 is the mirror image of consortium condition 1 (ie, the surrendering company is a trading company; it is owned by a consortium; the claimant company is a member of the consortium; both companies are UK-related (CTA 2010, s 188CH)). Consortium condition 4 is the mirror image of consortium condition 2 (ie, the surrendering company is a trading company; it is owned by a consortium; the claimant company is not a member of the consortium but a member of the same group as a link company; and both companies are UK-related (CTA 2010, s 188CH)).

3.140 Carry forward group relief is only possible if the surrendering company cannot itself make use of the losses: CTA 2010, s 188BE. While losses which are carried forward can be group relieved ('CF group relief'), each group company must set relevant profits against taxable profits of the source year before carrying forward any loss for group surrender. A company may not surrender group relief if at the end of the accounting period is has no income-producing assets: s 188BF.

3.141 No loss can be surrendered if it derives from a PE outside the UK: CTA 2010, s 188BH.

3.142 *Loss Relief*

3.142 A loss of a company which was non-UK resident in the loss-making period but was within the charge to UK corporation tax, so long as it is attributable to activities of the company which were subject to UK corporation tax, is not exempt under double taxation arrangements. Hence a non-UK company carrying on a trade of dealing in or developing land in the UK by a PE may only surrender a loss to the extent that it is attributable to its UK activity. If during the loss-making period the surrendering company was a non-resident company carrying on a trade of dealing in or developing UK land, or carrying on a trade in the UK through a PE, the UK related losses may be carried forward for surrender under CTA 2010, s 188BI.

Giving effect to carried-forward group loss relief

3.143 Where a claim is made under CTA 2010, ss 188CB or 188CC, the claimant company makes a deduction from its total profits for the claim period: s 188CK.

3.144 A company within the group or consortium must have carried-forward losses available for relief and must give notice of consent to surrender those losses to the claimant company before the loss relief claim is made: CTA 2010, s 188BB. The claimant company must make the claim for relief in its CTSA for the affected period (or by amendment of that return): CTA 2010, ss 188CB–188CC, 188CD.

Section R: The loss cap

3.145 The general principles as set out in CTA 2009, ss 45A–45H and CTA 2010, ss 188AA–188CK for single company and group relief for carried-forward losses are all subject to the overall limits on relief for carried-forward losses set out in ss 269ZA–269ZZB, which apply to standalone companies and groups alike. The loss cap only applies where carried-forward losses exceed the DA, which is the amount of current year taxable profits which may be offset without restriction against carried-forward losses. Broadly speaking, only 50% of the profits above the DA can be used to obtain tax relief for carried-forward losses.

3.146 Current-year reliefs must first be set against profits. Where it applies, the loss cap prevents a company from setting carried-forward losses against the balance of company profits (ie, after deducting current year reliefs) to nil. A proportion of the company's profits are carried forward to the following year.

3.147 This is achieved by establishing for both single companies and groups a 'relevant maximum' (RM) for each profit-making accounting period. The RM

Loss Relief **3.151**

is the total amount of current year profits against which carried-forward losses can be offset. The loss restriction applies at the individual company level. Each member of a group needs to work out its own RM, and its own relevant profits. So, there are multiple loss restriction calculations within a group, the results of which then must be aggregated to determine the overall group loss available for carry-forward relief.

3.148 In effect the carried-forward claim is in three stages for a single company:

(1) First, establish the amount of loss available to be carried forward, ignoring the possible application of the loss cap.

(2) Second, establish the tax capacity of the company in the accounting period to which the loss is carried forward (ie, the relevant profits).

(3) Third, having carried the losses forward, and ascertained what profits exist against which such losses may be relieved, establish whether the loss cap applies so as to limit the amount of relief which may be claimed in that accounting period. The loss cap means that carried forward trading losses can only be relieved to the extent of the 'relevant maximum', where this is less than the available profits in the carry forward year.

3.149 Within a group, the same broad stages apply. Each company must:

(i) ascertain separately what unutilised losses it has available for carry forward from the loss-making year;

(ii) establish to what extent it can itself utilise the carried forward loss, and what carried-forward losses are available for surrender within the group or consortium;

(iii) establish the extent to which it can absorb the available carried-forward losses of other group companies; and

(iv) separately ascertain its RM. For this purpose, the single company rules must be modified to apply in a group situation. There is no such thing as a 'group claim'.

3.150 All this means is that, for group relief purposes, the primary reality is that of the group, not the individual entities which belong to the group.

Section S: The key concepts in the loss cap

3.151 There are four key concepts in the loss cap:

- 'deductions allowance' (DA) (CTA 2010, s 269ZW);

3.152 *Loss Relief*

- 'relevant deductions' (RD) (CTA 2010, ss 269ZB(3)(4), 269ZC(2), 269ZD(3));
- 'relevant profits' (RP) (CTA 2010, ss 269ZD(5), 269ZF, 269ZFA) (Section T); and
- 'relevant maximum' (RM) (CTA 2010, ss 269ZB-269ZD) (Section U).

All these concepts exist solely for carried-forward loss relief purposes and have no wider application.

Deductions allowance

3.152 The deductions allowance (DA) is the key to enabling carried-forward losses to be used. It boosts the company's loss capacity by a fixed amount. Unless a company specifies the amount of DA available for utilisation each year, this is nil: CTA 2010, 269ZB(7), 269ZC(5), 269ZZ(2). The amount must be specified in 'a company's tax return for an accounting period': CTA 2010, s 269ZZ(1). This means that the notification must be made at the same time as the CTSA is submitted and be contained in or incorporated into it.

3.153 Every standalone company and every group of companies (as defined for the purposes of carried-forward loss relief) has a DA of £5m: CTA 2010, ss 269ZR, 269ZW. That means that losses of up to £5m can be carried forward from a loss-making year to a subsequent year without restriction. However, the DA must be divided into separate allowances for (i) streamed trading profits, (ii) streamed NTLRDs, and (iii) unrestricted profits. Post-1 April 2020 the DA also has to cover capital losses.

3.154 There is one DA for each accounting period. As soon as carried-forward losses exceed £5m, the loss cap applies when the carried-forward loss is offset against current year profits. The effect is to limit carried-forward loss offset to 50% of 'relevant profits'.

Example

Year	Profit	Unrelieved loss	Carried-forward	Loss cap applicable
1		(4,000,000)	(4,000,000)	No
2		(3,000,000)	(7,000,000)	No
3	10,000,000		(7,000,000)	Yes

3.155 CTA 2010, s 269ZD(6) states that a company's DA for an accounting period is £5m (s 269ZW) or, if the company is a member of a group, the

Loss Relief **3.159**

proportion of the group's DA which is allocated to it, plus any non-group DA (eg, where the company was not a member of the group for the whole accounting period) provided that the overall DA for all the members of the group cannot exceed £5m for that accounting period (s 269ZR).

3.156 The DA is a basic amount of current year profits (£5m) which, together with 50% of the excess of 'relevant profits' (being qualifying profits minus the DA), a company or group can set against carried-forward losses without triggering the loss cap. Broadly speaking, a company or group of companies can obtain current year relief for carried-forward losses (single company or group) of up to £5m (the DA) *plus* 50% of the relevant profits above £5m. When carried-forward losses > RM, a restriction on the amount of carried-forward losses which may be relieved in that accounting period will be triggered.

3.157 In the case of a single company CTA 2010, s 269ZW(2) defines the DA as £5m for each accounting period of 12 months. The DA is proportionately reduced for accounting periods of less than 12 months and may be increased where a company is required to bring into account a credit in respect of the reversal of an onerous lease provision: CTA 2010, ss 269ZX, 269ZY. Section 269ZW(2) states simply:

> '(2) the company's deductions allowance for an accounting period is £5,000,000.'

3.158 A separate restriction of profits available for relief has to be calculated for each type of carried-forward loss available to be relieved. If the company has carried-forward losses of a type that can only be deducted from a particular type of profit, then the company will need to show how it has divided its DA between its trading and non-trading profits: CTA 2010, ss 269ZB(7), 269ZC(5); CTM05080. A company only has to calculate a particular restriction if it has losses falling within that description.

3.159 This will apply if the company has carried-forward losses of any of the following types:

- non-trading loan relationship deficits (NTLRDs) carried-forward for deduction from non-trading profits only: CTA 2009, ss 457(3), 463H(5);
- trading losses carried-forward for deduction from profits of the same trade only: CTA2010, ss 45(4)(b), 45B(4); and
- deductions from trading profits under CTA 2010, ss 303B(4), 303D(5) for excess carried-forward non-decommissioning losses of a ring-fenced trade in the oil and gas industry, where certain conditions are met: CTA 2010, ss 269ZB(3)(b), (4).

3.160 Loss Relief

3.160 The DA accordingly comprises two components: (i) a 'trading profits deduction allowance' (TPDA) and (ii) a non-trading profits deduction allowance (NTPDA), depending upon whether the carried-forward losses qualify for deduction from (i) trading profits, being streamed trading losses; (ii) non-trading profits, being streamed NTLRDs; or (iii) total profits (being losses which qualify for flexible loss reliefs. The sum of (TPDA + NTPDA) must be ≤ £5m. If a company only has carried-forward losses which qualify for flexible relief, then it simply has a DA which, in turn, must be ≤ £5m. Post-1 April 2020, the NTPDA comprises the Non-Trading Income Deductions Allowance and the Chargeable Gains Deductions Allowance.

3.161 It follows that where a company has losses of a particular description, each category of category of loss restriction is set against a particular category of income and the RM will be the sum of 50% of the corresponding relevant profits and the allocated share of the DA:

- a company's maximum relievable losses for streamed trading losses is restricted by reference to 'qualifying trading profits': CTA 2010, s 269B;

- a company's maximum loss capacity for streamed NTLRDs is restricted by reference to 'qualifying non-trading profits': CTA 2010, s 269ZC; and

- a company's maximum loss capacity for flexible losses is worked out by reference to its 'qualifying profits': CTA 2010, s 269ZD.

3.162 If the company is making a claim for relief for carried-forward losses that can only be set against trading profits (CTA 2010, s 269ZB), it must specify the amount of any DA that it wants to use as the trading profits deduction allowance: CTA 2010, s 269ZB(7). The amount of the trading profits DA is then included when calculating the RM for trading profits.

3.163 If the company is making a claim for relief for carried-forward losses that can only be set against non-trading profits (CTA 2010, s 269ZC), it must specify the amount of any DA that it wants to use as the non-trading profits deduction allowance: CTA 2010, s 269ZC(5). This is then included when calculating the RM for non-trading profits.

3.164 A company which only has flexible losses will only have to consider the total profits restriction. From 1 April 2020, capital profits are included in total profits.

3.165 A company's CTSA for the carry-forward period must specify the amount of the DA it is entitled to for an accounting period, unless it is not claiming relief for carried-forward losses subject to the loss cap: CTA 2010, s 269ZZ(2). The company should state in its return the amount of its DA for

Loss Relief **3.171**

trading profits and non-trading profits, along with the total amount of its DA allowance. It can do this in its tax computations submitted as part of its return.

3.166 TPDA and NTPDA are the amounts specified in the company's CTSA. If no amount is specified, they are nil. Accordingly, the DA/TPDA/NTPDA must be specified in the CTSA for the carry-forward period: CTA 2010, s 269ZZ(1). Otherwise the DA is nil. The amount specified may not be greater that the difference between the DA less that for any non-trading profits specified in the return: CTA 2010, s 269ZB(8).

3.167 The company may choose how its DA should be allocated between trading profits and non-trading profits: CTA 2010, s 269ZB(7), 269ZC(5). For example, the whole amount could be apportioned to pre-1 April 2017 trading losses.

Deductions allowance – groups

3.168 The group DA is also £5m: CTA 2010, s 269ZR. This must be allocated amongst group companies, so that each group company with carried-forward losses will have its own DA of a fraction of £5m. The group must appoint a 'nominated company', which determines the allocation of the group DA and must notify HMRC of the apportionment: CTA 2010, s 269ZS; CTM05180. This is done by filing the 'group annual allowance statement' with HMRC: CTA 2010, s 269ZT.

Relevant deductions

3.169 The types of carried-forward losses that can be relieved against particular types of profits are known as 'relevant deductions' (CTA 2010, ss 269ZB(3)(4), 269ZC(2), 269ZD(3)). Relevant deductions are carried-forward losses which may be set against taxable total profits up to the RM. With effect from 1 April 2017, carried-forward losses (ie, relevant deductions) can only be relieved up to the amount of the RM, after allowing for relief for current year losses.

3.170 In-year reliefs are reduced, and so relevant deductions are increased by the CIR. This is explained in CTM05090 and CTM05240-CTM05260.

3.171 Under CTA 2010, s 269ZD(3), 'relevant deductions' are:

(i) losses which qualify for restricted relief under CTA 2010, s 45B;

(ii) NTLRDs which qualify for restricted relief under CTA 2009, ss 457(3), 463H(5); and

3.172 *Loss Relief*

(iii) losses which qualify for flexible relief under CTA 2009, ss 463G, 753; CTA 2010, ss 45A, 62(3), 1219.

3.172 CTA 2010, s 269ZD determines a company's 'taxable total profits' for an accounting period. Section 269ZD(2) says that the sum of any relevant deductions made by a company for an accounting period may not exceed the difference between the RM and the sum of carried forward RRLs. This means that the balance of the RM is available for offset against FRLs.

Section T: Relevant profits

3.173 Relevant profits' are defined in CTA 2010, ss 269ZD(5), 269ZF, 269ZFA. 'Relevant profits' are 'qualifying profits' less the DA: CTA 2010, s 269ZF(1). 'Qualifying profits' are defined and calculated in accordance with ss 269ZF and 269ZFA.

3.174 'Total profits' are modified to produce 'qualifying profits' by ignoring specified items of profit and losses which are exempt or fully relievable against current year profits. 'Qualifying profits' in turn allow 'relevant profits' to be calculated by the deduction of the DA. The purpose of calculating the loss cap by reference to 'relevant profits' rather than 'total profits' and by defining 'relevant profits' by reference to 'qualifying profits' is to exclude exempt profits and to ensure that losses already relievable by offset against current year profits (i) remain relievable in full, and (ii) are taken into account in the calculation of 'relevant profits' so as to prevent double-counting.

3.175 In summary:

(Total profits – excluded items) = Modified total profits

(Modified total profits – in-year reliefs) = Qualifying profits

(Qualifying profits – deductions allowance) = Relevant profits.

3.176 CTA 2009 s 269ZD(5) states that a company 'relevant profits' for an accounting period are the sum of (i) its 'relevant trading profits', (ii) its 'relevant non-trading profits and (iii) its 'relevant BLAGAB trade profits'. 'Relevant profits' are defined in terms of 'qualifying profits' (QP). 'Relevant trading profits' are (QTP – TPDA). 'Relevant non-trading profits are (QNTP – NTPDA): CTA 2010, s 269ZF(1)(2).

3.177 The various adjustments to 'total profits' to produce 'qualifying profits' and then 'relevant profits' are set out in CTA 2010, ss 269ZF, 269ZFA, which are explained in CTM05030–CTN05110. These are modified in the case of insurance companies by ss 269ZFB–269ZQ (CTM 05030–05110).

3.178 For companies other than life insurance companies, relevant profits are the sum of the relevant trading profits and the relevant non-trading profits: CTA 2019, s 269ZD(5). For life insurance companies relevant profits are the sum of relevant trading profits, relevant non-trading profits and BLAGAB trade profits: CTA 2010, s 269ZD(5).

3.179 'Relevant Profits' (RP) are defined in CTA 2010, s 269ZF for the period from 1 April 2017 to 5 July 2018. For periods commencing on and from 6 July 2018 (including notional accounting periods beginning on 6 July 2018 in years that straddle 6 July 2018), RP are calculated in accordance with the combination of s 269ZF and s 269ZFA, which use procedures set out in s 269ZF with certain modifications.

3.180 Sections 269ZF and s 269ZFA share four common features:

(i) 'Relevant profits' are divided into 'relevant trading profits' and 'relevant non-trading profits': s 269F(1)(2).

(ii) 'Relevant profits' are defined as 'qualifying profits'.

(iii) 'Qualifying profits' are computed by paragraph (1) of step 1 in section 269ZF(3) by reference to 'total profits'. This modifies total profits to give 'modified total profits' by leaving out some items and denying deductions for others, in accordance with s 269ZF(4).

(iv) Modified total profits are reduced by the amount given by paragraph (1) of step 2 in section 269ZF(3) in determining those profits for the accounting period to give 'qualifying profits'. The amounts in question are in-year reliefs, ignoring 'excluded deductions' as defined in s 269ZF(5), which include carried-forward trade losses which qualify for flexible relief.

3.181 There is no essential difference between CTA 2010, s 269ZF and 269ZFA. Section 269ZFA simply leaves out Steps 3 to 5 of s 269ZF(3). These are concerned with splitting qualifying profits into qualifying trading profits and qualifying non-trading profits.

3.182 Companies have software programs to calculate 'relevant profits', and the resultant RM. HMRC's approach is set out in CTM05030–CTM05110.

Relevant profits – Accounting periods 1 April 2017–6 July 2018

3.183 'Relevant profits' are 'Qualifying profits' less the DA: CTA 2010, s 269ZF(3), Step 5.

'Qualifying profits' are calculated in accordance with s 269ZF(3).

3.184 Loss Relief

3.184 The legislation (CTA 2010, s 269ZF) prescribes five steps:

Step 1: Calculate 'modified total profits' (MTP) by eliminating from total profits excluded profits, such as distributions (other than distributions which are treated as trading profits), and RRLs. If Step 1 leaves a positive figure, proceed to Step 2. If Step 1 leaves a negative figure, the relevant profits will be nil and no further steps are necessary.

Step 2: Calculate in-year reliefs deductible from modified total profits, taking no account of 'excluded deductions'.

Step 3: Divide MTP into TP and NTP. This is only necessary if a company has carried-forward losses which can only be relieved as RRLs.

Step 4: Allocate the in-year reliefs (Step 2) to TP and NTP provided that neither TP nor NTP can be < 0.

Step 5: Calculate the qualifying trading profits (QTP) and the qualifying non-trading profits (QNTP), being the Step 4 amounts less the Step 2 amounts (ie, the in-year reliefs)

QTP + QNTP = QP

RP = QP − DA.

If there are QTP and QNTP, RP = (QTP − TPDA) + (QNTP − NTPDA)).

It is then possible to calculate the RM.

3.185 In more detail:

Step 1

Calculate 'modified total profits' (MTP) in accordance with CTA 2010, s 269ZF(4) by disregarding all the items there listed which could otherwise be included in the calculation of total profits. These disregarded items are

- Distributions falling within CTA 2009, Part 9A, as these are exempt for corporation tax purposes.
- Ring fence profits of oil and gas companies.
- I–E profits of insurance companies
- Carried forward pre-1 April 2017 trading losses and restricted post-1 April 2017 trading losses (save in special cases of creative industry

Loss Relief **3.185**

losses, falling within (CTA 2009, ss 1210(5A), 1211(7A), 1216DA(3), 1216DB(5A), 1217DA(3), 1217DB(5A),1216DC(7A), 1217MA(3), 1217MC(9), 1217SA(3), 217SC(9), 1218ZDA(3) and 1218ZDC(9)).

- Losses of UK or European Economic Area (EEA) furnished holiday lettings (CTA 2010, s 65(4B), 67A(5A)).
- Insurance companies' shock losses (CTA 2010, s 269ZI(1)).
- Losses of oil and gas ring fence trades that are FLRs (CTA 2010, s 304(7)).
- Pre-1 April 2017 losses from oil contractor activities (CTA 2010, s 303B(4), 303D(5)).
- Carried forward NTDLRs which are RRLs (CTA 2009, ss 457(3), 463H(4)).

If MTP are nil, there are no relevant profits, so the company's DA is limited to £5m.

Step 2

In-year reliefs calculated at Step 2 are deducted from modified total profits when calculating qualifying profits at Step 5. If MTP > 0, calculate 'Step 2 amount': CTA 2010, s 269ZF(3) Step 2, (5). Calculate the amount of any deductions that can be made from total profits for any in-year reliefs: CTA 2010, ss 269ZF(3) and (5) (Step 2). If the MTP > Step 2 Amount, proceed to Step 3. If not, relevant trading profits and relevant non-trading profits are nil.

The Step 2 amount consists of profits which may be relieved by losses qualifying for current year reliefs, ignoring 'excluded deductions':

- carried-forward losses qualifying as FRLs
- carried back trading losses
- terminal losses
- excess capital allowances for special leasing carried back from a later accounting period (CAA 2001, s 260(3)).

Step 3

Divide MTP into trading profits and non-trading profits. If there are no RRLs, there is no need to calculate qualifying trading and qualifying non-trading profits separately.

3.186 *Loss Relief*

Step 4

Deduct in-year reliefs identified at Step 2 from either or both of the company's trading and non-trading profits as the company wishes (but so that neither amount is reduced below nil). The Step 2 amount is deducted from modified total profits, to give 'qualifying profits': CTA 2010, s 269ZF(4).

Step 5

The result is the company's QTPs and QNPTs (Step 5). Deduct the trading profits allowance and non-trading profits allowance from the QTPs and QNPTs respectively. The result is the company's relevant trading profit and relevant non-trading profit: CTA 2010, ss 269ZF(1)(2). A company's relevant profit for an accounting period is the sum of its relevant trading profit and relevant non-trading profit: CTA 2010, s 269ZD(5).

Relevant profits – Accounting periods from 6 July 2018

3.186 With effect from 6 July 2018 a modified definition of 'relevant profits' was introduced by Finance Act 2019 by the insertion of s 269ZFA. This is simpler in formulation than s 269ZF, but not substantially different.

3.187 For accounting periods including straddling periods commencing on or after 6 July 2018 (Finance Act 2019, Sch 10, paras 8, 32) ('post-6 July 2018 QP'), the basic method set out in s 269ZF is modified by s 269ZFA. The new section provides:

'(1) A company's "relevant profits" for an accounting period are –

   (a) the company's qualifying profits for the accounting period, less

   (b) the company's "deductions allowance" for the accounting period (see section 269ZD(6).

(2) A company's "qualifying profits" for an accounting period are –

   (a) the amount given by paragraph (1) of step 1 in section 269ZF(3) in determining the company's qualifying trading profits and non-trading profits for the accounting period, less

   (b) the amount given by paragraph (1) of step 2 in section 269ZF(3) in determining those profits for the accounting period.'

Loss Relief **3.188**

3.188 This requires:

(i) applying Step 1 of s 269ZF(3) to find modified total profits (though that term is no longer used; and

(ii) deducting from that figure current year reliefs.

The only change is that Step 3 (division of modified total profits into trading and non-trading profits) becomes redundant. There is no need to divide modified total profits into trading profits and non-trading profits.

Example 1

Item	Year to 31.03.17	Year to 31.03.18	Year to 31.03.19
Trading	(12,000,000)	6,000,000	8,000,000
NTLR	2,000,000	(1,000,000)	1,000,000
Distributions	2,000,000	1,000,000	2,000,000
Capital gains	2,000,000	2,000,000	3,000,000
Total profits	6,000,000	9,000,000	14,000,000
Excluded profits		(1,000,000)	(2,000,000)
Modified total profits		6,000,000	10,000,000
In-year reliefs	4,000,000	1,000,000	0
Modified trading profits		6,000,000	8,000,000
Modified non-trading profits		0	1,000,000
Deduct in-year reliefs	(4,000,000)	(1,000,000)	0
Qualifying profits		5,000,000	9,000,000
Deductions allowance		(5,000,000)	(5,000,000)
Relevant profits		0	4,000,000
Relevant maximum		5,000,000	7,000,000
Relief for carried-forward losses		(5,000,000)	(3,000,000)
Loss carried forward	(8,000,000)	(3,000,000)	0
Total taxable profits	0	2,000,000	9,000,000

3.189 *Loss Relief*

Example 2

Item	Year to 31.03.17	Year to 31.03.18	Year to 31.03.19
Trading	(15,000,000)	(8,000,000)	35,000,000
NTLR	(1,000,000)	(2,000,000)	(5,000,000)
Distributions	2,000,000	1,000,000	3,000,000
Capital gains	2,000,000		12,000,000
Total profits	6,000,000	9,000,000	50,000,000
Excluded profits		(1,000,000)	(2,000,000)
Modified total profits		6,000,000	48,000,000
In-year reliefs	4,000,000		2,000,000 (group relief) 5,000,000 (NTDLR)
Modified trading profits		6,000,000	35,000,000
Modified non-trading profits		0	13,000,000
Deduct in-year reliefs	(4,000,000)	0	(7,000,000)
Qualifying profits		6,000,000	41,000,000
Deductions allowance			(5,000,000)
Relevant profits			36,000,000
Relevant maximum		5,000,000	23,000,000
Relief for carried-forward losses		(5,000,000)	(3,000,000)
Loss carried forward	(8,000,000)	(3,000,000)	0
Total taxable profits	0	2,000,000	37,000,000

Section U: Relevant maximum

3.189 The 'relevant maximum' for trading and non-trading profits are set out in CTA 2010, ss 269ZA–269ZO. These provisions restrict the set off of carried-forward losses of all companies in accounting periods beginning on or after 1 April 2017 and running until 31 March 2020 to the relevant maximum (RM). The RM for total profits is the amount of carried-forward losses which can be set against current year profits. In both single companies and groups the amount of carried-forward losses which can be relieved in the accounting period following the loss-making period is restricted to the RM, unused losses being carried forward to the next accounting period. The DA does not determine the quantum of the relievable carried-forward losses, rather it is an element used to calculate the RM.

3.190 With effect from 1 April 2020, the RM was redefined to take account of the fact that part of the DA may be allocated by a company to chargeable gains. Accordingly, from that date, the DA may be split at the option of the company into:

- trading profits DA;
- total non-trading profits, which comprises the DA for:
    (i) non-trading income profits, and
    (ii) chargeable gains deductions allowance, and
- in the case of insurance companies, BLAGAB DA.

3.191 The RM is the maximum of carried-forward losses which may be set against current year profits. The 'sum of deductions' may not exceed the RM.

So:

$$RM = \frac{(QP - DA)}{2} + DA$$

Where:

RM = Relevant maximum

QP = Qualifying profits

DA = Deductions allowance

3.192 So, in the case of a single company with carried-forward losses of £8m, and QP for the current year of £7m (ie, RP of £2m),

$$RM = \frac{(QP - DA)}{2} + DA = \frac{(7,000,000 - 5,000,000)}{2} + 5,000,000 = 6,000,000$$

Relievable carried-forward loss = £6m

Loss cap = £(8m − 6m) = 2m

Alternatively:

$$RM = RP/2 + DA = 1 + 5 = £6m$$

3.193 *Loss Relief*

Example

Assume relevant deductions are £10m, and QP are £7m. Then relief for relevant deductions (ie, the RM, is restricted to £6m)

RP = (7m − 5m) = £2m

RM = ((2m/2) + 5m) = £6m

3.193 Where a company is subject to the loss cap, then

if current year profits = x,

the relevant maximum = y,

carried-forward losses = z, where z > y,

the unutilised carried forward loss taken forward to subsequent accounting periods is (z − y).

3.194 Under the pre-2017 system, the company would have been taxable on (x − z). Under the post-2017 system, the company is taxable on (x − y), the additional taxable profit being (z − y). For every £1 disallowed a company pays an additional (£1 × corporation tax rate) in corporation tax. If the company continues to make a profit, then the disallowed loss may become deductible in a later accounting period, with its value as a deferred tax asset suitably discounted.

3.195 As losses may be carried forward as streamed trade losses, streamed NTDLRs or on a flexible basis, there are three separate definitions of RM in CTA 2010, ss 269ZB(5), 269ZC(3) and 269ZD(4). Post-1 April 2017, carried-forward losses fall into three groups, each with its own RM:

CTA 2010	Relevant deductions	Loss carry forward	Relevant maximum	Notes
s 269ZB(5)	Trading losses which qualify for restricted relief	CTA 2010, s 45(4)(b), 45B, 45D, 303B(4),303D(5)	50% of 'relevant trading profits' + NTPDA	Losses only available for relief against trading profits
s 269ZC(3)	NTDLR which qualify for restricted relief	CTA 2009, ss 457(3), 463H(5)	50% of 'relevant non-trading profits' + NTPDA	Losses only available for relief against non-trading profits

Loss Relief **3.199**

CTA 2010	Relevant deductions	Loss carry forward	Relevant maximum	Notes
s 269ZD(4)	Losses which qualify for flexible relief	CTA 2009, ss 463G, 753; CTA 2010, ss 45A, 45C, 62(3), 1219, FA 2012, s 124B	50% of 'relevant trading profits' + TPDA	Losses available for relief against total profits

3.196 Hence CTA 2010, s 269ZB(5) states:

'(5) In this section the "relevant maximum" means the sum of –

    (a) 50% of the company's relevant trading profits for the accounting period, and

    (b) the amount of the company's trading profits deductions allowance for the accounting period.'

3.197 CTA 2010, s 269ZC(3) states that, where a company has relevant deductions which qualify for relief on a restricted basis under CTA 2009, ss 457(3), 463H(5) its RM is:

- 50% of 'relevant non-trading profits' plus
- NTPDA.

3.198 Section 269ZD(4) says that, where a company has relevant deductions which qualify for relief on a flexible basis under CTA 2009, ss 463G, 753; CTA 2010, ss 45A, 62(3), 1219 its RM is

- 50% of 'relevant profits' plus
- The company's DA for the accounting period.

This is a sweep-up provision dealing with carried-forward losses that do not fall under CTA 2010, ss 269ZB, 269ZC and which qualify as FRLs. This covers trading profits, non-trading profits and total profits that can be relieved by any type of carried-forward loss. This is the RM for total profits less the amount of any carried-forward trading losses (CTA 2010, s 262ZB(3)) and NTDLRs (CTA 2010, s 269ZC(2)) which are RRLs.

3.199 Accordingly, in cases where carried-forward losses comprise both FRLs and RRLs, the RM must be computed separately for trading and non-trading profits. Trade profits are profits of a trade of the company. Non-trade profits are all other profits, including capital gains (to be excluded from 1 April 2020). The 'relevant maximum' for an accounting period is defined by reference to the 'relevant profits' for the same accounting period. TPDA and NTPDA

3.200 Loss Relief

are taken into account in calculating 'relevant profits'. Thus, qualifying profits exceed the DA, which is taken into account twice, both as an absolute loss allowance and as part of a tapered loss allowance (being an element in the computation of 'relevant profits'). This is because 'relevant trading profits' are 'qualifying trading profits minus TPDA', and relevant non-trading profits are 'qualifying non-trading profits minus NTPDA'.

3.200 Where a company has to calculate separate DAs and RMs for (i) restricted relief trading losses, (ii) NTDLRs, and (iii) trading profits. If it does not use a particular RM to its full extent, the balance is transferred to the other RMs, provided that this sum does not exceed £5m.

Example 1

The results of Coffee Party plc are:

	31 March 2017	31 March 2018	31 March 2019
Trading	(10,000,000)	0	6,000,000
Non-trading loan relationships	0	1,000,000	0
Dividends	1,000,000	500,000	800,000
Loss relief	0	0	(5,500,000)
Carried-forward loss	10,000,000	10,000,000	4,500,000

- Qualifying profits: £6m
- Trading profits deductions allowance = £5m
- Qualifying profits: £6m
- Relevant maximum: = £(6m − 5m)/2 + 5m = £5.5m

Example 2

The results of Investment Ltd are:

	31 March 2017	31 March 2018	31 March 2019
Non-trading loan relationships	(10,000,000)	1,000,000	6,000,000
Dividends	1,000,000	500,000	800,000
Capital gains	1,000,000	0	1,000,000

	31 March 2017	*31 March 2018*	*31 March 2019*
Loss relief	0	(1,000,000)	(6,000,000)
Carried-forward loss	10,000,000	9,000,000	3,000.000

- Qualifying profits: £6m
- Non-trading profits deductions allowance = £5m
- Relevant profits: £(6m – 5m) = 1m
- Relevant maximum: 1,000,000/2 + 5,000,00 = £5.5m

Example 3

The results of Trader plc are:

	31 March 2018	*31 March 2019*
Trading profits	2,000,000	8,000,000
Non-trading loan relationships	(10,000,000)	1,000,000
Dividends	1,000,000	500,000
Capital gains	1,000,000	1,000,000
Loss relief	(3,000,000)	(7,000,000)
Taxable profits	0	3,000,000
Carried-forward loss	7,000,000	0

- Qualifying profits: £10m
- Total profits deductions allowance = £5m
- Relevant profits = £5m
- Relevant maximum: (5,000,000/2) + 5,000,000 = £7.5m

Example 4

The results of Manufacturing Ltd are:

	31 March 2017	*31 March 2018*
Trading profits	(1,000,000)	11,000,000
Non-trading loan relationships		(3,000,000)

3.201 *Loss Relief*

	31 March 2017	31 March 2018
Dividends	500,000	1,000,000
Capital gains	0	1,000,000
Loss relief – current year	0	(3,000,000)
Carried-forward loss pre-1 April 2017	1,000,000	(1,000,000)

- Qualifying profits: £12m – 3m (in-year reliefs) = £9m
- Specified trading profits deductions allowance = £5m
- Total profits deductions allowance = £5m – £5m = £0
- Relevant profits = £4m
- Relevant maximum: (4,000,000/2) + 5,000,000 = £7m

Relevant maximum – Groups

3.201 A group has a single 'group DA' of £5m for an accounting period, proportionally reduced if the nominated company's accounting period is less than 12 months or if the accounting period began before and ended after 1 April 2017: CTA 2010, s 269ZS(2)–(4).

3.202 Companies in a group must appoint one company to be responsible for allocating the group DA amongst the group companies: CTA 2010, s 269ZS. This will normally be the reporting company for CIR. Each company within the group within the charge to corporation tax must sign the nomination: CTA 2010, s 269ZS(1). The nominated company draws up a list of the group companies. The group DA is allocated amongst the listed companies by the nominated company appointed by the companies in the group ('the group allowance nomination'): CTA 2010, s 269ZS(1). The nominating company allocates the group DA amongst the group companies in accordance with a 'group allowance allocation statement': CTA 2010, s 269ZT. For each of the accounting periods in which it is the nominated company, it must submit a 'group allowance allocation statement': CTA 2010, s 269ZT–269ZU. This may be revised in accordance with s 269ZU. The statement must be received by HMRC within 12 months of the CTSA filing date: CTA 2010, s 269ZT(4)–(5). Subject to various time limits, a revised allocation statement may be submitted: CTA 2010, s 269ZU.

3.203 The nominated company's accounting period governs the proportions of the group DA which can be allocated. The accounting period for carry forward group relief is that of the nominated company. If the group allowance nomination takes effect for less than a full accounting period of the nominated company, the group DA is reduced proportionately: CTA 2010, s 269ZS. A group allowance nomination must state the date on which it takes effect and be signed by a proper officer of the company on behalf of each group member.

3.204 If the group allowance allocation statement is found to be inaccurate then, as in the case of the CIR, a revised statement must be submitted within 30 days: CTA 2010, s 269ZV(7).

To allocate the group DA amongst members of the group, the nominated company must submit a group allowance allocation statement for each of the accounting periods in which it is the nominated company (CTA10/S269ZT(1), CTM05200). It can submit the statement in PDF format as an attachment to its tax return. There is a template for the statement at CTM04836.

The nominated company lists one or more group companies on the group allowance allocations statement (the listed companies) (CTA10/S269ZV(3)(e)) and allocates the group DA between these companies.

There is no set proportion in which the DA has to be allocated amongst the listed companies; however, there is an overall maximum amount that can be allocated to a particular company for its accounting period (S269ZV(5), CTM05210).

The group allowance allocation statement must be signed by the appropriate person in relation to the nominated company (S269ZV(2)). An appropriate person is a proper officer of the company or another person who has the authority of the company to act on its behalf (S269ZS(9)). Proper officer takes the meaning given at TMA70/S108(3) and (4).

Requirements for individual companies in the group are set out below.

Companies with carried-forward losses that are members of a group

3.205 This applies to any individual company which is a member of a group.

The company's DA for an accounting period is whatever is allocated to it on the group allowance allocation statement or statements that relate to that period (CTA10/S269ZR, CTM05140).

The exception to this is if the company is only in a group for part of its accounting period, in which case it is entitled to an appropriate amount of non-group DA (S269ZR, CTM05150).

3.206 Loss Relief

The company should state the total amount of its DA for the accounting period on its tax return for that period (CTA10/S269ZZ).

If the company has carried-forward losses of a type that can only be deducted from a particular type of profit, it will need to show how it has divided its DA between its trading and non-trading profits (CTA10/S269ZB(7), S269SC(5)). This is the same as for companies that are not in a group.

3.206   Under CTA 2010, s 188DB, the amount of group relief on carried-forward losses in the claimant company is limited to the lesser of:

(a)   the unused parts of the surrenderable amounts; and

(b)   the RM for that company.

The unused part of the surrenderable amounts is the amount of carried-forward losses available for group relief less amounts already claimed (s 188DC). The RM is the claimant company's RM less a variety of specified reliefs which take precedence over carried forward group relief: s 188DD. The company's 'relevant profits' then have to be computed in accordance with CTA 2010, s 269ZD(5).

3.207   CTA 2010, s 269ZR(2) states:

'(2)   The company's deduction allowance for the accounting period is the sum of –

(a)   any amounts of group deductions allowance (£5 million) allocated to the company for the period in accordance with sections 269ZS to 269ZV, and

(b)   the appropriate amount of the non-group deductions allowance of the company for the period,

up to a limit of £5 million.'

The 'non-group DA' is the proportion of the annual period in which the company was concerned was not a member of the group. The aim is to prevent double relief for companies which change or join groups mid-year. An appropriate part of the non-group deductions allowance for a period is:

$$DNG/DAG \times £5,000,000$$

Where

DNG is the number of days in the period on which the company is not a member of a group, and

DAC is the total number of days in the period.

Loss Relief **3.209**

Example

In an accounting period ending 31 December X Ltd joins the Y PLC group on 7 September (day 219 of the accounting period). The nominated company allocates £2m of the group DA to X Ltd. The company's deduction allowance is ((219/365 x 5,000,000) + 2,000,000) = £5m

3.208 The nominated company's group allowance allocation statement must be received by HMRC within 12 months of the filing date for the submission of the nominated company's CTSA return. The calculation of the RM of claimant companies in a group has to be calculated in accordance with CTA 2010, ss 188ED, 269ZD(4), which in turn brings in ss 269ZF, 269ZFA (calculation of 'relevant profits'). If excess group DA is claimed, HMRC can assess to recover the excess: CTA 2010, s 269ZZA.

Section V: The cap on relievable carried-forward losses

3.209

Example 1

Year	1	2
Accounting period	01.01.18–31.12.18	01.01.19–31.12.19
Trading	(10,000,000)	10,000,000
Non-trading loan relationships (NTLR)	(500,000)	1,000,000

(i) Modified total profit for Year 2 is £11m.

(ii) There are no in-year reliefs (Step 2).

(iii) QTP £10m; QNTP £1m.

(iv) DA allocated £4.5m to QTP, £0.5m to QNTP.

(v) RM for QTP is (£10,000,000 – £4,500,00)/2 + £4,500,000 = £7.25m

(vi) RM for QNTP is (£1,000,000 – £500,000)/2 + £500,000 = £750,000

(vii) Taxable profit in Year 2 (£10,500,000 – £7,750,000) = £2.75m (x – y)

(viii) Taxable trading profit in Year 2 (£10,000,000 – £7,250,000) = £2.75m

3.209 Loss Relief

(ix) Taxable non-trading profit in Year 2 is (£1,000,000 − £500,000) = £500,000

(x) RM taxable total profit is (£11,000,000 − £5,000,000) + £5,000,000 = £8m (ie, 7,250,000 + 750,000).

Example 2

Developer Ltd's results are:

Accounting period	Ending 31 March 2019	Loss relief	Ending 31 March 2020
Trading	(10,000,000)	500,000 (CTA 2010, s 37(3)(a))	8,000,000
NTLR	500,000		
Capital gains			1,000,000
Trading loss c/f	(9,500,000)	CTA 2010, s 45A	
Relevant profits			9,000,000

RM:

(£9,000,000 − £5,000,000)/2 + £5,000,000 = £7m

Trading loss carried forward at end of Year 2: £9,500,000 − £7,000,000 = £2.5m

---

Example 3

(all losses post-1 April 2017/single company)

Year 1			Year 2				Year 3	
CFL	RP	Less DA	50%	Add DA	RM	S45A relief	Loss c/f	
£m	£m							
(10)	20	5	7.50	5	12.50	(10)	0	
(20)	10	5	2.50	5	7.50	(7.50)	12.50	
(10)	15	5	5	5	10	(10)	0	
(100)	150	5	72.50	5	77.50	(77.50)	72.50	

Loss Relief **3.209**

Hence, if RM ≥ CFL, losses are relievable in full.

If RM < CFL, the ratio RM: CFL gives the rate of loss relief.

Example 4

Year	Source	Profits £'000,000	Taxable	C/f losses post-01.04.17	C/f losses pre-01.04.17
Year 00					
01.04.16–31.03.17	Trading	(10)			(10)
Year 1					
Year1 01.04.17–31.03.18	Non-trading loan relationships	(10)			
	Trading	(10)			
			0	(20)	
Year 2					
01.04.18–31.03.19	Non-trading loan relationships	10			
	RM	(7.5)			
			2.5	(12.5)	

Example 5

Year	Source	Profits £'000,000	Taxable	C/f losses post-01.04.17	C/f losses pre-01.04.17
Year 00					
01.04.16–31.03.17	Trading	(10)			(10)
Year 1					
01.04.17–31.03.18	Non-trading loan relationships	(1)			

3.210 Loss Relief

Year	Source	Profits £'000,000	Taxable	C/f losses post-01.04.17	C/f losses pre-01.04.17
	Trading	(1)			
			0	(2)	
Year 2 01.04.18–31.03.19	Non-trading loan relationships	10			
	Relief – first £5m	(5)			
	Excess over £5m (50% relievable)	(2.5)			
			2.5	(0)	(4.5)

Targeted anti-avoidance rule

3.210 The legislation contains a number of targeted anti-avoidance rules (TAAR):

(i) CTA 2010, Part 14 applies to selling losses, where a person buys a trading company wholly or partly for its unused losses;

(ii) CTA Part 14A applies to selling latent losses, where a person buys a company wholly or partly for the sake of expenditure which will only be recognised at a future date under normal commercial accounting;

(iii) CTA 2010, Part 14, Ch 2A states that on a change of ownership, pre-acquisition forward losses cannot be surrendered into the new group for a period of five years; and

(iv) CTA 2010, s 730F states that groups cannot enter into arrangements which turn carried-forward losses into current year losses. These restrictions extend to losses of a UK property business and NTLIFAs.

Section W: Corporate capital loss restriction

3.211 For the period from 1 April 2017 to 31 March 2020, flexible relief meant that carried-forward income losses could be set against corporate capital gains. Finance Act 2020 enacted the corporate capital loss restriction (CCLR), which imposes an equivalent restriction of the proportion of carried

Loss Relief **3.215**

forward capital losses which can be offset against current year capital gains. There is a single DA which can be set against income and/or capital losses. For accounting periods ending on or after 1 April 2020 (i) the DA will apply to capital and income losses together; (ii) carried-forward capital losses can only be relieved against capital gains up to the RM; and (iii) the RM is defined separately for capital gains and income gains.

3.212 TCGA 1992, s 2A states that the amount of chargeable gains to be included in a company's total profits for an accounting period is the total amount of chargeable gains accruing to the company in the period less allowable losses incurred in the period and brought forward unrelieved losses. However, with effect from 1 April 2020, CTA 2010, s 269ZBA(2) provides that brought forward losses are only deductible up to the amount of the RM.

3.213 In the case of corporate chargeable gains, the RM is '50% of relevant chargeable gains and the amount of the company's chargeable deductions allowance for the account period'. A company's chargeable DA is 'so much of the company's deductions allowance for the period as is specified in the company's tax return as its chargeable gains deductions allowance for the period' (CTA 2010, s 269ZBA(5)). If no amount is specified, this is nil. The amount specified as the chargeable gains DA may not exceed the difference between the company's DA for the period (which will be £5m in the case of a single company for a 12-month accounting period or the proportion allocated to it by the reporting company in a group) and the sum of

- the trading profits DA (s 269ZB(7)(a));
- the non-trading income profits DA (s 269ZC(5)(a)); and
- the BLAGAB DA (s 269ZFC(5)(a).

3.214 Chargeable gains and losses of life insurers' BLAGAB business are ring-fenced by TCGA 1992, ss 204–213A. Life insurers' BLAGAB gains and losses are excluded from the restriction, which also does not apply to companies with ring-fenced trade from oil-related activities where chargeable gains are realised within that restriction. REITs are exempt from capital gains tax.

3.215 The company/group DA remains fixed at £5m and must be allocated between income profits and capital gains. Companies/groups are free to choose how to allocate the allowance between the DA of:

- trading profits,
- non-trading income profits,

3.216 *Loss Relief*

- chargeable gains, and
- BLAGAB,

provided that the total of these cannot exceed £5m for a 12-month accounting period for a single company or a group. All these amounts must be specified in the CTSA return. Otherwise the amount is nil.

3.216 The CCLR only applies to capital losses realised after 1 April 2020. Pre-commencement capital losses are set against post-commencement capital gains. Where accounting periods straddle 1 April 2020, the accounting period is divided into two notional accounting periods: a pre-commencement accounting period and a post-accounting period in accordance with the normal date of disposal rules for capital gains tax.

The key concepts are:

- Qualifying chargeable gains are capital gains for the accounting period less in-year reliefs.
- Relevant chargeable gains are qualifying chargeable gains less the chargeable gains DA.
- Qualifying non-trading profits are:
  - Qualifying non-trading income profits plus
  - Qualifying chargeable gains.
- Qualifying total profits are the sum of
  - Qualifying trading profits
  - Qualifying non-trading income profits
  - Qualifying chargeable gains.
- The chargeable gains DA is that proportion of the company/group DA which is allocated to capital gains.
- Relevant chargeable gains are (qualifying chargeable gains – chargeable gains DA).
- The RM is 50% of (qualifying chargeable gains – chargeable gains DA) + chargeable gains DA.

3.217 Accordingly, the RM is computed on the same basis as for qualifying/relevant income: see the formula at para 3.197.

Loss Relief **3.218**

The RM formula for capital gains is:

$$RM = \frac{(QCG - CGDA)}{2} + CGDA$$

Where

RM = Relevant maximum

QCG = Qualifying chargeable gains

CGDA = Chargeable gains deductions allowance

3.218 The calculation of RM for chargeable gains follows the procedure for the calculation of RM for Relevant Profits with various modifications to take account of the CCLR. See Section T, paras 3.173–3.188, and the steps at para 3.186. *With effect from 1 April 2020, CTA 2010, s 269ZF is amended to take into account the CCLR.*

Step 1: Calculate 'modified profits' by eliminating from total profits:

- excluded profits, such as distributions (other than distributions which are treated as trading profits)
- RRLs
- carried-forward capital losses.

    If Step 1 leaves a positive figure, proceed to Step 2. If Step 1 leaves a negative figure, the relevant profits will be nil and no further steps are necessary.

Step 2: Calculate in-year reliefs deductible from modified profits, taking no account of 'excluded deductions' (*Step 2 Amounts*).

Step 3: Divide modified profits into:

- trading profits
- non-trading income profits
- chargeable gains.

These are the *Step 3 Amounts*

If there are no carried-forward capital losses, there is no need to separate chargeable gains from non-trading income profits.

3.218 *Loss Relief*

Step 4: Allocate the Step 2 Amounts between

- trading profits
- non-trading income profits
- chargeable gains.

This can be on any basis, provided that none of these amounts can be < 0. No deductions can be made under TCGA 1992, s 2A(1)(b) in respect of losses accruing in earlier accounting periods.

These are the *Step 4 Amounts*

Step 5: Deduct the Step 4 Amounts from the Step 3 Amounts to give the company's

- qualifying trading profits
- qualifying non-trading income profits
- qualifying chargeable gains.

The sum of these amounts constitutes qualifying total profits.

Step 6: Allocate the company's DA (or share of DA) between:

- trading profits
- non-trading income profits
- chargeable gains
- BLAGAB.

This can be on any basis, provided that the total DA ≤ £5m.

Step 7: Deduct from the qualifying chargeable gains (Step 5) the chargeable gains DA (Step 6) to give the relevant chargeable cains.

Step 8: The RM for capital gains is:

$$RM = \frac{QCG - CGDA}{2} + CGDA$$

Where

RM = Relevant maximum

QCG = Qualifying chargeable gains

CGDA = Chargeable gains deductions allowance

Loss Relief **3.219**

3.219 Carried forward capital losses up to the RM may be deducted in computing chargeable gains. Carried-forward trading losses are restricted in accordance with CTA 2010, s 269ZB. Carried-forward non-trading income losses are restricted in accordance with s 269ZC.

The RM for total profits is (Qualifying total profits /2) + the company's DA. See Step 5 for qualifying total profits.

This sets the overall limit for carried-forward loss relief.

Example

(i) In the accounting ending on 31 March 2021 Cerberus International plc has unrelieved losses of:

	£m
Trading losses (pre-01.04.17)	15
NTLRD (pre-01.04.17)	9
Capital losses (post-01.04.20)	20

In the accounting period to 31 March 2022 the total profits of Cerberus plc are as follows:

Trading profits	30
Non-trading income profits (property)	15
NTLRD	(5)
Distributions	10
Capital gains	12
Capital losses	(2)

(iii) Find RM

Step 1	Find modified profits	67–10 (distributions)	57
Step 2	In-year reliefs	NTLRD (5)	5
Step 3	Find Step 3 amounts	Trading profits	30
		Non-trading income profits	15
		Chargeable gains 12–2	10

153

3.220 *Loss Relief*

Step 4	Allocate Step 2 amounts	NTLRD set against	5
		Non-trading income profits (2) trading profits	(2)
		Chargeable gains (3) (Step 4 Amounts)	(3)
Step 5	Find qualifying profits by deducting Step 4 amounts from Step 3 amounts	Qualifying trading profits 30–0	30
		Qualifying non-trading income profits 15–2	13
		Qualifying chargeable gains 10–3	7
Step 6	Allocate DA	Trading profits	1
		Non-trading income profits	1
		Chargeable gains	3
Step 7	Deduct chargeable gains DA to give relevant chargeable gains	7–3	4
Step 8	Find RM	Trading: (30–1)/2 + 0	15.5
		Non-trading: (20–4)/2 + 4	12
		Capital gains (7–3)/2 + 3	5

(i) Find RM for carried-forward losses:

	Loss carried-forward	RM	Taxable	Loss carried-forward
Trading	15	15.5	0	0
NTLRD (RRL)	9	$12 - 7^1 = 5$	9	4
Capital gains	20	5	7	2
Total profits RM		27.5^2		

[1] 7 of RM for qualifying non-trading profits set against carried-forward capital loss.

[2] $\dfrac{(50-5)}{2} + 5 = 27.5$

Clogged capital losses

3.220 'Clogged' losses are losses in disposal between connected persons, which can only be deducted from gains arising from disposals between the same persons: TCGA 1992, s 18(3). In the case of capital gains tax groups, disposals will be on a no gain/no loss basis in accordance with TCGA 1992, s 171. However, one company may be connected with another under TCGA 1992, 286(5) (controlling shareholding) without having the 75% holding required for group membership. In such cases s 18(3) will apply, so that any losses are 'clogged' and can only be set against capital gains on transactions between the same parties and carried-forward clogged losses must be separated from other capital losses. TCGA 1992, s 18(9)–(12) provide that in the case of clogged losses a company may make a claim for the clogged loss to be treated as an allowable loss accruing in the accounting period, so as to displace a corresponding amount of non-clogged loss to be carried forward for future relief.

Insolvent companies–deductions allowance

3.221 With effect from 1 April 2020, CTA 2010, ss 269ZWA, 269ZYA, 269ZYB apply where a company has gone into insolvent liquidation. The company's DA for the winding-up period is increased by the amount of chargeable gains accruing to the company during this period.

Pre-entry losses

3.222 Relief for pre-entry losses (ie, capital losses incurred before a company joins a capital gains tax group) are in any event restricted by TCGA 1992, Sch 7A. While they do not form part of the general carried-forward losses of a company, they nevertheless come within the CCLR. They must be left out of account in calculating the CCLR unless the company opts that they should displace losses which would otherwise form part of the calculation.

Section X: Corporate acquisitions followed by transfer of trades and assets

3.223 Within a group, or on a company reconstruction falling within TCGA ss 136, 139, a trade may be transferred from one company to another. There is a cessation of the transferor company's trade, but it is treated as carried on by the transferee company, provided that the 'ownership condition' and 'tax condition' are satisfied. The conditions are that:

(a) on, and within two years after the cessation, the trade is at least 75% owned by the same persons as owned a similar interest within one year before the cessation, and

3.224 *Loss Relief*

(b) throughout these periods the trade is carried on by a company within the charge to corporation tax.

(CTA 2010, ss 940A–943.)

3.224 While termination relief under CTA 2010, s 45F is not available on cessation of the predecessor's trade, such loss is treated as incurred by the successor company in the accounting period in which it began to carry on the predecessor's trade.

3.225 The carried-forward losses are reduced where relevant liabilities exceed the market value of relevant assets at the time of transfer. 'Relevant assets' are assets retained by the predecessor; relevant liabilities are liabilities of the predecessor assumed by the successor.

3.226 A common situation occurs where:

- T Ltd is carrying on a loss-making trade;
- A Ltd acquires all the shares in T Ltd;
- T Ltd transfers its trade to A Ltd; and
- A Ltd seeks to relieve its profits from tax by setting against the profits of the combined trade the losses accumulated by T Ltd.

3.227 The policy of the law is that A Ltd should acquire T Ltd for commercial reasons and should not buy T Ltd for its losses. If, therefore, within a specified period within which the change of ownership occurs, there is also a major change in the nature of conduct of the transferred trade or that trade becomes small or insignificant, no carry forward of losses incurred before the change of ownership to the period following the change of ownership is allowed. Further, the transferred trade may be regarded as a separate trade, and past losses are only relievable against future profits of that notional separate trade.

3.228 The issue was summed by Greene MR in *Laycock v Freeman, Hardy & Willis Ltd* 22 TC 288 at 299:

'Is it possible to put the finger upon some taxable profits arising from a trade, and say of those profits that they arise from the trade which was taken over?'

In *Falmer Jeans Ltd v Rodin* [1990] STC 270 Millett J held that, where there had been a succession to a trade, the combined trade would be regarded as two notionally separate trades.

3.229 In *Leekes Ltd v R & C Comrs* [2018] STC 1245:

(i) L a retailer bought all the share capital of C, a retailer. C owned a retail trade. L held the shares of C for one day (to establish common ownership before and after the trade transfer) before hiving up the trade of C to L; and

(ii) L merged the trade of C with its own and sought to set the pre-transfer losses of C against the profits of the combined trade under ICTA 1988, s 343.

The Court of Appeal held that L was only entitled to set those losses against the post-transfer profits of C, regarded as a separate business, notwithstanding that C's former trade was carried on as part of an enlarged business:

'The amount of the relief is confined to that which the predecessor would have been entitled to obtain, on the hypothesis that it had continued to carry on the predecessor's trade.'

(Henderson LJ at (43).)

3.230 From 1 April 2017, CTA 2010, s 672 ff applies the carried-forward loss rules in cases of reconstructions to which ss 940A–943 apply. The period in which the change of ownership rules apply are expanded from three to five years in relation to the period post change of ownership. There is also a new limb to the change of ownership definition. The concern was that, with the introduction of flexible relief (i) trading losses of the target company could be set against capital gains of the acquiring company, and (ii) the transferor company would surrender carried-forward losses to other group companies. Hence the scope of existing restrictions on the use of transferred losses was expanded and refined.

3.231 The rules in CTA 2010, ss 673–676 and 677–691 take precedence over the rules in ss 676AA–676AL (s 676AB). Accordingly, the order in which the provisions need to be considered is:

(i) ss 673–676;

(ii) ss 677–691; and

(iii) ss 676AA–676ED.

(i) Ss 673–676

3.232 Carried-forward loss relief is restricted in cases where (i) there is a change in ownership of a company, and (ii) within a period of five years

3.233 Loss Relief

(previously three years) beginning not earlier than three years prior to the change in ownership there is a major change in the trade or conduct of a trade carried on by the company: CTA 2010, ss 673–676. It is necessary to look back to the nature and conduct of the company from which the trade was transferred to the company that eventually carries it on, to establish whether or not carried-forward losses should be restricted.

(ii) Ss 677–691

3.233 Where there is a change in the ownership of a company with investment business, and

- after the change of ownership there is a significant increase in capital or
- within eight years beginning three years before the change of ownership there is a major change in the nature or conduct of the business or
- the change in ownership occurs after the business has become small or negligible,

then losses of the business incurred before the change of ownership cannot be set against income received after the change of ownership: ss 677–691.

(iii) Ss 676AA–676ED

3.234 Section 676AA, which applies both to trading companies and companies with investment business, specifies a number of 'required periods' during which there must be no change in the nature or conduct of the business of the transferred company, for losses to remain available for carry forward. In the case of pre-1 April 2017 trading losses, the required period is a period of five years beginning no earlier than three years before the change of ownership (s 676AF). In respect of loan relationship debits (s 676AG), non-trading loan relationship deficits (s 676AH), losses on non-trading intangible fixed assets (s 676AI), unrelieved expenses of management (s 676AJ) and losses of a UK property business (s 676AK), the required period is eight years.

3.235 Section 676AC elaborates the concepts of:

- 'major change in the business';
- 'major change in the scale of any trade or business'; and
- 'beginning or ceasing to carry on a particular trade or business'.

The approach adopted is explained more fully in SP 10/91.

3.236 Section 676AD and 676AE set out the approach adopted where the change of ownership occurs in the middle of an accounting period, and how losses are to be allocated to the two notional periods.

3.237 'Affected profits' are profits of the acquired company arising in the five-year period prior to the change of ownership, attributable to the trade which has undergone the major change (s 676AE). A company is not allowed to deduct carried-forward trading losses from total profits of the company so far as they are 'affected profits' carried forward under CTA 2010, ss 45A, 45F (s 676AF). There are similar rules for the other types of carried-forward losses.

3.238 Where, after the change of ownership, assets are transferred within a group from the target (acquired) company to another company in the acquiring group on a no gain/no loss basis under TCGA s 171, and the asset is disposed of within five years of the period beginning with the change of ownership, group relief for carried-forward losses (CTA 2010, ss 188CA–188EK) is not available against the capital gain then realised (Chapter 2B, ss 676BA–676BE).

3.239 Losses arising to a company before it joins a group cannot be claimed by other members of the group in the five years after the loss-making company joins the group (Chapter 2C, ss 676CA–676CI). Similar rules apply to the surrender and claiming of group relief by consortium companies. However, the restrictions do not apply amongst co-transferred companies (ie, where a group of companies is acquired).

3.240 Where, after 1 April 2017, (i) there is a change of ownership of a company, (ii) a capital asset or intangible fixed asset is transferred intra-group and (iii) a chargeable gain is realised on disposal of the asset within five years of the change of ownership, group relief cannot be claimed against the capital gain (Chapter 2D, ss 676DA–676DE).

3.241 Where, after 1 April 2017, (i) there is a change of ownership of a company ('the transferred company'), (ii) within a period of eight years beginning three years before the change of ownership the transferred company transfers a trade intra-group, and (iii) the transferred company and successor company were not related immediately before the change of ownership, trading losses carried forward in the transferred trade cannot be deducted from the 'relevant profits' of the successor company. This will apply to hives down/cross of trades within purchaser group (Chapter 2E, ss 676EA–676EE).

3.242 All these restrictions are detailed, intricate and apply for a long time after company acquisitions have been made. Accordingly, the computation of available loss reliefs in situations where these multiple and overlapping restrictions potentially is complex and requires careful and detailed working out.

Chapter 4

Capital Instruments

Chapter Contents

Section	Topic	Paragraphs
A	Capital instruments rules	4.1
B	Hybrid mismatches	4.2–4.16
C	BEPS Action Points 2 and 15	4.17–4.22
D	Conditions for D/NI mismatch	4.23–4.31
E	Other types of mismatch	4.32–4.36
F	Regulatory capital	4.37–4.49
G	Hybrid capital instruments	4.50–4.61

Section A: Capital instruments rules

4.1 The loan relationships rules are overlaid by two sets of special rules relating to capital instruments. These are:

(1) The hybrid mismatch rules in TIOPA 2010, Part 6A, ss 259A–259E, introduced by FA 2016, Sch 10 to implement BEPS Action 2, but wider in scope than the BEPS requirement.

(2) The hybrid capital instruments rules in FA 2019, Sch 20 and CTA 2009, ss 320B, 420A, 475C.

The hybrid and other mismatch legislation can apply to deny a company within the charge to corporation tax relief for interest payable on a loan relationship in the circumstances set out in TIOPA Part 6A. The hybrid capital instruments rules, by contrast, allow companies, principally banks and insurance companies, to treat instruments as equity but obtain a tax deduction for interest paid in respect of them, thereby achieving the alchemist's gold of tax deductible equity.

Capital Instruments **4.5**

Section B: Hybrid mismatches

4.2 With effect from 1 January 2017, the hybrid mismatch rules replicate the arbitrage rules formerly contained in TIOPA 2010, ss 231–259. They apply to 'hybrid mismatch' arrangements. Typically these are arrangements which give rise to a deduction for one party in one jurisdiction without a corresponding charge in the other party in another jurisdiction, because the instrument is classified for tax purposes as debt in the payer's jurisdiction and equity in the payee's jurisdiction. Alternatively, both parties may claim a deduction for the same economic expenditure.

Interaction

4.3 Rules to address hybrid mismatch arrangements are applied to an entity before the CIR to determine the entity's total net tax-interest expense. The hybrid instrument rules take precedence over the CIR (TIOPA 2010, s 259NEA), and qualify the operation of the loan relationship and derivative contracts rules, in particular those relating to debits (ie, 'a relevant debt relief provision' under the loan relationship rules where the deduction claimed by a UK company exceeds the corresponding charge to tax in the payee, which is a company in another jurisdiction TIOPA 2010, s 259CB(3)). Once the total net tax-interest expense figure has been determined, the fixed ratio and group ratio rules are applied to determine what percentage of the finance costs is deductible and what percentage is disallowed. The distribution exemption provisions will in practice take priority over the hybrid mismatch rules.

4.4 The rules take effect in priority to the unallowable purpose rule (CTA 2009, ss 444, 690) and the transfer pricing rulings (of which the hybrid mismatch rules may be regarded as a special application): TIOPA 2010, s 259CB(6).

Application

4.5 The core application of the rules is to financial instruments and derivative contracts, as defined in the loan relationships and derivative contracts legislation: TIOPA 2010, s 259N. However, the legislation also applies more widely to royalties, rent and payments for goods and services. 'Financial instruments' are defined in s 259N as loan relationships, derivative contracts and anything which is a financial instrument within GAAP. The definition covers:

- arrangements and contracts which would, on the assumption that the person to whom they arise, is within the charge to corporation tax on loan relationships and derivative contracts;

4.6 Capital Instruments

- 'finance arrangements' falling within CTA 2010, ss 758–776; and
- a share or instrument giving economic rights equivalent to a share.

4.6 The rules apply in relation to 'tax' which includes foreign tax. The definition of 'tax' in TIOPA 2010, s 259B excludes withholding tax, which accordingly is not 'tax' contemplated by the regime and so should be ignored in considering whether a mismatch arises.

4.7 Under TIOPA 2010, s 259A(1), the hybrid mismatch rules counteract cases which *'it is reasonable to suppose that would otherwise give rise to'* either:

(a) a deduction/non-inclusion mismatch [s 259A(2)] (D/NI); or

(b) a double deduction mismatch [s 259A(3)] (DD).

4.8 To know whether there is a mismatch, it is usually necessary to know how the receipt is taxed in the foreign jurisdiction. 'Otherwise' means 'if the hybrid mismatch rules had not been enacted'.

4.9 The 'reasonable to suppose' test is objective and does not depend upon purpose. The rules are designed to operate in a purely mechanical fashion. It is found throughout much of the recent legislation, eg in relation to the DPT rules (FA 2015, s 82(5) (*'the alternative provision which it is just and reasonable to assume would have been made ...'*).

4.10 There are a number of safe harbours in the rules. They will apply if both parties are UK resident. So, in practice, the rules only apply to cases where the payer is in one jurisdiction and the payee is in a different jurisdiction, provided that one of those jurisdictions is the UK. Further, (i) the payer and payee must be related or in the same control group (TIOPA 2010, ss 259NB, 259NC), or (ii) the arrangement must be a 'structured arrangement' (ie, one designed to secure the mismatch) see 4.24.

4.11 A deduction/non-inclusion mismatch is predicated on the assumption that if A Co, the UK payer, obtains a deduction of x in its UK jurisdiction, B Co, the payee, should be taxed on x in its jurisdiction. The policy aim is to eliminate tax asymmetries. If B Co is taxed in its jurisdiction on y (which is < x), then the mismatch is counteracted by limiting A Co's deduction for tax purposes to $(x - y)$, which is that 'mismatch amount'.

4.12 A double deduction mismatch occurs if X (resident in State A) is not taxed on income of amount p, because State A attributes the income to Y (an investor in X resident in State B), but State B attributes the income to X. So, X deducts Y's income from his taxable income in State A and Y is not taxed on the income in State B. It is counteracted by requiring X to include Y's income in his own, unless State A and State B both recognise the income of amount p as belonging to both X and Y ('dual inclusion income': TIOPA 2010, s 259IC(10) – see below).

4.13 The legislation is concerned with cases involving:

- *'payments or quasi-payments under or in connection with financial instruments or repos or lending arrangements or other transfers of financial instruments'* (TIOPA 2010, s 259A(7));
- hybrid entities;
- permanent establishments; and
- dual-resident companies.

4.14 A 'payment' means a transfer of funds giving rise to a tax deduction. A 'quasi-payment' is an accounting entry not requiring a transfer of funds but producing the same effect: TIOPA 2010, s 259BB. A quasi-payment is a payment arising in an arrangement where tax relief is given on an accruals rather than a paid basis.

4.15 'Hybrid entity' is defined in TIOPA 2010, s 259BE as a legal person, some of whose profits or income are attributed to another person, and which is regarded as transparent in another jurisdiction. A 'hybrid entity' is an entity which meets two conditions (s 259BE):

- Condition A is that the law of any territory (a D Territory) categorises the entity as a distinct and separate legal person; and
- Condition B is that the law of any territory other than a D Territory (a non-D territory) the entity is not regarded as a distinct and separate entity and some or all of its income is regarded as the income of a person other than the entity recognised in law by the D Territories.

Example

Z LLP is a UK body corporate. It has two equal members, X and Y. It is transparent for UK tax purposes. Half the income belongs to X and Y respectively.

In the US under tick the box it is classified as a distinct and separate entity, and all the income belongs to Z.

The UK is the non-D territory; the US is the D territory.

4.16 *Capital Instruments*

4.16 'Dual inclusion income' of a hybrid entity means an amount that is both ordinary income of the hybrid entity for corporation tax purposes and ordinary income of an investor in the hybrid entity (TIOPA 2010, s 259IC(10)).

Section C: BEPS Action Points 2 and 15

4.17 The rules trespass on matters already covered by double taxation agreements and the question arises whether they are consistent with a given double taxation treaty or function as treaty overrides. The Final Report of the OECD on 'Neutralising the Effects of Hybrid Mismatch Arrangements' is referred to in TIOPA 2010, s 259BA(2). This provides that a charge can arise on a company within the charge to corporation tax if and to the extent that no corresponding charge arises under equivalent legislation in a non-UK jurisdiction. However, when – as in common with so many of the BEPS Actions – so much discretion is vested in the tax authority, the meaning 'provision *under the law* of a territory outside the United Kingdom' may be extremely broad or quite restricted. Whether 'law' has a substantive meaning or is purely a formal concept ('This law provides that everything which X does is legal') is one of the questions of principle which is regarded as secondary to pragmatic considerations.

4.18 The policy aim is to eliminate international tax asymmetries, where this is regarded as impermissible. The situation is not like that under double taxation treaties, where asymmetric results may be the consequence of the normal operation of the treaty (eg, State A assigns the taxation right in respect of x to State B, but State B may not tax the item in question: see *Fowler v R & C Comrs* [2020] UK SC 22). However, the Supreme Court in that case somewhat surprisingly limited the scope of deeming provisions in tax legislation, to the effect that a deeming provision could not cut down the UK's taxing right, if no corresponding charge in the other treaty state resulted from the allocation of taxing rights (ie, where there would otherwise be a tax mismatch).

4.19 The rules are related to transfer pricing, for which provision is made in double taxation agreements under the 'associated enterprises' article. However, the rules do not depend upon the application of the ALP or in general on whether the parties are related (though they normally will be) but on the actual tax treatment in B Co's jurisdiction.

4.20 These rules in TIOPA 2010, Part 6A are designed to implement various parts of BEPS Action 2, but also extend more widely so that some Chapters derive from Action 2, while others have a different origin:

(i) ss 259C–259CE (Chapter 3 of Part 6A, Hybrid and other mismatches from financial instruments) implements Action 2, Recommendation 1, first part;

(ii) ss 259D–259DG (Chapter 4, Hybrid transfer deduction/non-inclusion mismatches) implements Action 2, Recommendation 1, second part;

(iii) ss 259E–259ED (Chapter 5, Hybrid payer deduction/non-inclusion mismatches);

(iv) ss 259F–259FB (Chapter 6, Deduction/non-inclusion mismatches relating to transfers by permanent establishments);

(v) ss 259G–259GE (Chapter 7, Hybrid payee deduction/non-inclusion mismatch) implements Action 2, Recommendation 4;

(vi) ss 259H–259HC (Chapter 8, Multinational payee deductions/non-inclusion mismatches);

(vii) ss 259I–259ID (Chapter 9, Hybrid entity double deduction mismatches) implements Action 2, Recommendation 6;

(viii) ss 259J–259JD (Chapter 10, Dual territory double deduction cases) implements Action 2, Recommendation 7; and

(ix) ss 259K–259KD (Chapter 11, Imported mismatches) implements Action 2, Recommendation 8.

4.21 BEPS Action Point 15 called for the development of a multilateral instrument (MLI) to enable states to amend bilateral tax treaties quickly and simply, so as to give effect to the treaty-related BEPS measures, in particular Action Points 2, 7 and 14. The changes set out in the MLI are modelled on the changes introduced into the 2017 OECD Model Convention. The purpose of the MLI is to align existing double taxation treaties with domestic provisions on hybrid mismatches designed to give effect to Action Point 2.

4.22 The UK has ratified the MLI. In accordance with TIOPA 2010, s 6 (the non obstante rule) the UK has incorporated it into UK domestic law under the Double Taxation Relief (Base Erosion and Profit Shifting) Order 2018 (SI 2018/630). The UK signed the Multilateral Instrument (MLI) in June 2017 and deposited its instrument of ratification on 29 June 2018. It came into force on 1 October 2018.

Section D: Conditions for D/NI mismatch

4.23 The conditions giving rise to a hybrid or otherwise impermissible deduction/non-inclusion mismatch, from financial instruments, all of which must be fulfilled for the legislation to be potentially applicable, are (TIOPA 2010, ss 259C–259CD):

- Condition A: there is a payment or quasi-payment in respect of a financial instrument.

4.24 *Capital Instruments*

- Condition B: the payer is within the charge to UK corporation tax.
- Condition C: it would be reasonable to suppose that there would otherwise be a deduction/non-inclusion mismatch.
- Condition D: in the case of a quasi-payment the payer and payee are related, and the financial instrument, or any arrangement connected with it, is a structured arrangement.

4.24 Two persons are related if (a) they are in the same control group (one controls the other or both are under common control), (b) one has a 25% investment in the other, or (c) a common investor has a 25% investment in each: TIOPA 2010, ss 259NB, 259NC, 259ND.

4.25 A 'structured arrangement' exists if (a) it is reasonable to suppose that the hybrid transfer arrangement is designed to secure a hybrid transfer deduction/non-inclusion mismatch, or (b) the terms of the hybrid transfer arrangement share the economic benefit of the mismatch between the parties: TIOPA 2010, s 259CA(6), (7).

4.26 If the conditions for the legislation are satisfied, there will be an actual hybrid or otherwise impermissible deduction/non-inclusion mismatch, if either of two further conditions is fulfilled (TIOPA 2010, s 259CB):

(i) Case 1: A Co claims a deduction of x, and B Co as payee only brings y, being <x, the excess of the deduction over the chargeable amount is brought into charge to tax: TIOPA 2010, s 259CB(2). In other words, the relevant deduction exceeds the ordinary income taken into account in computing the payee's profits for a permitted taxable period, and this situation is attributable to the terms or any other feature of the financial instrument: TIOPA 2010, s 259CB(10). The UK tax charge is increased by reference to the non-payment of tax in the non-UK jurisdiction.

(ii) Case 2: In respect of a payment by A Co to B Co, B Co is undertaxed by reason of the terms or any other feature of the financial instrument, i.e. the rate of tax on the payment in B Co is less than its marginal rate for the period: TIOPA 2010, s 259CB(11). 'Undertaxed' is defined in s 259CB(7).

4.27 If B Co is taxed in its jurisdiction on y (which is < x), then the mismatch is counteracted by limiting A Co's deduction for tax purposes to (x – y). If the payer is within the charge to UK corporation, the counteraction is specified in TIOPA 2010, s 259CD as a restriction of the deduction to (x – y). Section 259CD(3)(a) says that the 'relevant amount' is *'an amount equal to the hybrid or otherwise impermissible deduction/non-inclusion mismatch specified in section 259CA(4)'*. This simply means (x – y).

4.28 If the payee is within the charge to UK corporation tax, then TIOPA 2010, s 259CE states that they are subject to an additional charge of $(x - y)$. A payer can also be a payee if an entity is treated as the payer under UK law but is treated as a separate entity under the law of a non-UK legislation, so that he can be regarded as making the payment in one legal capacity and receiving it in another.

4.29 The basic rule is that amounts to which the legislation applies are brought into charge to corporation tax as 'ordinary income': TIOPA 2010, s 259BC. 'Ordinary income' is defined as 'income that is brought into account before any deductions, for the purpose of calculating the income or profits a relevant tax charge is imposed ("taxable profits")': TIOPA 2010, s 259BC(2). Amounts charged to tax at a zero rate or are refunded are not 'ordinary income'.

4.30 In case 2, the amount of the hybrid deduction/non-inclusion mismatch is given by the formula in TIOPA 2010, s 269CB(10):

$$\frac{UTA \times (FMR - R)}{FMR}$$

where:

UTA = under-taxed amount

FMR = payee's full marginal rate

R = highest percentage rate at which payee is liable to tax on taxable profits.

4.31 The unallowable purpose rule does not apply: TIOPA 2010, s 259CB(6). In computing the excess of the deduction in the payer over the ordinary income amount of the payee, 'relevant debt relief provisions' (ie, CTA 2009, ss 322, 357–359, 361C, 361D, 362A) are ignored: TIOPA 2010, ss 259CB(3), 259CC(3).

Section E: Other types of mismatch

4.32 The legislation sets out in details a number of similar arrangements which also give rise to hybrid mismatches. For example, Chapter 4 is concerned with repos and stock lending, which are classified as 'hybrid transfer arrangements'. The conditions for its application follow that of TIOPA 2010, s 259C, with the additional condition that there must be a hybrid transfer arrangement in relation to the underlying instrument.

4.33 A hybrid transfer arrangement is defined in TIOPA 2010, s 259DB. It is a repo, stock lending or similar arrangement, which is equivalent to the

4.34 *Capital Instruments*

lending of money at interest, and in relation to which either (a) one party treats it as a loan and the other does not ('the dual payment condition'), or (b) a payment or quasi-payment is made that is representative of the underlying return and is paid to someone other than the person to whom the underlying return arises ('the substitute payment condition').

4.34 There is a financial trader exemption (TIOPA 2010, s 259DD) which applies under the following conditions:

- Condition A: The mismatch arises because the payment or quasi-payment is a substitute payment which the financial trader brings into account for corporation tax purposes.
- Condition B: The financial trader also brings any associated payments into account.
- Condition C: If the underlying return arose directly to the payee neither Chapter 3 nor the equivalent non-UK law would apply and the hybrid transfer arrangement is not a structured arrangement.

4.35 The remaining chapters follow the same model and can be summarised as follows:

Chapter	Sections	Mismatch	Sphere of application	Impact if mismatch – UK payer	Impact of mismatch – UK payee
3	259C–259CE	D/NI	Financial instruments	Restrict deduction of UK payer	Include as ordinary income
4	259D–259DG	D/NI	Repos and stock lending (hybrid transfer arrangements)	Restrict deduction of UK payer	Include as ordinary income
5	259E–259ED	D/NI	Payers which are hybrid entities	Restrict deduction of UK payer	Include as ordinary income
6	259F–259FC	D/NI	Transfers by UK PE to head office	Restrict deduction of UK PE	Not applicable
7	259G–259GE	D/NI	Payment to a hybrid entity	Restrict deduction of UK payer	Include as ordinary income

Capital Instruments **4.36**

Chapter	Sections	Mismatch	Sphere of application	Impact if mismatch – UK payer	Impact of mismatch – UK payee
8	259H–259HC	D/NI	Payment to part of a MNE	Restrict deduction of UK payer	No applicable
9	259I–259ID	DD	Payment by company which is a hybrid entity	Restrict deduction if UK is the investor in the hybrid, unless deduction is deducted from dual inclusion income	Restrict UK deduction where the hybrid entity is within the charge to UK CT and the investor does not include amounts as dual inclusion income
10	259J–259JC	DD	Hybrid entity which is a dual resident company of a multinational company	Restrict deduction unless it forms dual inclusion income	
11	259K–259KD	Indirect D/NI	Imported mismatches	Counteract on just and reasonable basis	

4.36 Examples of D/NI

Example 1

A Co (UK resident) issues convertible bonds to B Co (resident in State B). The interest payments are taxable in the UK pending conversion, but classified as a distribution in B's jurisdiction.

Example 2

1   A Subco issues preference shares to Parent (both resident in jurisdiction A).

4.37 *Capital Instruments*

2   P repos the Subco preference shares to unrelated interim holder (H) in jurisdiction B.

3   Subco pays a dividend to H and H is not required to make a substitute payment to P.

4   P accounts for the transaction as a borrowing, the finance cost being the Subco dividend, and claims a deduction for the finance cost.

5   H treats the repo as giving rise to a gain or loss on the repurchase and is not liable for tax on the pref dividend.

Example 3

1   A non-UK tax exempt fund makes a stock loan of debt securities to a UK bank.

2   The UK bank receives a coupon and makes a substitute payment to the stock lender.

3   The non-UK fund is not liable to tax on the substitute payment.

Section F: Regulatory capital

4.37   Convertible bonds are a classic form of hybrid capital instrument, having both debt- and equity-like features. Securities which are convertible into shares at the option of the holder are subject to a special tax treatment, being divisible on issue into a notional loan (a loan relationship) and a derivative contract (the separated-out share option). The procedure is known as bifurcation: CTA 2009, ss 415, 577, 585, 640, 652, 653 and 670. (See 10th edition, Chapter 15).

4.38   Securities which are convertible into shares, otherwise than at the option of the issuer, are quite different because there is no embedded share option. These are simply debt until conversion, shares after conversion. They are generally known as 'contingent convertibles' (CoCos), because they are convertible on the occurrence of a contingency.

4.39   As regards the potential tax charge on conversion of the bond or bond element into shares, and disregarding the position in relation to embedded derivatives:

(a)   the reorganisation provisions in TCGA 1992, ss 116, 126–132 may be applicable; and

(b)   in any event, the conversion of hybrid capital instruments into shares remains protected from tax charge by the safe harbour of CTA 2009, s 322(4).

The issue of contingent convertibles had, until 1 January 2019, been confined to the raising and maintenance of regulatory capital.

4.40 Capital adequacy rules (a) define what counts as capital or 'own funds', and (b) prescribe the minimum solvency ratio which banks and insurance companies must maintain. Banks are required to maintain regulatory capital which constitutes a prescribed proportion of their risk-weighted assets. Capital adequacy standards for international banks are laid down by the Basel Committee on Banking Supervision of the Bank for International Settlements (BIS). These are given legislative force within the UK by EU and UK legislation. In particular, FSMA 2000 requires all authorised institutions to conduct their business in a prudent manner, which includes complying with capital adequacy requirements. An overview of capital regulation of banks and insurance companies is contained in IF-BEPS, pp 191–196.

4.41 Under the *Second Capital Adequacy Directive* (93/6/EEC) a bank's assets are divided into 'trading book' and 'banking book'. On the banking side, a specified amount of capital must be allocated to each risk-weighted lending balance.

Example

A bank lends £1 million to a company. The asset is risk-weighted at 100% (= 1). If the bank's solvency ratio is 10%, capital of £100,000 will have to be allocated to the loan. The bank's gross profit will be (interest + fees received) − (cost of capital + cost of funds).

4.42 Bank capital comprises Tier 1, Tier 2 and Tier 3 capital. There are no limits on Tier 1 capital. Tier 2 capital cannot exceed Tier 1, so surplus Tier 2 capital will not be 'capital' for capital adequacy purposes. Tier 3 capital can only be used to meet trading book requirements.

4.43 The guidelines in the Basel III accord (Capital Requirement Directive III) were implemented from 2013. These divide regulatory capital into:

- Tier 1 common equity (CET1);
- Additional Tier 1 (AT1);
- Tier 2; and
- Tier 3.

4.44 *Capital Instruments*

4.44 CET1 must be accounted for as equity. AT1 must meet 14 criteria to be accounted for as equity, such as:

- callable only by issuer with consent of regulator;
- perpetual (ie, no fixed redemption date);
- any dividend or coupon must be discretionary and non-cumulative; and
- automatically convertible into common equity if trigger event occurs.

4.45 Additional Tier 1 capital features as part of equity accounting, as opposed to liability accounting. Innovative Tier 1 capital is a finance structure designed to provide tax deductible funding costs in respect of hybrid securities which count as Additional Tier 1 regulatory capital (equity) for banks. Such securities are referred to as 'preferred securities' or 'perpetuals'.

4.46 If all these requirements are met, the preferred securities will be debt for tax purposes, allowing interest to be tax deductible, but count as shares for regulatory purposes. Accordingly, the finance cost of Additional Tier 1 capital will be lower than that of common equity (ie, share capital). Preferred securities are thus a special category of hybrid instrument.

4.47 Under Basel III, such securities will be Co-cos. Additional Tier 1 capital will have a trigger point above the non-viability point, so that they will have potential for loss absorption. Conversion is likely to constitute a release of debt. In that case, liability write-down will produce a taxable profit. It is unlikely that the issuer would be required to bifurcate the bond into a loan relationship and an equity instrument under IAS 39, because there is no way in which a premium or discount on redemption can be derived from the instrument. Co-cos will be Eurobonds, to take advantage of the gross payment facility.

4.48 The issuer of a perpetual has a contingent obligation to repay the principal. Perpetuals are accordingly loan relationships: CTA 2009, ss 303(1)(a), 476(1); *Reed International Ltd v IRC* (1975) STC 427. Interest payable on such securities are not 'results dependent' within CTA 2010, s 1015(4), so cannot be re-characterised as a distribution. The 'equity notes' rules in CTA 2010, ss 1015(6) and 1016 apply because interest on such securities is only liable to tax re-characterisation if held by a person funding or associated with the issuer.

4.49 The Taxation of Regulatory Capital Securities Regulations (SI 2013/3209) provided that a 'regulatory capital security' (ie, a security which qualifies as AT1 or T2) is to be treated as a loan relationship from 1 January 2014. No credit or debit is to be allowed for tax purposes on conversion or write down, in the case of the issuer or a connected creditor. For group relief purposes the security is treated as a 'normal commercial loan'. There is no duty to deduct withholding tax on interest under ITA 2007, ss 874, 889. These rules were repealed with effect from 1 January 2019 (FA 2009, s 89, Sch 20, para 1(1)).

Section G: Hybrid capital instruments rules

4.50 In June 2018, the Bank of England issued a Statement of Policy on its approach to setting minimum requirements for own funds and eligible liabilities (MREL) of banks, to take effect on 1 January 2019. This produced changes to regulatory requirements. Further, the Regulatory Capital Securities Regulations were thought to constitute possible state aid to banks and insurance companies. Sectors outside banking and insurance also needed to issue securities which had debt and equity features. For accounting periods beginning on or after 1 January 2019, these rules are replaced by the hybrid capital instruments rules in CTA 2009, ss 320B, 420A, 475C. These were introduced by FA 2019, Sch 20. The new rules apply to companies generally.

4.51 The hybrid capital instruments rules share the central feature of the former rules, namely, coupon deductibility for convertible instruments.

4.52 CTA 2009, s 475C defines the circumstances in which a loan relationship can be classified as a 'hybrid capital instrument' at the option of the issuer. Only loan relationships as defined by CTA 2009, ss 302–303, 479–480 and 585 can be hybrid capital instruments. A loan relationship can only be a hybrid capital instrument if:

(a) the issuer makes an irrevocable election to that effect (CTA 2009, s 475C(1)(c),(8)(9)) within six months of entering into the loan relationship; and

(b) the loan relationship has all the features prescribed in CTA 2009, s 475C.

4.53 The features prescribe by CTA 2009, s 475C are as follows:

- The debtor is entitled to defer or cancel a payment of interest.

- The security has no other significant equity features, provided a facility to convert the debt into shares or write-down the debt on the occurrence of a 'qualifying case' is not a significant equity feature.

- The only circumstances in which the creditor can receive any return other than either interest or repayment are confined to 'qualifying cases'.

- The terms of the security make provision for 'qualifying cases', being provision either (i) going concern insolvency; (ii) balance sheet

4.54 *Capital Instruments*

insolvency; or (iii) the need to satisfy a regulatory (MREL) or other legal requirement.

- The power to determine that a qualifying case applies is not exercisable by the creditor.

- In the event of conversion, the securities are only convertible into ordinary share capital of the debtor or the ordinary share capital of the debtor's quoted parent company.

- The only voting rights which the creditor holds are confined to one vote per creditor in relation to matters affecting the debtor generally.

- The creditor has no right to exercise a dominant influence over the debtor, being the right to give operating/financial policy directions with which the debtor must comply.

4.54 If the debt is not converted but simply cancelled, the rules do not cover this and there will be a tax charge on the debtor subject to CTA 2009, ss 322(3) (Condition A), (5) (Condition C), (5A) (Condition D), (5B) (Condition E), 323.

4.55 As a result of these changes the following are no longer financial instruments:

(i) AT1 instruments as defined by Banking Act 2009, s 3(1);

(ii) T2 instruments within the same definition;

(iii) Own funds and eligible liabilities within the same definition, subject to certain exclusions; and

(iv) T1 and T2 securities issued by insurance companies.

4.56 CTA 2009, s 420A provides that a 'qualifying amount' (ie interest) in respect of a hybrid capital instrument remains a payment under a loan relationship, notwithstanding the ability to cancel or withhold interest. This feature could otherwise have brought the instrument into the category of 'special securities'. Hybrid capital securities are excluded from categorisation as 'special securities' (ie, return dependent on results of business) within CTA 2010, s 1015 (s 1015(1A)). Further, hybrid capital instruments are normal commercial loans within CTA 2010, s 162, notwithstanding the possibility of conversion: CTA 2010, s 162(1B).

4.57 Notwithstanding the ability to withhold interest, hybrid capital instruments can be quoted Eurobonds within ITA 2007, s 987.

4.58 If a creditor has a 25% interest in the debtor, then the hybrid instrument rules become potentially applicable.

4.59 If in accordance with GAAP an amount in relation to a hybrid capital instrument is recognised in OCI or equity, these amounts – other than exchange gains and losses relating to hedged items – are to be regarded as recognised in the income statement for tax purposes: CTA 2009, s 320B; SI 2004/3256, reg 3(5)(c).

4.60 The rules apply for accounting periods commencing on or after 1 January 2019. Where an accounting period straddles 1 January 2019, it is divided into two notional periods.

4.61 HMRC may refuse to recognise an election for the rules to apply if it is made for tax avoidance reasons (CTA 2009, s 475C(9)), but the purpose of seeking to benefit from the facility provided by the rules is not tax avoidance.

Chapter 5

Transfer Pricing

Chapter Contents

Section	Topic	Paragraphs
A	The ALP and separate entity principle	5.1–5.14
B	Passive association	5.15–5.19
C	The transfer pricing hypothesis	5.20–5.26
D	Incorporation of BEPS	5.27–5.33
E	Thin capitalisation	5.34–5.40
F	The EU context	5.41–5.50
G	The UK rules	5.51–5.58
H	Application to financing arrangements	5.59–5.68
I	Securities	5.69–5.72
J	Guarantees	5.73–5.78
K	Economic substance re-characterisation	5.79–5.81
L	Corresponding adjustments	5.82–5.85
M	Balancing payments	5.86–5.87
N	Withholding tax	5.88–5.89
O	Centrally provided services	5.90–5.92
P	Exemptions	5.93–5.96
Q	Compliance aspects	5.97–5.98
R	Diverted profits tax	5.99–5.122

Section A: The ALP and separate entity principle

5.1 Transfer pricing is about shifting profits from one business to a related business by charging 'transfer prices' (ie, prices which do not conform to an arm's-length principle (ALP)). Transfer pricing rules apply to 'controlled transactions' (ie, transactions between related parties). The fundamental objective of transfer pricing is to establish tax parity between controlled and uncontrolled transactions, where a causal connection can be established

Transfer Pricing **5.6**

between the control relationship and transactional price distortion. This involves a comparison between the actual transaction into which related parties have entered, and the options realistically available to them for achieving the same commercial goals. This is achieved by application of the ALP which, since the 1920s, has been the gold standard of transfer pricing. This appears in articles 7 and 9 of the OECD Model Convention. Article 7 applies to permanent establishments, and article 9 to transfer pricing. The aim is to adjust the price for the actual transaction to the arm's-length price for tax purposes.

5.2 The assumption behind transfer pricing is that control relationships between enterprises distort market forces. However, from an economics point of view, it is market forces which produce groups of companies. When enterprises are linked by ownership and control to produce a linked and co-ordinated business, this provides superior efficiencies to those achievable in the market between independent enterprises.

5.3 This highlights the artificiality of the ALP. Nevertheless, even though the OECD itself raises questions in relation to it, including Pillar 1 of its Two Pillars proposal of January 2020, it remains the keystone of transfer pricing.

5.4 The purpose of transfer pricing rules is to prevent tax loss by the charging of transfer prices. This is only likely to occur between enterprises that are commercially linked and located in different jurisdictions. Transfer pricing rules substitute, for tax purposes, the 'arm's-length provision' for the 'actual provision' in transactions between related parties. Where the rules apply, all transactions between related parties, including financing transactions and transactions between related parties who are both taxable UK residents, must be conducted for tax purposes on an arm's-length basis. In other words, uncontrolled prices are, for tax purposes, to be substituted for controlled prices. Like state aids, transfer prices are seen as distortive of the economic relationships which would have existed had there been no distortive transactions. They are a half-way house between economic nationalism and world government. Hence the leading role played in transfer pricing by the OECD and the earlier work of the League of Nations.

5.5 As in relation to the corporate interest restriction (CIR), the impact of BEPS on transfer pricing has been extensive (see Richard Collier and Joseph Andrus, *Transfer Pricing and the Arm's Length Principle after BEPS* (Oxford University Press, 2017).

5.6 The fundamental objective of transfer pricing is to establish tax parity between controlled and uncontrolled transactions. Transfer pricing starts with the assumption that related parties will behave as if they were dealing with each other at arm's length. In other words, members of a group are treated as if they were standalone entities.

5.7 Transfer Pricing

5.7 The ALP is embodied in art 9(1) of the OECD Model Convention which provides:

'Where

(a) an enterprise of a Contracting State participates directly or indirectly in the management, control or capital of an enterprise of the other Contracting State, or

(b) the same persons participate directly or indirectly in the management, control or capital of an enterprise of a Contracting State and an enterprise of the other Contracting State,

and in either case conditions are made or imposed between the two enterprises in their commercial or financial relations which differ from those which would be made between independent enterprises, then any profits which would, but for those conditions, have accrued to one of the enterprises, but, by reason of those conditions, have not so accrued may be included in the profits of the enterprise and taxed accordingly ...'

This illustrates a basic feature of transfer pricing: it only provides for upwards-only adjustments which increase the tax charge. For the taxpayer, it is a game of snakes and ladders without the ladders.

5.8 The *OECD Transfer Pricing Guidelines for Multinational Enterprises and Tax Administrations* (TPG) of 10 July 2017 provide guidance on the application of the ALP and represent an international consensus on transfer pricing. 'Arm's-length pricing' has the meaning attached to it under art 9(1). It is specifically provided that the UK legislation *'is to be read in such manner as best secures consistency with'* the TPG: TIOPA 2010, s 164(1).

5.9 There is specific guidance in relation to financial transactions in the Transfer Pricing Guidance on Financial Transactions, Inclusive framework on BEPS: Actions 4, 8–10 (see 5.61).

5.10 The corollary of the arm's-length principles is the separate entity principle. Each member of a group is to be treated as an independent business, dealing with connected companies as if they were all independent parties rather than parts of a unified or co-ordinated business: TPG, para 1.6. This is expressed in the 'distinct and separate enterprise' treatment of permanent establishments: OECD MC, art 7; CTA 2009, ss 21, 22. This is difficult to reconcile with the approach of the CIR, which starts with the finance expense of a worldwide group as established from the UK and worldwide consolidated accounts.

5.11 The words in art 9(1) *'conditions are imposed'* (*'conditions are made or imposed between the two enterprises in commercial or financial relations which differ from those which would be made by independent enterprises'*) are crucial. The special relationship has to be the cause of the 'conditions' which are imposed, and those conditions have to lead to the distortive pricing. If these conditions exist, then the commercial accounts may not show the 'true' commercial profits.

5.12 This involves making a series of counterfactual assumptions. The assumption has to be made that the companies are not related, when, in fact, they are not only related but are related for sound commercial reasons. We have to say what companies would have done if they had not been related, when, in fact, they are, and what the accounts would have recorded if they had reflected the true accounting position, rather than the actual position. As Tweedledee puts it:

> 'If it was so, it might be; and if it were so, it would be; but as it isn't, it ain't. That's logic.'

5.13 Transfer pricing is based on the legal definition of a firm (ie, a business, rather than an economic definition). According to economists, the whole point of forming groups of companies and obtaining goods and services intra-group is to obtain such goods and services more efficiently and more economically than they can be supplied in the market. The integration of various businesses allows costs and market uncertainties to be reduced. The economy is co-ordinated (ie, resources are allocated) both through the price mechanism (adjusting supply to demand, and production to consumption) and the entrepreneur co-ordinator. There is a price for operating in the market. The firm replaces market costs by internal costs. According to R.H. Coase:

> 'the distinguishing mark of the first is the supersession of the price mechanism ... A firm ... consists of the system of relationships which comes into existence when the direction of resources is dependent on an entrepreneur'.

The internal market can be superior to out-sourcing.

5.14 Having recognised the economic unity of a group and thus the synergies produced by group membership, transfer pricing adopts, as its basic model, a standalone taxation of each group company as a single entity. Each entity will, on this hypothesis, deal with each other as if they were not related. Each company must report its self-assessed tax position, taking into account transfer pricing adjustments.

5.15 *Transfer Pricing*

Section B: Passive association

5.15 Transfer pricing methodology may, in some measure, seek to take account of this factor by the recognition of 'affiliation benefit', 'passive association' or the 'halo effect' in the transfer pricing analysis of transactions between such members (ie, the extent to which notions of 'implicit support' between members of a group of companies may be taken into account in applying the arm's-length principle). This reflects the synergies between members of a multinational group of companies, and the fact that the membership of a group may reasonably give rise to an inference that the parent would provide financial support in the event that the subsidiary experienced financial difficulties. For example, if Group Co A lends funds to Group Co B, it may take into account the fact that Group Co B has implicit credit support because it is a subsidiary of Group Co P. Indeed, any external lender might also take account of this. This is the 'halo effect'. To this extent, group synergies must be taken into account when evaluating intra-group financial payments.

5.16 However, this does not alter the basic application of the ALP or separate entity principle. The definitive study of this topic was made by Dr Murray Clayson (Freshfields Bruckhaus Deringer) in 'The Recognition of the Effect of Passive Association on Controlled Transactions for Transfer Pricing Purposes' (Unpublished doctoral thesis, 2016).

5.17 The UK has hitherto not recognised passive association, the rationale for this approach being drawn from a literal reading of TPG. However, the 2017 TPG marked a distinct shift in the approach of the OECD. Sections 1.158 and 1.164 of the 2017 TPG make express reference to the 'incidental benefits' which may arise by reason of group affiliation, even in the absence of express actions leading to such benefits.

5.18 In *Chevron Australia Holdings Pty Ltd v Commissioner of Taxation (No 4)* [2015] FCA 1092 and *General Electric Canada Inc v The Queen* [2010] FCA 344, courts outside the UK recognised implicit support as a factor in transfer pricing analysis. It should now be recognised as an essential element in the transfer pricing analysis. However, it does not displace it.

5.19 Self-assessed arm's-length transfer pricing provisions must be re-evaluated to take account of passive association. This may then be tested by seeking agreement with HMRC through the Advance Thin Capitalisation Agreement (ATCA) procedure.

Section C: The transfer pricing hypothesis

5.20 Accounting and tax generally take, as the basis of their computations, the price used by parties to commercial transactions (subjective basis) rather than market values (normative basis). This is a pragmatic rather than a doctrinal approach. The alternative would be to reopen every bargain and rewrite everyone's accounts according to what people should have paid according to some hypothetical standard, rather than what they actually paid. Where they apply, the transfer pricing rules do just that. The starting point is always the actual transaction into which the parties enter. The question is: Does it meet the arm's-length standard? That is purely a matter of evidence. If the transaction does not satisfy the arm's-length standard, then the accounts figures must be adjusted to meet it. For transfer pricing purposes, companies are required to *measure* profits. This is purely a tax requirement which has nothing to do with accounts. An arm's-length rate needs to be imputed for tax purposes.

5.21 This is the 'transfer pricing hypothesis'. We are bidden to postulate an imaginary state of affairs in which the arm's-length provision applies, rather than the actual provision made in the transaction between related enterprises. The fact that the transaction would not have taken place at all if the parties had been unrelated does not take the transaction outside the transfer pricing provisions (TIOPA 2010, s 151). This is why the starting point is always the actual transaction and the hypothesis must be applied to that transaction.

5.22 The arm's-length principle rests on a comparability exercise – to analyse what would have happened between unrelated parties. It has much in common with the 'comparables' which every valuer invokes to justify his valuations. This, in turn, raises the need to take into account the relevant circumstances of the parties. In applying the transfer pricing hypothesis, extensive use is made – as in the case of any valuation exercise – of internal and external comparables, generic data and benchmarks. The perpetual search is for comparable transactions in comparable circumstances between unconnected parties.

5.23 Transfer pricing adjustments are upwards only, while compensating adjustments are downwards only. Only the profits, but not the losses, of the potentially advantaged person are to be computed for tax purposes as if an arm's-length provision had been imposed instead of the actual provision (TIOPA 2010, s 147(3)). The transfer pricing rules require all dealings between related companies to be adjusted for tax purposes to conform to an arm's-length standard, where to do so would produce a larger charge to UK tax, either by increasing the profits or reducing the costs of the potentially advantaged person.

5.24 Under the self-assessment system, companies are required to make adjustments for tax purposes, but upwards-only adjustments (ie, adjustments which increase revenue or decrease expenses). If the other party to the transaction is in another jurisdiction, the state requiring the tax adjustment is not concerned with the other end of the transaction. In a domestic context, however, it is necessary to look at both ends of the transaction.

5.25 *Transfer Pricing*

5.25 The transaction should be examined on the basis of the transaction actually undertaken by the associated enterprises, as it has been structured by them (TPG, para 1.36). The proper application of the arm's-length principle requires the determination of a price which would have been agreed had the parties, in fact, been independent.

5.26 In a domestic context, this may have little economic effect because, on consolidation, the pricing advantage enjoyed by one company will be cancelled out by the equivalent disadvantage suffered by the other company. In an international context, however, transfer pricing may transfer taxable profits from one jurisdiction, where they are more heavily taxed, to another jurisdiction where they are taxed more favourably. In such a case, where parties to a transaction are connected, for policy reasons tax may diverge from the accounting treatment and require the use of market values in place of the actual prices charged by the parties. In the absence of tax sharing, states take measures to protect the national tax base in the form of transfer pricing rules.

Section D: Incorporation of BEPS

5.27 BEPS has made wide-ranging changes in relation to transfer pricing:

- Action 5 applies to countering harmful tax practices. These include intellectual property (IP) regimes. The recommendation is that there should be a nexus between income-receiving benefits and expenditure contributing to that income.

- Action 6 seeks to prevent the granting of treaty benefits in inappropriate circumstances (treaty shopping).

- Action 7 is concerned with preventing artificial avoidance of the permanent establishment (PE) status.

- Actions 8–10 deal with changes to the Transfer Pricing Guidelines.

- Action 13 is concerned with 'transfer pricing documentation and country-by-country reporting (CBCR). For groups with an annual revenue of more than €750 million, this requires the filing of information on activities and tax paid in particular countries.

- Action 14 seeks to make dispute resolution procedures more effective.

- Action 15 provides for a multilateral instrument to facilitate the modification of bilateral tax treaties.

5.28 Transfer pricing has been central to the BEPS but has then been overlaid and displaced by the formulaic approach of Action 4. Actions 8 to 10 in the BEPS Action Plan aim to ensure that transfer pricing outcomes better align with the value creation of multinational enterprises (MNEs). The OECD Guidelines have been revised, with particular emphasis on determining arm's-length conditions, for transactions involving intangibles. A function and comparability exercise must be conducted to determine the arm's-length conditions for transactions involving intangibles. The changes aim to base taxation on economic substance rather than legal form.

5.29 However, unless the legal arrangements are a sham or a result of mislabelling, they have to provide the essential starting point. As TPG, para 1.42 says:

> 'Where a transaction has been formalised by associated enterprises through written contractual agreements, those agreements form the starting point for delineating the transaction between them ...'

5.30 The legal form is then compared with the economic reality, by reference to five comparability factors; where the two differ, economic reality prevails (para 1.45). The five comparability factors are (para 1.36):

- Contractual terms.
- Functions of the parties including allocation of risk.
- Characteristics of property transferred or services provided.
- Economic circumstances and environment of the parties.
- Business strategies of the parties.

Section D1.2 sets out the requirements for a functional analysis of the roles of the parties by reference to the economically relevant characteristics of their relationships.

5.31 The revised TPG and CBCR requirements have been incorporated by reference into UK law by means of the Taxes Base (Base Erosion and Profit Shifting) (Country-by-Country Reporting) Regulations, SI 2016/237 (as modified by SI 2017/497). The main regulations came into force on 18 March 2016. The amended regulations came into force on 20 April 2017. The modifications reflect the revised OECD Guidance.

5.32 The main shift occasioned by BEPS has been to move the application of the ALP to value-chain analysis in order to determine the relative value – and hence the arm's-length price – for each activity in the value chain. The mantra of BEPS is to align transfer pricing and value creation.

5.33 The updated guidelines require arm's-length price to be driven by economic substance rather than legal ownership. From a functional point of view, the focus is on the component activities which create intangible

5.34 *Transfer Pricing*

value – Development, Enhancement, Maintenance, Protection and Exploitation (DEMPE). Functions associated with the DEMPE of intangible assets may need to be unbundled and allocated to different jurisdictions. The focus has shifted to people-based functions. Hence, if there are no personnel where the intellectual property (IP) is located, no deduction for IP royalties is allowed. This accords with permanent establishment (PE) profit attribution. The 2010 OECD Report, *Report on the attribution of profits to permanent establishments* focused on the roles of significant people functions and entrepreneurial risk taking. Risk and reward go together. It sets out the Authorised OECD Approach (AOA).

Section E: Thin capitalisation

5.34 Intragroup financial transactions have been one of the principal and most contentious areas for the application of transfer pricing. The 1987 OECD Report, *Thin Capitalisation* placed great emphasis on 'excessive' debt (ie, debt which exceeded the amount which a commercial lender would have been prepared to lend in an arm's-length situation). This is the essence of thin capitalisation.

5.35 The purpose of thin capitalisation rules is to support an ALP quantum of debt, including specifically supporting the interest rate and the terms of the borrowing transaction. The leverage and interest cover of the Borrowing Unit require benchmarking, often by reference to generic data and market trends.

5.36 The paradox of BEPS is that is has largely replaced transfer pricing for financial transactions with the rigid formulaic approach of the CIR which, in most cases, imposes an additional charge on top of any transfer pricing adjustments. Thus, transfer pricing continues alongside the CIR, but rather like an old steam train which has run out of steam and is being carried along by the rails or an old duffer who has been elbowed out by his younger, more dynamic colleagues.

5.37 Accordingly, as a result of BEPS 4 and its over-enthusiastic and over-elaborate implementation in the UK, the ALP-based thin capitalisation approach has little role to play. The future belongs to CIR, which is entirely different in approach. In relation to PEs, IP and services, the importance of transfer pricing is much enhanced post-BEPS.

5.38 Thin capitalisation is an application of transfer pricing, where a parent seeks to extract untaxed profits from a subsidiary by capitalising the subsidiary with interest-bearing debt rather than equity. Thin capitalisation is concerned with leverage and interest cover of the Borrowing Unit. A company is said to be 'thinly capitalised' if the level of intra-group debt exceeds that which an unconnected third-party lender would have loaned to

Transfer Pricing **5.42**

the borrower. The 'excessive loan' may be re-characterised as a 'disguised equity contribution'. Where a company located in one country receives capital from a parent company or associated company located in another jurisdiction, capital may be provided in the form of equity, loans, or a capital contribution. Where capital is provided by way of share capital (including preference shares) rather than debt, the return on the share capital will be by way of dividends. In the case of the UK (and most other countries), dividends are not an allowable deduction in calculating corporate profits of the paying company. There may also be withholding tax, or an irrecoverable tax credit, on the dividends paid abroad. By contrast, interest expense is deductible for UK tax purposes. Although the payment of interest to a foreign parent company or associate may be subject to withholding tax, in practice such taxes are often reduced or eliminated under the terms of the interest article in a double taxation treaty between the payer and payee countries.

5.39 Hence, a parent in one jurisdiction may capitalise a subsidiary in another jurisdiction with debt rather than equity. The subsidiary will then, in the absence of legal barriers, pay tax-deductible interest to its parent, eliminating its profits in its state of residence. In the absence of countervailing rules, the subsidiary obtains an interest deduction for tax purposes in excess of that which would have been available if all its borrowing had been on arm's-length terms with unconnected commercial lenders. Thin capitalisation rules, like transfer-pricing rules generally, are designed to ensure an arm's-length allocation of the tax base between different states.

5.40 The 'authorised OECD approach' requires a PE to be treated as if it were a distinct and separate enterprise: OECD Model Convention, art 7(2); CTA 2009, ss 21, 22. This is broadly to secure comparability of treatment between PEs and subsidiaries. However, the creditworthiness of the business as a whole is attributed to the PE.

Section F: The EU context

5.41 Though it is now bad form to discuss the EU in the UK, it is important to understand the EU context to understand the evolution of the UK thin capitalisation rules.

5.42 Such measures in an EU context may lead to a conflict between national law provisions and EU law. A national rule will be contrary to EU law where its effect is to discriminate directly or indirectly between parties on the ground of nationality and thereby render less attractive the exercise of fundamental freedoms by nationals of Member States, in particular the freedom of establishment (TFEU, art 49). The view of the court is

5.43 *Transfer Pricing*

that it is only the single market as a whole – the EU-wide position – that matters. This is in line with para 32 of the Advocate General's Opinion in *Metallgesellschaft Ltd v IRC; Hoechst AG v IRC (Cases C-397/98 and C-410/98)* (2001) STC 452 at 469:

> '32 ... it would seem that the true scope for fiscal cohesion as a justification for the differential treatment of non-residents would concern only situations in which there is a real and substantial risk that extending equal treatment in respect of a particular benefit would potentially facilitate tax evasion in both the host member state and the member state of residence of the claimant non-resident taxpayer.'

5.43 A similar problem arose with Dutch rules, which linked the tax deduction for financing costs with taxability of the companies thereby financed. *Bosal Holdings BV v Staatssecretaris van Financien (Case C-168/01)* (2003) STC 1483 concerned a Dutch holding company, which borrowed money to finance subsidiaries in other Member States. The Dutch participation exemption freed profits derived from these subsidiaries from tax, as long as the subsidiary itself was subject to Dutch tax. Bosal claimed a deduction for all the financing costs of its subsidiaries, whether or not the profits of those subsidiaries were subject to taxation in the Netherlands. Bosal claimed that the Dutch rule penalised the creation of subsidiaries in other Member States and so made less attractive the exercise of the right of freedom of establishment (EC Treaty). Article 4(2) of the Mergers Directive (90/434/EEC) permitted a Member State to refuse to a parent company deduction of finance costs incurred in connection with holdings in the capital of their subsidiaries. Nevertheless, the ECJ held that this possibility could only be exercised to the extent that it complied with the fundamental freedoms of the EC Treaty. The 'coherence' argument could not be upheld, because the grant of a tax advantage to a parent has no direct link to the taxation regime that applies to its subsidiary (*Bosal*, para 32):

> '... parent companies and their subsidiaries are distinct legal persons, each being subject to a tax liability of its own, so that a direct link in the context of the same liability to tax is lacking and the coherence of the tax system cannot be relied upon'.

5.44 In *Lankhorst-Hohorst GmbH v Finanzamt Steinfurt (Case C-324/00)* (2003) STC 607, a Dutch company capitalised its German subsidiary using debt. German law said that, if the loan was made by a substantial shareholder 'not entitled to a corporation tax credit' (which included non-resident shareholders) and could not have been obtained on the same terms from a commercial lender, the excess interest would be regarded as a concealed distribution of profits (*verdeckte Gewinnauschüttung*). German law allowed a debt: equity safe haven of 3:1. The company alleged that its freedom of establishment (EC Treaty, art 43; TFEU, art 49) was infringed by this rule. The court concluded:

'32. Such a difference in treatment between resident subsidiary companies according to the seat of their parent companies constitutes an obstacle to the freedom of establishment which is in principle prohibited by art 43 EC. The tax measure ... makes it less attractive for companies established in other member states to exercise freedom of establishment and they may, in practice, refrain from acquiring, creating or maintaining a subsidiary in the state which adopts that measure.'

'Coherence' could only be established as a justification for a discriminatory tax measure if there was a strict correlation between the tax advantage and the unfavourable tax treatment in one and the same person (para 84 of Advocate General's Opinion; para 42 of the judgment).

5.45 In *Société de Gestion Industrielle SA v Belgium* (Case C-311/08), a Belgian company granted a loan on favourable terms to a French subsidiary. While recognising the need to deny recognition to wholly artificial arrangements, the CJEU had to consider reviewing the legality of intra-EU transfer pricing rules as to whether this was a proportionate national restriction on the freedom of establishment.

5.46 Notwithstanding the general adherence to transfer pricing within the EU, the proposed Common Consolidated Corporate Tax Base ('CCCTB') proposes formulary apportionment as a form of tax pooling between Member States.

5.47 By reason of ICTA 1988, s 212(1), the UK thin capitalisation rules in ICTA 1988, s 209(2)(da) only applied where the borrower and the related lender were resident in different jurisdictions. The operation of this rule was considered by the Advocate General in *Test Claimants in the Thin Cap Group Litigation (Case C-524/04)*. The UK government concluded from the ECJ decisions that the UK transfer pricing and thin capitalisation rules might not be compliant with EU law, where the subsidiary was resident in the UK and the parent company was resident in another Member State. The Advocate General confirmed that the rules did constitute a disadvantageous tax treatment, incompatible with EC Treaty, art 43, but held that it could constitute a proportionate anti-abuse measure (Opinion, paras 42 and 66).

5.48 The UK solution adopted to overcome the potential inapplicability of thin capitalisation rules in an EU context was to harmonise downwards (ie, extend transfer pricing to purely domestic situations). This involved two steps:

(a) to transfer the thin capitalisation rules into the transfer pricing rules, into which they are integrated as a sub-set of the transfer pricing rules; and

5.49 *Transfer Pricing*

(b) to extend the transfer pricing rules to intra-UK structures and international structures alike.

5.49 In *Test Claimants in the Thin Cap Group Litigation*, the Advocate General expressed the view that this reaction went further than what was required:

> '68. Nor am I of the view that, in order to conform with Article 43, Member States should necessarily be obliged to extend thin cap legislation to purely domestic situations where no possible risk of abuse exists. I find it extremely regrettable that the lack of clarity as to the scope of the Article 43 EC justification on abuse grounds has led to a situation where Member States, unclear of the extent to which they may enact prime facie "discriminatory" anti-abuse laws, have felt obliged to "play safe" by extending the scope of their rules to purely domestic situations where no possible risk of abuse exists. Such an extension of legislation to situations falling wholly outwith its rationale, for purely formalistic ends and causing considerable extra administrative burden for domestic companies and tax authorities, is quite pointless and indeed counterproductive for economic efficiency. As such, it is anathema to the internal market.'

5.50 Accordingly, the UK rules apply both in an international and in a purely UK context.

Section G: The UK rules

5.51 UK rules on transfer pricing were first introduced by the Finance (No 2) Act 2015, s 31: *Gillette Safety Razor Ltd v IRC* [1920] 3 KB 358. UK transfer pricing rules incorporating the ALP were first included in the Finance Act 1951, s 37, which in turn became ICTA 1988, s 770.

5.52 The rules are set out in TIOPA 2010, Part 4, ss 146–217. Transfer pricing adjustments only apply in a limited range of circumstances. They only apply if four conditions are fulfilled:

(1) There are two connected enterprises. One enterprise must be 'directly or indirectly participating in the management, control or capital of the other', or the same person must be 'directly or indirectly participating in the management, control or capital of each of the affected persons' (TIOPA 2010, s 148).

(2) There is a transaction between the two enterprises, in which an 'actual provision' is made by one enterprise in the transaction which differs from the 'arm's-length provision' (ie, the provision which would have

Transfer Pricing **5.55**

been made between independent enterprises). This is the UK equivalent of 'conditions made or imposed' in OECD Model Convention art 9(1).

(3) The non-arm's-length provision confers a potential UK tax advantage on one of the affected persons ('the potentially advantaged person').

(4) If both parties are UK resident, the non-adjusted party may be able to decrease its profits or increase its losses to mirror the adjustment made in the adjustment party. This is called a 'compensating adjustment'. As an alternative to making a compensating adjustment, the disadvantaged party can make a 'balancing payment'. In either case, the additional tax payable by the potentially advantaged person is neutralised by the saving of tax in the disadvantaged person.

5.53 Where these conditions apply, the basic rule is in TIOPA 2010s 147(3), (5), namely, that tax calculation must be based on the ALP and not on the actual provision:

'(3) The profits and losses of the potentially advantaged person are to be calculated for tax purposes as if the arm's length provision had been made or imposed instead of the actual provision.

...

(5) The profits and losses of each of the affected persons are to be calculated for tax purposes as if the arm's length provision had been or imposed instead of the actual provision.'

'Actual provision' and 'affected persons' are defined in TIOPA 2010, s 147(1), 'arm's-length provision' is defined in s 151 and 'potential advantage' is defined in s 155.

5.54 The connection which must exist for the rules to apply is that one of the affected persons must be 'directly or indirectly participating in the management, control or capital of the other', or the same person must be 'directly or indirectly participating in the management, control or capital of each of the affected persons' (TIOPA 2010, s 148(3)). 'Participation' is elaborately defined and extends to a 'direct participant' (s 157), 'indirect participant' (s 158) and a 'potential direct participant' (s 159). 'Control' is construed in accordance with the definition contained in CTA 2010, s 1124 (TIOPA 2010, s 217(1)). This is the 'majority of voting power' test.

5.55 Participation for transfer pricing purposes will exist in two situations:

(1) One person controls the other or both are under common control.

5.56 *Transfer Pricing*

(2) One person is a 'major participant' in another. A 'potential major participant' is a 40% shareholder (or holder of a 40% share in a partnership) where two participators each own a 40% interest.

A joint venture owned in proportions 40:40:20 will be regarded as controlled by each of the two 40% owners (TIOPA 2010, s 160). A 39.9% interest will be outside the transfer-pricing rules, as will a 45:25:30 ownership structure.

Members of corporate groups will be enterprises; a holding of investments will be an enterprise; a partnership will be an enterprise. Participation in management or control of a company, or holding investments in a close investment holding company, will not be enterprises.

5.56 TIOPA 2010, s 164(4) requires Part 7 to be interpreted in accordance with the TPG.

(4) In this section "the transfer pricing guidelines" means–

(a) the version of the Transfer Pricing Guidelines for Multinational Enterprises and Tax Administrations approved by the Organisation for Economic Co-operation and Development on 22 July 2010 as revised by the report, *Aligning Transfer Pricing Outcomes with Valuation Creation, Actions 8–10* – 2015 Final Reports, published by the OECD on 5 October 2015, or

(b) such other document approved and published by the OECD in place of that (or a later) version or in place of those Guidelines as is designated for the time being by order made by the Treasury, including, in either case, material which is published by the OECD as part of (or by way of update or supplement to) the version or other document concerned and which is designated for the time being by order made by the Treasury).

5.57 The OECD MC art 9(1) concept of 'conditions made or imposed' between connected parties is transposed into UK tax law by s 147(1). The UK provisions apply to apply domestic transactions and cross-border transactions alike. However, where there is a wholly UK transaction, the ability for the non-affected party to make a 'corresponding adjustment' will, in many cases, ensure that there is no net tax charge in group situations. However, the increased compliance burden is considerable.

5.58 There are exemptions for small and medium-sized enterprises (SMEs), subject to certain exclusions, in TIOPA 2010, ss 166–168. Share transactions generally fall outside the transfer pricing rules.

In *Abbey National Treasury Services plc v R & C Comrs* [2015] SFTD 929 at (98a)–(110) Tracker Shares were issued by a subsidiary to its parent for their nominal value of £1,000, when their market value was £161 million. The question was considered whether a subscription price for shares was a 'provision' falling within the scope of the transfer pricing rules. In *Union Castle Mail Steamship Co Ltd v R & C Comrs* [2018] STC 2034, the Upper Tribunal concluded that this did constitute a provision for these purposes.

Section H: Application to financing arrangements

5.59 Transfer pricing guidelines regarding the pricing of related party financial transactions, including financial and performance guarantees, derivatives (including internal derivatives used in intrabank dealings) and captive insurance arrangements, take priority over the loan relationship rules: TIOPA 2010, s 146. The one exception is that CTA 2009, s 340 takes precedence over the transfer pricing rules. The only circumstance where transfer pricing will not apply to the transfer or novation of a loan relationship on non-arm's-length terms is where the transferor and the transferee are members of a capital gains tax group and both are within the charge to corporation tax in respect of the loan relationship. Transfer pricing does not take precedence of foreign exchange movements on non-arm's-length term loan relationships: CTA 2009, s 445(2), 464(3)(a). Further, CTA 2009, s 465(2) provides that nothing in s 464(1) is to prevent the disregard in computing loan relationship profits of amounts which are not brought into account under the transfer pricing rules.

5.60 In relation to financing arrangements, transfer pricing focuses on:

(i) the rationale and basis for the debt finance;
(ii) the commercial position of the connected parties regarded as separate and independent enterprises;
(iii) the borrowing capacity and debt servicing capability of the lender; and
(iv) whether enterprises dealing with each other at arm's length would have entered into comparable arrangements.

5.61 In February 2020, the OECD issued its *Transfer Pricing Guidance on Financial Transactions: Inclusive Framework on BEPS Actions 4, 8–10* to be incorporated into the guidance on transfer pricing of related party financial transactions in TPG.

5.62 *Transfer Pricing*

Para 10.23 emphasises the importance of a functional analysis:

'10.23 In accurately delineating the actual financial transaction, a functional analysis is necessary. This analysis seeks to identify the functions performed, the assets used and the risk assumed by the parties that controlled transaction.'

Risk analysis is central:

'10.25 When under accurate delineation, the lender is not exercising control over the risks associated to an advance of funds, or does not have the financial capacity to assume the risks, such risks should be allocated to the enterprise exercising control and having the financial capacity to assume the risk …'

The overall financing policy of an MNE must be considered:

'10.36 The analysis of the business strategies will also include consideration of the MNE group's global financing policy …'

The role of passive association in the transfer pricing analysis is acknowledged:

'10.77 In the context of intra-group loans, this incidental benefit that the MNE is assumed to receive solely by virtue of group affiliation, is referred to as implicit support.'

One area where there is no third-party equivalent transaction is constituted by cash pooling:

'10.115 As cash pooling is not undertaken regularly, if at all, by independent enterprises, the application of transfer pricing principles requires careful consideration.'

The link with the OECD *Report on the Attribution of Profits to Permanent Establishments* is noted in relation to captive insurance companies:

'10.209 … the economically relevant risks associated with issuing insurance policies, i.e. underwriting, must be identified … the Report … identifies those risks, that include, inter alia, insurance risk, commercial risk or investment risk …'

5.62 In establishing the quantum of debt and interest which may give rise to deductible amounts for tax purposes, the transfer pricing rules and CIR adopt a fundamentally different approach. The transfer pricing rules adopt the ALP. By contrast, CIR is based on a formulaic approach, while the transfer pricing rules

Transfer Pricing **5.65**

take precedence over the loan relationship rules, the derivative contracts rules, the CIR rules and the DPT rules alike. In accordance with BEPS Action 4, the UK introduced general restrictions on interest deductibility in the form of either (i) mandatory fixed ratio method, or (ii) the optional group ratio method (see Chapter 2). Accordingly, the significance of the transfer pricing rules for thin capitalisation has been considerably reduced, because the debtor's interest expense will be cut down for tax purposes before the transfer pricing rules come into effect. By contrast, the creditor's income receipts will remain undiminished, producing unfavourable tax asymmetries for MNEs.

5.63 Where there is a 'special relationship' (as defined in TIOPA 2010, s 154(3), ie a relationship in which the 'participation condition' is fulfilled) between two companies, the transfer pricing rules apply in two sets of circumstances:

(i) where one company has lent money to the other or left a debt outstanding; and

(ii) where the debt is entered into between independent parties, but where credit support is given by one or more associates of the borrower.

5.64 The following financial transactions lend themselves most readily to a transfer pricing analysis.

- related party lending;
- thin capitalisation;
- intra-group guarantees;
- bank loans guaranteed by a parent;
- bank loans which are back to back with a deposit by the borrower or a related company;
- use of a UK group finance company; and
- any debt with related party credit support.

5.65 The comparable uncontrolled price method is normally applicable to financing transactions. In the case of financing arrangements, a series of special rules supplement and displace the general transfer pricing rule. In relation to financing transactions, the sort of adjustments that are possible under the transfer-pricing rules include:

(a) increasing or decreasing the rate of interest;

(b) inserting a rate of interest on an interest-free loan;

(c) increasing or decreasing the amount of a loan;

5.66 *Transfer Pricing*

(d) increasing or decreasing a guarantee fee or similar expense; and

(e) interpolating a guarantee fee or similar expense where no provision is made for one.

5.66 The UK relies solely on an arm's-length test in relation to limiting interest deductibility on related party debt. In the case of thin capitalisation, the allowable UK level of commercial gearing is very low by international standards. HMRC broadly adhere to the rule of thumb that, in order to be outside the transfer pricing rules, the debt: equity safe harbour ratio must be 1:1. The UK also expects an interest cover of 3:1 (see Inland Revenue *Tax Bulletin No 17*, June 1995, p 218; *No 35*, June 1998, p 554; *Issue 37*, October 1998, p 580). Where a company has loans, as a result of which it is regarded as thinly capitalised, any interest arising is treated as a cost disallowable for corporation tax computation purposes. *Tax Bulletin No 17* says:

> 'We have in recent years tended to accept that, where a loan otherwise meets the arm's length test, if the UK grouping remains geared at something less than 1:1 and its interest cover is at least 3:1, its financing should be regarded as satisfying the arm's length test as a whole.'

It was stated that HMRC may negotiate a forward agreement on interest deductibility with a company, giving a measure of certainty for up to five years (*Tax Bulletin No 37;* SP 165/99).

5.67 There are exceptions to the UK target ratio of 1:1. In the case of financial businesses, a gearing between 10:1 and 20:1 is acceptable. Property and shipping companies may have a 3:1 ratio. Start-ups and mergers are allowed three to five years to reach the target ratio.

5.68 Transfer pricing documentation is fundamental to transfer pricing. HMRC have stated that documentation should be in place to show that a review of thin capitalisation has been undertaken; otherwise, any tax lost may be attributable to 'a careless inaccuracy' and a penalty consequently charged under FA 2007, Sch 23, para 1.

Section I: Securities

5.69 TIOPA 2010, s 152 contains special rules for financing arrangements where a 'security' is issued. Section 153 applies where a 'security' is issued and a guarantee provided. The special rules in ss 152 and 153 are subcategories within the general rule in s 147(3). Each contains particular expressions of the ALP in relation to securities. The significance of ss 152, 153 is not so much in the application of the arm's-length rule but rather to determine how corresponding adjustments are to be made by a disadvantaged person, whether under s 174 in the case of adjustments under s 147, or under s 175 for adjustments under ss 152 and 153.

5.70 TIOPA 2010, s 152 applies where a 'security' (used in an extended sense) is issued by one of the controlled parties to another. In considering whether a financing transaction between related parties is priced on an arm's-length basis, it is necessary to have regard to all factors, in particular:

(a) whether the loan would have been made at all in the absence of a special relationship;

(b) the amount which the loan would have been in the absence of a special relationship; and

(c) the rate of interest and other terms which would have been agreed in the absence of a special relationship.

These are the three factors listed in TIOPA 2010, s 152(2). Hence all intra-group lending and intra-group balances left outstanding may require modification for tax purposes, notwithstanding that the overall incidence of UK tax is not affected.

5.71 The transfer pricing rules define 'security' as including instruments which do not create or evidence a charge: TIOPA 2010, s 154(6). 'Potential advantage in relation to UK taxation' is defined in s 155 as a decrease in UK taxable profits or an increase in UK allowable losses. Where a transfer-pricing adjustment is made by a company, imputed interest will have to be brought into account as a loan relationship credit or debit.

5.72 The creditworthiness of a borrower is determined in isolation for its constituent group looking upwards, but taking into account the value of its assets, including holdings in subsidiaries, because an unrelated lender would have taken these assets into consideration in assessing borrowing capacity (TIOPA 2010, s 152(5), (6)). The question is whether the UK borrower has sufficient creditworthiness to support the debt and whether the lender is connected with it. A positive act is required to justify the inference of an enhanced expectation of repayment; thus, for example, a passive association between one company and its parent, so that a lender will have a higher expectation of repayment or a credit-rating agency will accord a higher rating to a debt, will not be relevant for tax purposes. In considering the three factors listed in s 152(2), any guarantee or letter of comfort provided by another related company is to be disregarded. The aim is to ensure that the creditworthiness of the borrower is considered in isolation from the rest of the group, particularly where the loan is ostensibly at arm's length because the

5.73 *Transfer Pricing*

lender is an independent bank. Hence, cross-guarantees, where every group member guarantees the borrowings of other group members, will not enhance creditworthiness when it comes to applying the transfer pricing rules.

Section J: Guarantees

5.73 If the transaction is characterised as involving the issue of a security, the provisions relating to guarantees in TIOPA 2010, s 153 are also brought into play. Where there is a loan from an unrelated lender, but the loan is guaranteed by a party related to the borrower, the question of whether the guarantee has been provided on arm's-length terms must be analysed in the same way as the question of whether a loan of a similar amount would have been made by an unrelated lender. If an adjustment is made, reducing a borrower's interest expense, the connected guarantor can claim a compensating adjustment, as if the guarantor had borrowed money from and paid interest to the unrelated lender. Under TIOPA 2010, s 192, the guarantor may claim to be treated as being party to the non-arm's-length element of the borrowing, as if he were the borrower. In that case, the guarantor will be deemed to be a party to a non-trading loan relationship.

5.74 Guarantees are dealt with in TIOPA 2010, s 152(5). This requires any guarantee given by a related company to be ignored in determining the arm's-length price. Transfer pricing includes thinly capitalised companies paying interest to third parties under finance arrangements guaranteed by affiliates. The effect of the rules may be to treat the guarantor as having taken out part of the loan and paid the interest. Two situations arise:

(a) the effect of the guarantee is to reduce the interest rate otherwise payable; and

(b) without the guarantee, the loan would not have been made at all or would have been made in a smaller amount.

5.75 TIOPA 2010, s 153 addresses indirect thin capitalisation, where a borrower borrows money from a non-connected party, but the loan is guaranteed by the borrower's parent. In those situations, the guarantee has to be ignored. All kinds of UK multinationals need to apply thin capitalisation principles to loans within the UK part of the group, as do UK groups with no overseas subsidiaries.

5.76 'Guarantee' is extremely broadly defined in s 154(4) to include:

'any other relationship, arrangements, connection or understanding (whether formal or informal) such that the person making the loan to the issuing company has a reasonable expectation that in the event of a default by the issuing company he will be paid by or out of the assets of, one or more companies'.

5.77 One effect of a guarantee, in the transfer pricing context, is to increase the amount that the borrower is able to borrow. This increases the amount of deductible interest permitted under TIOPA 2010, s 147. Section 152(5), however, restricts the interest in respect of a security where a guarantee is given by a related company to the arm's-length amount payable in the absence of such a guarantee. However, where the effect of the guarantee is to reduce the amount of the deductible interest (because the guarantee allows the borrower to borrow at a more favourable rate), a claim by the guarantor may be treated as if it had issued the security and paid any interest or other amounts pursuant to it (TIOPA 2010, s 192). Where there is more than one guarantor, the amount may be shared among them. The creditor is permitted to pay an arm's-length guarantee fee to the companies providing the guarantee. The guarantors are required to include that amount in their taxable income pursuant to s 153(1).

5.78 The question is, whether the base case proposition should be to assess the stand-alone creditworthiness of the borrower and then to consider whether that creditworthiness should be adjusted to reflect the degree to which independent third parties would regard the borrower's standing as enhanced by its affiliations. TIOPA s 152(5) states:

> 'Section 147(1)(d) is to be read as requiring that, in the determination of any of the matters mentioned in subsection (6), no account is to be taken of (or of any inference capable of being drawn from) any guarantee provided by a company of which the issuing company has a participatory relationship.'

The ignoring of 'inferences' only applies where there is a formal guarantee. It would appear, therefore, that, in pricing the loan, implicit support which would be taken into account by third parties should be regarded as relevant, thus potentially reducing, in relative terms, the pricing of the guarantee.

Section K: Economic substance re-characterisation

5.79 The 2017 TPG exceptionally allow the financing structure adopted by the taxpayer to be disregarded and to be re-characterised in accordance with its substance. In the context of thin capitalisation, it may be appropriate to characterise the investment in accordance with its economic substance, with the result that it may be treated as a subscription of capital (Guidelines, para 1.37). The issue concerns the extent to which a financing structure between unrelated parties would represent equity or debt. In the case of debt, the rate of interest will also need to be determined. HMRC accept that a transaction structured as a debt may have an equity function in the context of outward

5.80 *Transfer Pricing*

financing in limited circumstances (IM503000). In the context of inward financing, this is regarded as thin capitalisation (ie, the company is funded by more debt than would be agreed in arm's-length circumstances (IM504050)).

5.80 An equity function is often supported by treatment of an amount as a capital contribution. In the UK, there is no specific company law provision relating to capital contributions. A capital contribution in a conventional sense is simply a gift of money. It is not a loan and creates no obligation to transfer economic benefit to the maker of the contribution.

5.81 Foreign exchange gains and losses are excluded from the rules because these are separately charged and relieved under CTA 2009. Where profits are recomputed by transfer pricing adjustments, the whole or, as the case may be, a proportionate part of any exchange gains and losses resulting from the adjustment are left out of account for tax purposes.

The CBCR requirements apply where a group has a consolidated turnover in excess of €750 million per year.

The alignment of form and substance must be documented in Transfer Pricing Documentation. This will ordinarily comprise a master file and a local file structure.

Section L: Corresponding adjustments

5.82 Other UK companies may claim adjustments for the deductions disallowed in the borrower if the company claiming the compensating adjustment:

(a) is related to the borrower;

(b) has given guarantees for the borrower's debt; and

(c) has sufficient creditworthiness to support that guarantee.

It is not necessary for the borrower and the guarantor to have a common UK parent. The compensating adjustment can be allocated to whichever UK company wants to claim it.

5.83 Hence, if a UK company has given a guarantee of a related company borrowing, and the debtor company has had a tax deduction disallowed under the transfer pricing rules, a deduction can be allowed to the guarantor company by way of compensating adjustment if it could have borrowed, on an arm's-length basis, the debt in respect of which the interest deduction has been denied. Thus, while the existence of a guarantee is not taken into account in determining the amount of interest (if any) to be imputed to the lender under

TIOPA 2010, s 152, group companies providing the guarantee are permitted to make corresponding adjustments. In the domestic context, this may cause a proportion of the cost of servicing the debt to be tax deductible by the guarantor, as opposed to the borrower. Where the effect of a transfer pricing adjustment in a domestic transaction is to create a loss, that loss may be surrendered under the group relief provisions. In the context of s 147, a corresponding adjustment can only be claimed by the counterparty disadvantaged as a result of the adjustment. This is made by the disadvantaged party after an adjustment and within the time limits of s 174.

5.84 In the context of a claim under TIOPA 2010, s 152, a corresponding adjustment may be made by either party under s 181, including an adjustment before any adjustment is made in the CTSA return (s 182(3)). This permits automatic adjustment for the borrower if interest is imputed or increased in the hands of the lender.

Example 1

X Ltd borrows £1,000 at 6% from an unrelated bank. X Ltd issues a debenture. A guarantee is provided by X Ltd's 75% parent Holdco. In the absence of the guarantee, they would only have lent £700. X Ltd is potentially advantaged and has to adjust its interest deduction by £(60 – 42) = 18. Holdco is treated as having borrowed £300 at 6% and claims a corresponding adjustment by way of a deduction from its profits of £18.

Example 2

X Ltd borrows £1,000 at 6% from an unrelated bank. X Ltd issues a debenture. A guarantee is provided by X Ltd's 75% parent, Holdco. In the absence of the guarantee, the bank would still have lent £1,000, but have charged interest at 8%. X Ltd would have had to pay £20 a year for the guarantee.

(1) Holdco is potentially advantaged and has to bring in additional income of £20.

(2) X Ltd is a disadvantaged person. It makes a corresponding adjustment of £20. This gives X Ltd a loss of £10. It surrenders the loss to Holdco.

5.85 In the case of cross-border transactions, the corresponding adjustment is made via the relevant double taxation treaty (DTT) (eg, OECD Model Convention, art 25). Some DTTs allow the creditor to make an adjustment to reduce the amount of interest which is otherwise taxable. This is also possible

5.86 *Transfer Pricing*

where both the creditor and the debtor are subject to UK corporation tax: TIOPA 2010, s 181.

Section M: Balancing payments

5.86 Where a compensating adjustment is made, a payment may be made between the two companies in respect of the tax adjustment, being an amount not exceeding the gross amount of the adjustment. The net effect, in most UK cases, will be to put the two companies back into the same cash position as they were in before the transfer pricing adjustment was made. Provided that the amount of such a 'balancing payment' does not exceed the transfer pricing adjustment, it will be ignored for tax purposes: TIOPA 2010, s 195.

5.87 In the case of capital market arrangements, a company entitled to a compensating adjustment can elect not to make a balancing payment to the company which would suffer the adverse transfer pricing adjustment, but instead to undertake sole responsibility for paying the additional tax liability of that company: TIOPA 2010, s 199. This will improve the credit rating of the instruments.

The conditions for the availability of the election are:

- an election can only be made in relation to inter-company debt which forms 'part of a capital markets arrangement';
- the capital markets arrangement must include the issue of capital markets investments that are issued wholly or mainly to independent persons; and
- the total value of the capital markets investments made under the capital markets arrangement must be at least £50 million.

An election must be made in the tax return relating to the accounting period in which the relevant security was issued.

Section N: Withholding tax

5.88 Article 11 of the OECD Model Convention (the interest article) normally provides for reduced or no tax withholding on interest paid by a person in one treaty country to a person resident in the other. Article 11(6) excludes from the provisions of this article that amount of interest which 'by reason of a special relationship between the payer and the beneficial owner or between both of them and some other person ... exceeds the amount which would have been' payable in the absence of such a relationship. A question arises whether this provision applies only to the rate of interest or can also extend to the amount of debt. The reclassification of interest as a dividend is only permitted where the applicable article in a double taxation treaty contains a provision to this effect (eg, UK-Canada Convention, art 11(9) and the UK-Bolivia Convention, art 11(6)). Recent UK treaties contain such wording, but older ones do not. A parent company guarantee may create a 'special relationship'. Where interest is disallowed, it will no longer be treated as a distribution but as a disallowable expense. Thus, there will be no question of non-residents claiming tax credits.

5.89 If interest payable to a non-resident is disallowed as a deduction by reason of a transfer pricing adjustment, no withholding tax need be imposed on the disallowed deduction. TIOPA 2010, s 187 gives the lender the right to make a claim that will remove the liability to withholding tax. It will continue to be necessary for overseas lenders to apply for advance clearance to receive interest gross. The applicant will be asking HMRC to confirm their acceptance that the arm's-length portion of the interest is protected by the interest article in the relevant DTT and that the non-arm's-length portion is protected by s 187. Except in cases where the DTT allows a rate of withholding tax on arm's-length interest, it will be unnecessary, for withholding tax purposes, to determine how much of the interest is non-arm's length.

The interest article in DTTs continues to apply to thin cap interest, unless this is disapplied by a 'special relationship' clause. In that case, thin cap interest may be governed by the 'other income' article or be outside the scope of the DTT.

Section O: Centrally provided services

5.90 In the case of centrally provided services, the service should be provided for cost plus a profit mark-up.

A number of factors should be considered in calculating mark-up:

- The cost base should include overheads on an absorption (not marginal) basis.

- Employee costs should include associated overheads, such as accommodation, management, IT.

- For bought-in costs, no mark-up is required for the bought-in element; but a mark-up is required for the internal element.

- For internally provided services, a mark-up should be charged to reflect the profit margin a third party would make.

5.91 *Transfer Pricing*

- Where a service is recharged to a number of companies, the allocation should reflect the benefit to each.

The same approach should be used consistently year to year.

5.91 Because of the greater degree of risk by the provider and potential profit, the 'cost plus' method is considered unlikely to give an arm's-length result in the case of:

- financial services such as treasury services; or
- services creating, enhancing, or using intellectual property (including research and development, product design, brand development and management).

5.92 The effect of these rules can be illustrated in the following examples:

Example 3

A UK resident insurance company X Co owns 55% of the shares in a Bahamas resident reinsurance company Y Co. X lends £5m to Y at 5%. In completing its corporation tax self-assessment, X takes the view that it would have charged 8% interest to Y if interest was charged on a commercial, arm's-length basis. X is required to add the imputed interest to its loan relationship credits.

Example 4

A UK parent makes an interest free loan to a subsidiary, repayable on demand. Fair value recognition will require the difference between the fair value of the loan and the cash received to be accounted for as a gift. Assuming that the subsidiary is adequately capitalised, an interest rate will have to be attributed to the loan, so reversing for tax purposes the accounts entries. If the parent subsequently writes off the loan, the accounting entries will again be ignored for tax purposes under the connected party debt rules.

Example 5

The subsidiary borrows money from a bank. The parent gives a guarantee without making a charge. A higher rate of interest would have been charged in the absence of the guarantee. On initial recognition, the premium which the parent would have received on arm's-length terms will have to be amortised to profit and loss account over the life of the guarantee in both companies for tax purposes. If there is a 20% possibility that the parent will have to make a payment under the guarantee, the parent will measure the financial liability at 20% of the outstanding amount payable to the bank by the subsidiary. If a payment has to be made by the parent, the parent will, by virtue of its payment under the guarantee, acquire the bank's rights as creditor against the subsidiary. However, because the debt asset it acquires is connected party debt, it will obtain no tax relief for its payment.

Section P: Exemptions

5.93 There are a number of exemptions from the basic rule in TIOPA 2010, s 147(3), (5) designed to reduce the regulatory impact of the rules.

The first exemption is for small and medium-sized enterprises (SMEs): TIOPA 2010, ss 166–168. These are defined in s 172 by reference to the EU definition in *Commission Recommendation 2003/361/EC* (research and development tax credits/transfer pricing). A company is an SME if it satisfies the employee test and at least one of the turnover or balance sheet tests. An SME is an undertaking with two of the following three characteristics:

Two of:	(i) Number of employees	and	(ii) Turnover	or	(iii) Balance sheet total
Small	< 50		≤ €10 million		≤ €10 million
Medium	< 250		≤ € 50 million		≤ € 43 million

Associated companies, called 'partner enterprises', are included in applying the limits. Two companies will be 'partner enterprises' where one holds (either solely or jointly with any linked company) 25% or more of the capital or voting rights of the other company. Two enterprises will be linked where one holds the majority of voting rights, has the right to appoint or dismiss the management, or can exercise a dominant influence. Partnership interests are also included when deciding whether an enterprise is an SME and cover situations where one party holds 25% or more of the capital or voting rights of the other and the two parties are not linked enterprises.

This means that, no matter how small a company may be, it cannot benefit from the exemption unless its entire worldwide group meets the thresholds on a consolidated basis. Certain specified investors, such as venture capital companies, local authorities and public bodies, are ignored for the purposes of the test.

These thresholds are applied on a current year, annual basis. Hence a company may go in and out of the transfer pricing regime.

5.94 *Transfer Pricing*

5.94 Companies may elect to be brought within the transfer pricing rules: TIOPA 2010, s 167(1).

The exclusion does not apply to transactions where the other affected person party is a resident of certain countries ('non-qualifying territories'). In the case of a composite transaction, the exemption is disapplied if any of the parties are resident in a non-qualifying country: TIOPA 2010, s 167(3). 'Qualifying territory' and 'non-qualifying territory' are defined in s 173: a 'qualifying territory' is the UK or a country with which the UK has a DTT, the DTT contains a non-discrimination clause, and the Treasury has so designated the country in question; a 'non-qualifying territory' is any other country.

5.95 As regards medium-sized enterprises, the same conditions apply as for the small enterprise exclusion, save that HMRC have the power to withdraw the exemption by giving a 'transfer pricing notice': TIOPA 2010, ss 168–170. Groups of taxpayers who meet the medium-sized test may file their tax returns without being required to apply the arm's-length test. However, once the return has been filed, HMRC have the power to issue a 'transfer pricing notice' if significant amounts of tax are thought to be at stake. This will require the taxpayer to revise the return for any understatement of profits arising from non-arm's-length pricing. Taxpayers will then have 90 days to file an amended return.

5.96 A further exemption is for dormant companies: TIOPA, 2020, s 165. Dormant companies are often kept in existence to avoid 'phantom' degrouping charges under TCGA 1992, s 179, or the costs of a formal liquidation. Banks, insurance companies and companies providing financial services cannot be dormant.

Section Q: Compliance aspects

5.97 HMRC guidance notes (available at www.hmrc.gov.uk/international/transfer-pricing.htm) relate to the following topics:

- Small and medium-sized enterprises.
- Dormant companies.
- Documentation.
- Risk assessment.
- Centrally provided services.
- Thin capitalisation.
- Securitisation.
- Foreign exchange gains and losses on matching loans.

- Scope of rules – enterprises.
- Trading stock.
- Corresponding adjustments.
- Employee share schemes.

5.98 There is a penalty for failure to keep adequate transfer pricing records which:

- identify transactions to which the transfer pricing rules apply; and
- provide evidence of an arm's-length price.

There are penalties for careless or deliberate inaccuracies as a result of a failure to apply transfer pricing rules.

Large groups can apply for advance pricing agreements (APAs): TIOPA 2010, ss 218–230.

HMRC guidance lists seven categories of documents required for transfer pricing purposes, labelled (a)–(g).

Section R: Diverted profits tax

5.99 CTA 2009, s 5(1) states that a UK-resident company is chargeable to corporation tax on its worldwide profits. Section 5(2) provides that a non-UK resident company is only within the scope of corporation tax if it carries on a trade in the UK through a permanent establishment, or carries on a trade of dealing in or developing land in the UK other than through a permanent establishment.

5.100 Taxation is national. The economy is international. This tension lies at the heart of the globalisation issue, as noted in Chapter 1. The mantra of the BEPS project has been that the traditional international law definition of company residence is no longer capable of capturing modern forms of economic activity. Residence encompasses the legal rights vested in a person. The BEPS Action Plan also expressed the concern that taxation according to legal ownership might shift taxation away from the jurisdiction where, in substance, economic activities were carried on. Multinationals could use or misapply the transfer pricing rules to separate income from the economic activities which produce that income and shift it to low-tax environments. Likewise, companies without a formal tax presence in a particular jurisdiction could, in substance, carry on economic activity in that jurisdiction, without incurring that country's taxation on profits earned there, by artificially avoiding the creation of a PE in that jurisdiction.

5.101 *Transfer Pricing*

5.101 The notion of 'shifting' profits presupposes that profits have some sort of 'natural' home where they 'belong' other than that afforded by residence or physical presence. Before BEPS, the UK had already explored a looser and more flexible concept than that of tax residence in the form of the concept of 'tax presence'. This is not a statutory term but was invented by Charles Potter QC in *Clark v Oceanic Contractors Incorporated* [1983] STC 35.

5.102 The question in that case was whether a non-resident employer was required to operate PAYE in respect of North Sea employees taxable under Sch E (now 'employment income'), when the payments were made by a non-resident employer outside the UK to non-resident employees. By a majority of 3:2 the House of Lords held that the collection mechanism of PAYE was applicable, because the employer had sufficient 'tax presence' in the UK. Lord Scarman said that the employing company was brought within PAYE because it had a '*UK tax presence*':

> 'My Lords, I find nothing anomalous or contrary to principle in a "tax presence" being the determinant of the s 204 (ICTA 1970) liability.'

In a global context, this is an expansive concept.

5.103 The diverted profits tax (DPT) was introduced in 2015 as a means of taxing both resident and non-resident companies outside the framework of corporation tax. It echoes and reinforces BEPS Action policy aims. The charge is separate from corporation tax and cannot be relieved under a DTT. It is widely drafted and applies across all commercial sectors.

5.104 The DPT is a unilateral UK response to BEPS. Like the CIR, it is superimposed on the transfer pricing rules. However, it differs fundamentally from the transfer pricing rules:

(a) it operates outside the self-assessment system;

(b) whereas companies self-assess transfer pricing adjustments, tax payable under DPT is '*the amount of tax charged by a notice*' issued by a HMRC officer (s 79(2)(i));

(c) transfer pricing adjustments result from the application of the ALP, whereas DPT is quantified by calculating the 'diverted profits'; and

(d) whereas corporation tax is charged at the standard corporation tax rate, DPT is imposed at the rate of 25% on the 'taxable diverted profits' (ie, profits which would have been taxable in the UK, if they had not been 'diverted' to another jurisdiction). This rises to 33% ('notional banking surcharge profits') and 55% ('notional adjusted ring fence profits')(profits 'diverted' from the UK: FA 2015, s 77(1)).

(e) transfer pricing is aimed at allocating tax revenues between two jurisdictions, where the pricing in a controlled transaction does not correspond to the ALP. DPT It is aimed at protecting the national tax base where the legal situation does not correspond to the economic reality of where profits are generated;

(f) tax on transfer pricing can be relieved under a DTT but DPT cannot be so relieved;

(g) transfer pricing operates within the procedural norms of the appeal system while DPT operates outside these norms;

(h) the fictions on which transfer pricing is based derive from the ALP, while DPT depends upon what it is 'reasonable to assume' which, translated into English, means what the tax authority thinks it is reasonable to assume; and

(i) DPT is, in effect, a short-cut which by-passes transfer pricing procedures.

5.105 DPT was introduced with effect from 1 April 2015 under legislation in FA 2015, ss 77–116. The statutory framework and purpose of the legislation is set out by Green J (as he then was) in *Glencore Energy UK Ltd v R & C Comrs* [2017] STC 1824.

5.106 It targets groups in two situations:

(i) Case 1: *UK company: involvement of entities or transactions lacking economic substance* (FA 2015, s 80). This operates if the arrangements produce an effective tax mismatch outcome (ss 80(1)(d), 107, 108). Where a UK company ('C') enters into arrangements with insufficient economic substance (s 80(1)(f), 110) under which it then pays to a related non-UK company ('P') management fees, rent or royalties, which reduce the UK company's taxable profits by the amount of the charges, the 'diverted profits' being the difference between tax at the UK corporation tax rate, and tax at the rate paid by the non-resident company. The insufficient economic substance test is met if it is reasonable to assume that the transaction was designed to achieve the tax reduction (s 110(4)(5)). In some cases, it is also necessary to show that the fiscal benefits exceed the non-fiscal benefits (s 110(5)–(9)).

(ii) Case 2: *Non-UK company avoiding a UK taxable presence* (FA 2015, ss 81, 86). Where a non-UK company ('the foreign company') carries on trading activity in the UK through a person with whom it is connected ('the avoided PE'), it is reasonable to assume that the activity of the avoided PE is designed to ensure that the foreign company does not have a UK PE (in most cases relying on the principle that an independent agent is not a PE) and there is *'an effective tax mismatch outcome'*, the profits which the foreign company would have earned in the UK

5.107 *Transfer Pricing*

(being the profits of the avoided PE), are 'diverted profits' for which the foreign company is liable to corporation tax. The 'mismatch condition' is that the 'material provisions' made between the foreign company and the avoided PE are such that The company will be deemed to have a UK PE, to which profits will be attributed in accordance with the 2008 OECD Report on the Attribution of Profits to Permanent Establishments.

5.107 An *effective tax mismatch outcome* occurs if the tax payable by the non-UK company is 80% or less than the tax on the diverted profits which would have been payable by the UK company, but for the arrangements (eg, if the UK rate of corporation tax is 19%, an overseas company must be paying tax at 16% or less on the additional profits it obtains as a result of the arrangements). The reduction of UK corporation tax must be a minimum of 20% (eg, the DPT will only apply if the rate of foreign tax rate on the diverted profits is less than 80% of the UK rate (16%) (ss 107, 108)).

5.108 If the outcome is an 'excepted loan relationship outcome', the transaction will not meet the 'effective tax mismatch outcome' condition. An 'excepted loan relationship outcome' means that all the debits and credits arising to C from the arrangements are loan relationship debits and credits (s 109). The s 80 charge also does not apply if either C or P is an SME within TIOPA s 172 (see 5.93).

5.109 Where FA 2015 ss 80 or 81 apply, HMRC can re-characterise the supply chain under ss 82–85 by reference to the hypothetical alternative arrangements ('the relevant alternative provision', RAP) which, it is reasonable to assume would have been agreed between the relevant companies, had they not had an intention to divert profits away from the UK.

5.110 The procedures for imposing the tax are closely modelled on and follow the procedures for accelerated payment notices contained in FA 2014, ss 214–233. Attempts to challenge the validity of these procedures through judicial review have been unsuccessful: *R (on the application of Rowe) v R & C Comrs* [2017] EWCA Civ 2105, [2018] STC 462.

5.111 Companies have an obligation to notify HMRC if they are potentially within the DPT regime within three months of the end of their accounting period, unless it is 'reasonable to conclude' that no DPT charge would arise (s 92). HMRC then have 24 months to issue a charging notice (four years in the absence of a notification of potential liability) (s 93). This is the preliminary notice, in respect of which the taxpayer company can make representations of a limited nature. If no representations are made, or and to the extent that the notice is confirmed after representations, it becomes definitive (Charging Notice) and the amount charged on the notice becomes immediately payable, without any right of appeal against payment. The company has 30 days in which to make very limited 'representations'.

5.112 The taxable diverted profits are *'such amount (if any) as the designated HMRC officer issuing the notice determines on the basis of the best estimate that can reasonably be made at that time, to be the amount calculated in accordance with sections 84 or 85 (as the case may be)'*: s 96(2). However, ss 82–85 themselves incorporate large elements of conditionality, hypothesis and a counterfactual scenario, so each step towards the conclusion builds hypothesis upon hypothesis, and erects an ever-taller tower on an ever-more strained foundation.

5.113 Interest is payable for the period beginning six months after the end of the accounting period to which the DPT relates and ending with the date of issue of the charging notice.

5.114 Tax can be assessed on the non-UK company's representative in the UK and can be recovered from any affiliates with assets in the UK. The representative will be deemed to have been paid a royalty by the avoided PE.

5.115 Section 101 provides that HMRC can conduct a review of the charging notice. Section 102 provides a right of appeal against a charging notice, to be exercised at the end of the review period.

5.116 The type of situations which are seen as being within the scope of DPT include cases where legal contracts allocate risks to related non-UK companies but the substantive control of the risk area remains with UK entities. Examples provided by HMRC include commissionaire structures, management services, contract manufacturing, research & development, captive insurance and, in particular, the vesting of IP in entities in lower-taxation jurisdictions.

5.117 Judicial review was sought of a charging notice in *R (on the application of Glencore Energy UK Ltd) v R & C Comrs* [2017] STC 1824; [2018] STC 51. The background was:

(a) Glencore Energy UK traded in the UK in oil and gas products.

(b) In order to enable it to carry on its trade, it was provided with facilities by its Swiss parent, GIAG, in return for 80% of its net profits.

(c) Glencore and HMRC had been considering transfer pricing issues in relation to the facilities agreement for several years.

(d) A charging notice was issued on the basis that the arrangements fell within s 80 (inadequate economic substance).

5.118 *Transfer Pricing*

5.118 Judicial review is only available if there is no suitable alternative remedy. As Sales LJ (as he then was) observed in the Court of Appeal at [2018] STC 51 at (55):

> '... judicial review in the High Court is ordinarily a remedy of last resort, to ensure the rule of law is respected where no other procedure is suitable to achieve that objective'.

5.119 In the High Court, Green J held that the combined review procedure under s 101 and right of appeal under s 102 provided a suitable alternative remedy and leave to seek judicial review was refused. He concluded:

> '(7) FA 2015 provides a comprehensive two-stage dispute resolution mechanism which first facilitates and encourages negotiation between the taxpayers and HMRC and then, if this is unproductive, allows for an appeal to a specialist tribunal.'

His reasoning and conclusion were confirmed by the Court of Appeal.

5.120 On 10 January 2019, HMRC set up a revised disclosure facility known as the Profit Diversion Compliance Facility (PDCF), to enhance FA 2015, s 92 and related transfer pricing compliance.

5.121 The difficulty with the PDCF is that, in effect, it requires a group to declare and quantify a liability to DPT, which may be to beg the question whether the group is liable at all. It is a safe general assumption that there is always someone, somewhere who is engaged in dirty work at the crossroads. However, there are several intervening steps which have to be gone through before liability in individual cases can be established.

5.122 This illustrates the fundamental problem of the DPT, namely, the inherent uncertainty of its scope, which is not cured by increasing the length and density of the legislation and imposing an additional layer of hypothesis. The courts are concerned to remove the scenery and get to the reality behind it: *'when the outer garments are peeled back the true substance is revealed'*: Green J, [2017] STC 1824 at (7). However, that approach is capable of being applied two ways. If the reality of DPT is examined, after removing the carefully crafted scenery, it may appear that a Designated Officer makes a demand for tax, in an amount which is justified based on a number of hypothetical assumptions. Dignified objections are raised. However, that sum becomes immediately payable, no shriving time is allowed, no right of appeal exists against the order for payment and the alternative remedy of judicial review is barred. The procedure exactly follows that provided for in relation to accelerated payment notices under FA 2014. Experience in that area indicates that the rights of appeal against the liability itself are, in most cases, of limited practical value. The DPT, it may be argued, pushes transfer pricing beyond its legitimate bounds. Such procedures, while highly effective, resemble taxation by executive fiat. That is the system of Danelaw, which, as the Domesday Book exemplified, William the Conqueror was anxious to supersede: see para 1.1. And thus, the whirligig of time brings in its changes.

Chapter 6

Controlled Foreign Companies

Chapter Contents

Section	Topic	Paragraphs
A	BEPS	6.1–6.3
B	The UK rules	6.4–6.14
C	Definition of CFC	6.15–6.17
D	Control	6.18–6.25
E	The exemptions	6.26–6.34
F	The CFC Gateways	6.35–6.54
G	Computation of CFC profits	6.55–6.58

Section A: BEPS

6.1 A further aim of the BEPS project was to strengthen and amend domestic rules on controlled foreign companies (CFCs). The Final Report recommended six building blocks.

- The definition of CFC should apply both a legal and economic control test.
- CFC exemptions and a low-tax threshold.
- Defining CFC income.
- Computing CFC income.
- Attributing CFC income.
- Preventing and eliminating double taxation.

6.2 The OECD recommended that the CFC rules should only apply to CFCs subject to a 'meaningfully lower' rate of tax that the rate to which it would be subject if resident in the jurisdiction of the parent company. This simply confirmed the practice of most jurisdictions, including the UK, to exempt CFCs from the rules if the effective local tax rate is at least 75% of the parent country rate.

6.3 If the CFC is established in a low-tax jurisdiction, that would lead to the attribution of part of its profits to the parent company. A 'territorial' basis of taxing foreign profits should be applied to prevent profit shifting. The income of CFCs should be aligned with the territory where the income arose. The parent country should apply its domestic rules to compute the income of the CFC. The amount of income attributed to each participator should be calculated according to their participation in the CFC. Inappropriate treaty benefits should be denied. For payments by the CFC to be treated as dividends, the participator should hold shares for a minimum 12-month period.

Section B: The UK rules

6.4 In the UK, CFC finance companies have been commonly used by UK companies to finance overseas operations. The UK company lends money to the CFC finance company, which invests the funds in overseas operations and pays tax-exempt dividends to the UK parent (see para 2.12). However, the CIR reduces the potential benefit of CFC finance companies because, in computing the group ratio, interest paid by the CFC to the UK will be excluded from qualifying net group-interest expense (QNGIE).

6.5 Accordingly, many CFCs are finance companies and are often group treasury companies. In general, the CFC rules are targeted at CFCs with significant non-trading finance profits (ie, profits from non-trading loan relationships which, if taxable in the UK, would be taxable under CTA 2009, s 299, or as profits of a finance lease).

6.6 Life insurance companies have a large number of offshore investment funds which take the form of CFCs. These will generally be outside the CFC rules (TIOPA 2010, ss 371CA(11), 371VI).

6.7 Profits are also within the CFC rules to the extent that they derive from assets or risks that relate to activities carried out in the UK. This excludes trading activities in the UK carried on through a PE, because they will be independently liable to UK tax. Profits will also be excluded if there is a commercial, non-tax reason for the arrangements.

6.8 When a company establishes a foreign subsidiary, the profits of the non-resident subsidiary are only taxed when repatriated to the UK and, as a rule, qualify as exempt distributions. If the CFC rules apply, however, the profits of the foreign subsidiary are attributed to the UK parent as they arise and, notwithstanding, that the UK shareholder has received no income. Credit is given for foreign tax paid by the subsidiary.

6.9 Controlled Foreign Companies

6.9 The UK rules are set against the background of the jurisprudence of the European Court in *Cadbury Schweppes plc v IRC (Case C-196/04)* [2006] STC 1908. Cadbury Schweppes plc, a UK incorporated and resident company, established two indirect 100% subsidiaries in Ireland in order to benefit from the special 10% rate of tax available for companies established in the International Financial Services Centre (IFSC) in Dublin. The companies performed treasury functions by raising finance and lending it on to other members of the group. The Inland Revenue Commissioners applied the CFC rules to Cadbury Schweppes. Cadbury Schweppes argued that this was incompatible with the principle of freedom of establishment, one of the basic freedoms established by EU law.

6.10 The CJEU held that the CFC rules can be compatible with the freedom of establishment principle enshrined in EU law, provided they are targeted at wholly artificial arrangements intended to escape the national tax normally payable. However, the Court held that the CFC rules could not be applied if, despite the tax motivation in establishing it, the CFC established in a host Member State '*carries on genuine economic activities there*' [75].

6.11 As a result, the UK rules were reformulated to remove 'motive' tests and seek to apply – not unlike the corporate interest restriction (CIR) rules – objective, mechanical tests. The UK CFC rules were further revised to take account of these BEPS requirements and were incorporated in TIOPA 2010, Part 9A, ss 371AA–371VJ. These adopt a specific transfer pricing methodology, in relation to UK source profits. For the legislation to apply to attribute the profits of the CFC to a UK participator, the non-resident company must be a CFC and its profits must pass through the 'CFC charge gateway', which comprises five individual charge gateways. As TIOPA 2010, s 371AA(4)(a) explains, the sieve is '*the CFC charge gateway through which the profits of a CFC must pass in order to be chargeable profits*'.

6.12 TIOPA 2010, s 371AA(3) defines a CFC as a non-resident company which is controlled by a UK person or persons. The UK companies which own the CFC are 'relevant persons' and their interests are 'relevant interests'. The profits of the CFC can, in circumstances falling within the charge, be allocated proportionately to UK relevant persons, which are accordingly 'chargeable companies' (CCs). A chargeable company is one which has a relevant interest in the CFC of at least 25%: TIOPA 2010, ss 371BC, 371BD.

6.13 UK companies with relevant interests in CFCs should review annually whether CFC profits need to be included in their taxable total profits for UK corporation tax purposes.

6.14 There are a wide range of exemptions from the charge. If none of these apply then, to the extent that the CFC profits so ascertained pass through one of the five 'CFC charge gateways', the profits will be apportioned to UK shareholders. If 25% or more of the profits are apportioned to a UK-resident company then, under corporation tax self-assessment, the UK company is required to include the whole or part of the profits of the CFC in their own profits for corporation tax purposes.

Section C: Definition of CFC

6.15 The CFC rules apply where a UK company is a 'controller' of a non-UK subsidiary (a CFC), in circumstances where a proportionate share of the profits, being 25% or more, of the CFC can be attributed to the UK controller for tax purposes, and no exemption applies. CFC profits can be attributed to a 'relevant person'. A relevant person is person with a 25% interest: TIOPA 2010, ss 371OA–371OE.

6.16 In determining the residence of a CFC, the usual rules apply (place of registration, otherwise place of central management and control; place of effective management under tie-breaker in double taxation treaty): CTA 2009, ss 14–18; TIOPA 2010, ss 371TA–371TC. However, art 4 of the Multilateral Instrument (BEPS Action 15) provides that, in the case of covered treaties, the place of effective management tie-breaker will be replaced by a mutual agreement procedure, which will give a much more active role to tax administrations in determining the place of residence of a CFC. As regards the application of the excluded territories exemption, if there are two or more non-UK territories in which the CFC is liable to tax, the company can elect a specific reference (TIOPA 2010, s 371KC). An election for territory of residence can only be made by persons with a controlling influence in the CFC.

6.17 Where there is a foreign permanent establishment (PE), exempt from corporation tax by reason of CTA 2009, s 18A, it is treated as a CFC, where, if a company, it would have been classified as a CFC (eg, a Jersey or Guernsey cell company).

Section D: The control test

6.18 The control test rests on a blend of legal and economic control and is much the same as for the participation test for transfer pricing purposes. Control will exist in two situations:

(a)   one person controls the company; and

6.19 *Controlled Foreign Companies*

(b) one UK-resident person is a is a 40% shareholder (or holder of a 40% share in a partnership) and a non-resident owns a 40–55% interest.

6.19 A person controls the company if they have the power to secure that the affairs of the company are conducted in accordance with their wishes:

(a) by means of the holding of shares or the possession of voting power in that or any other company; or

(b) by virtue of the powers conferred by the articles of association or other document regulating the affairs of the company.

6.20 A person controls a company if they hold, or are entitled to acquire, rights that would entitle them to receive the greater part (50%+) of the:

(a) profits available for distribution to ordinary shareholders;

(b) proceeds if the whole of the company's share capital were sold; and

(c) assets available for distribution to ordinary shareholders on a winding up.

6.21 A person will also control a company if he is required to prepare consolidated financial statements in respect of the subsidiary.

6.22 For the purposes of economic and legal control, where two or more persons taken together have control, they are taken to control the company.

6.23 Where together a UK resident company and its associated enterprises directly or indirectly satisfy the control conditions, the UK resident company is a controller. An associated enterprise is a company in which another company has a 25% investment (ie, the same test as for 'related parties' under the CIR): TIOPA 2010, ss 259ND, 463.

6.24 A bank is not a controller if it satisfies the control tests by reason of an ordinary banking relationship.

6.25 A person is connected to a CFC if he is an 'associate' within CTA 2010, s 882 or 'connected' within CTA 2010, s 1122. A person and a body of persons of which the person has control are 'associates', as are a person or a body of persons associated with the person having control. A company is connected with another company if the same person controls both or one controls the other: TIOPA 2010, s 371VF.

Section E: The exemptions

Excluded territories exemption (TIOPA 210, ss 371KA–371KJ)

6.26 Most foreign subsidiaries are excluded from the CFC by a wide range of specific exclusions. These are:

- excluded territories exemption;
- exempt period exemption;
- low profits exemption (£500,000, of which not more than £50,000 can be non-trading income);
- low profit margin exemption (< 10% of relevant operating expenditure); and
- tax exemption.

6.27 The primary requirement for the application of the rules is that the controlled subsidiary should be resident in a country with a 'lower level of taxation' (ie, <75% of UK rates). If the controlled subsidiary is resident in a country without a lower level of taxation, it is excluded from the rules. Whether a controlled company is resident in a jurisdiction with a 'lower level of taxation' is determined by regulation: Controlled Foreign Companies (Excluded Territories) Regulations 2012 (SI 2012/3024).

6.28 The exemption applies without restriction to companies who are resident in Australia, Canada, France, Germany, Japan and the United States.

6.29 If it is resident in any other exempt country (ie, a country which does not have a lower level of taxation (a 'specified territory')), non-resident income and gains do not qualify for the excluded countries exemption for an accounting period if its non-local source income ('threshold amount') exceeds the greater of £50,000 and 10% of its commercially quantified income (reg 5). This is intended to prevent the routing of profits from non-excluded territories to excluded territories. Further, it will only be excluded if no intellectual property has been transferred to the company from the UK in the previous six years and it is not party to any arrangements whose main purpose is to secure a tax advantage.

6.30 For this purpose, the income of the CFC is divided into four categories:

- Category A: Income brought into account for accounting purposes (ss 371KE–371KF).
- Category B: Notional interest deducted from the income of a PE as attributable to notional free capital but not deducted in computing the

6.31 *Controlled Foreign Companies*

PE's assumed taxable profits (s 371KG). See: *Irish Bank Resolution Corporation Ltd v R & C Comrs* [2020] EWCA Civ 1128.

- Category C: Income accruing under a trust or partnership (s 371KH).
- Category D: Tax-favoured income (s 371KI).

Exempt period exemption (TIOPA 2010, ss 371JA–371JG)

6.31 The excluded period exemption excludes CFCs from the rules for a period of up to 12 months where:

(a) the company was carrying on business before the relevant time;

(b) was formed for the purpose of controlling one or more CFCs which meet this condition; and

(c) in either case there would be a chargeable company in respect of the CFC charge but for the excluded period exemption.

Low profits exemption (TIOPA 2010, ss 371LA–371LC)

6.32 The low profits exemption applies where the CFC profits are < £50,000 or < £500,000 of which no more than £50,000 represents non-trading income. The low profits exemption does not apply where:

- there are arrangements in place to secure the exemption;
- the CFC's business is the provision of 'UK intermediary services' (ie, where the CFC enters into a contract with a UK client to provide the services of a UK resident individual); and
- the CFC's assumed total profits reflect the use of a group mismatch scheme (10th edition, paras 9.93, 16.103–109).

Low profit margin exemption (TIOPA 2010, ss 371MA–371MC)

6.33 The low profit margin exemption applies where accounting profits are no more than 10% of operating costs.

Tax exemption (TIOPA 2010, ss 371NA–371NE)

6.34 The tax exemption applies where a company is not resident in an excluded territory but, in the country where it is resident, the local tax rate is at least 75% of the UK tax. However, this does not apply if the local tax is charged under 'designer tax provisions' (ie, designed to keep a company outside the CFC regime).

Section F: The CFC gateways

6.35 TIOPA 2010, s 371BB contains a 'CFC charge gateway' test, to determine:

(a) the assets, risks and profits of a CFC;

(b) the identification of significant people functions and key entrepreneurial risk-taking functions (SPFs) to determine cases where there is an artificial separation of assets and risks from people functions; and

(c) a profit attribution to a deemed UK permanent establishment.

This determines which of the 'CFC's assumed total profits' pass through this particular 'CFC charge gateway' to require inclusion in the profits of the UK controller.

6.36 The profits of a non-exempt CFC are liable to attribution to a UK controller only to the extent that they pass through the CFC charge gateway to form part of the CFC's assumed total profits. There are five gateways:

- profits attributable to UK activities;
- non-trading finance profits;
- trading finance profits;
- captive insurance companies; and
- sub-consolidation.

Gateway 1: Profits attributable to UK activities (TIOPA 2010, ss 371DA–371DL)

6.37 This gateway does not apply if any of the following conditions are met (TIOPA 2010, s 371CA):

- Condition A is that the CFC does not have UK tax minimisation as a main purpose.
- Condition B is that the CFC has no UK managed assets or risks.
- Condition C is that the CFC would remain commercially viable if its UK managed assets or risks ceased to be UK managed.
- Condition D is that the CFC's assumed total profits only consist of one or both of non-trading finance profits or property business.

6.38 *Controlled Foreign Companies*

6.38 Activities are attributable to the UK in accordance with the *OECD Report on Attribution of Profits to Permanent Establishments* (22 July 2010): TIOPA 2010, s 371DA(3)(a). Terms used in the legislation have the same meaning as the terms used in the Report. In particular, 'SPF' means 'a significant people function or a key entrepreneurial risk-taking function': s 371DA(3)(f). The latter is usually referred to as 'KERT'. Profits are to be attributed to the UK if the SPF is located there. The steps in determining the SPF are set out in TIOPA 2010, s 371DB.

6.39 The steps are:

(a) Identify relevant assets and risk from which the CFC.s assumed total profits have arisen.

(b) Identify SPFs relevant to economic ownership of profits and assets.

(c) Identify which of the SPFs are carried on in the UK by CFC or a connected company.

(d) Assume that the UK SPFs are carried on by a UK PE

(e) Exclude from the gross assets those where the UK activities are a minority of the total activities.

(f) Exclude profits where substantial economic value, other than tax savings, arises to CFC or where profits arise from arrangements that an independent commercial company would have entered into.

(g) Exclude all profits which meet safe harbour conditions, namely:

- CFC has premises with a reasonable degree of permanence in residence state;

- no more than 20% of relevant trading profits derive directly or indirectly from UK resident persons or UK Pes other than from sale of goods in the UK manufactured in the CFC's territory of residence;

- the UK-related management expenditure is no more than 20% of total management expenditure;

- there has been no transfer of intellectual property from the UK to the CFC in the previous six years; and

- no more than 20% of profits of CFC arise from sale of goods exported from the UK.

6.40 If the profits arise in the territory where SPFs and key entrepreneurial risk-taking functions are located, the profits do not pass through the gateway.

Gateway 2 – Non-trading finance profits

6.41 As the CFC rules are mainly targeted at finance subsidiaries, this is the most elaborate gateway.

6.42 'Non-trading finance profits' are defined in ITOPA 2010, s 371VG as profits from non-trading loan relationships (CTA 2009, s 299), non-exempt distributions and profits from relevant finance leases. Profits arising from the investment of funds held for the purposes of a trade or a property business are excluded if that trade is carried on by the CFC and none of the profits pass through the CFC charge gateway.

6.43 Non-trading finance profits pass through this gateway if they fall within the following categories:

(a) non-trading finance profits attributable to UK activities;

(b) non-trading finance profits arising from the investment of 'relevant UK and other assets' (ie, capital contributions from UK companies) and any funds received directly or indirectly from a UK connected company;

(c) non-trading finance profits arising directly or indirectly from arrangements with a UK connected company or the UK PE of a non-UK resident connected company where it would be reasonable to assume that the arrangements are an alternative to paying a distribution; and

(d) non-trading profits where they arise from the direct or indirect finance lease of an asset to a UK resident company or a UK PE funds represent a concealed distribution.

6.44 This gateway does not apply if the CFC has (i) trading or property income, and/or (ii) exempt dividend income from a 51% subsidiary, and its non-trading finance profits are not more than 5% of either of these amounts or the total of both: TIOPA 2010, ss 371CC, 371CD.

6.45 On election there is a partial exemption regime for financial profits derived from CFCs. The finance company partial exemption (FCPE) gives a special regime for financing activities involving 'qualifying loan relationships'. This election applies to all qualifying loans of all CFCs of the chargeable company making the election.

6.46 Qualifying loan relationship profits are profits from loan relationships which derive from UK capital investment but not from (i) UK monetary or (ii) UK activities, where the debtor is a company connected with the CFC and controlled by the same persons: TIOPA 2010, s 371IA. The authorised OECD

6.47 *Controlled Foreign Companies*

Approach (AOA) (as set out in the 2010 Report – see 6.37) identifies the SPF and KERT functions.

6.47 Where CFC profits pass through the non-trading finance profits gateway, the UK company to which the profits would be allocated can claim exemption from tax on the grounds that the attributed profits are '*qualifying loan relationship profits*'.

6.48 The exempt profits of the UK controller are the profits covered by the qualifying resources rule or the 75% exemption rule. Where the qualifying resources rule applies, the exempt profits are such proportion (X%) of the attributable profits as derive from a loan funded by the CFC from its 'qualifying resources', and the ultimate debtor's country of residence does not change. 'Qualifying resources' are CFC profits derived from making loans to other members of the CFC group in the relevant territory or funds received by the CFC which derive from shares held by the CFC: TIOPA 2010, s 371IB(6)(7). The 'relevant territory' is the country of residence of the ultimate debtor: TOIPA 2010, s 371IB(10(c). Hence, the funds must also derive from that territory.

6.49 If no claim under the qualifying resources rule is made, then 75% of the attributed profits are exempt.

6.50 Attributed profits from qualifying loan relationships which are still taxable after the qualifying resources or 75% rule has been applied, come within the matched interest rule. If the aggregate net tax-interest expense (ANTIE) of the worldwide group (WWG) to which the CFC belongs for the same accounting period are nil, then the attributed profits ('the matched interest profits') are also nil. Otherwise, a relevant proportion of those profits are exempt.

Gateway 3: Trading finance profits

6.51 If the CFC is financed from the UK, its trading finance profits pass through the CFC gateway: TIOPA 2010, 371CE. The profits which are chargeable profits arising from an excess of 'free capital' (ie, capital in excess of the regulatory capital which the CFC is required to maintain and which does not give rise to deductible interest).

6.52 The Controlled Foreign Companies (Excluded Banking Business Profits) Regulations 2012 (SI 2012/3041) provide exclusion from the CFC charge on trading finance profits, where the CFC is a member of a regulated UK banking group, and its Tier One capital ratio does not exceed 125% of the Tier One ratio of its parent.

Gateway 4: Captive insurance company

6.53 This gateway applies to the profits of a captive insurance company, which insures the risk of a UK enterprise: TIOPA 2010, s 371CF.

Gateway 5 – Solo consolidation

6.54 This gateway applies to banking profits of a CFC subsidiary of a UK resident bank which has applied for a solo consolidation waiver, so that the subsidiary is treated as a division of the bank: TIOPA 2010, s 371AH.

Section G: Computation of CFC profits

6.55 In calculating the attributable profits of a CFC, the assumption is made that the CFC is UK resident, and its taxable total profits are its 'assumed total profits': what those profits would be, if it were subject to corporation tax. Various assumptions are made (eg, that it is not a close company). Profits for CFC purposes do not include capital gains. There are no special rules as far as the loan relationship rules are concerned and the normal 'connected party' provisions apply.

6.56 The CFC's *chargeable profits* are for an accounting period are its *assumed taxable total profits* plus losses deductible from current year profits based on the assumption that it is UK resident and its profits are calculated as for UK corporation tax purposes, subject to a number of adjustments: TIOPA 2010, ss 371BA(3), 371SB.

6.57 The assumed total profits are limited to those that pass through the CFC gateway. Chargeable gains are not included in total profits. The various supplementary assumptions include an assumption that the designated currency election for investment companies has been made and that no claim for reinvestment relief in respect of intangible fixed assets will be made. The deductions allowance for carried-forward losses is taken to be nil.

6.58 For the purposes of the CIR, the CFC is assumed to be the sole member of a WWG: TIOPA 2010, ss 371SC–371SK. It is assumed that the CFC is not a member of a group or a consortium, so that no group loss relief is available. The CFC is taken not to be a close company. The profits to be apportioned include creditable tax (ie, double taxation relief and UK tax are charged on the CFC profits): TIOPA 2010, s 371PA.

Index

[All references are to paragraph number.]

Accounting periods
loss relief, and, 3.68–3.75
Accounts adjustments
corporate interest restriction, and, 2.54–2.63
Adjusted net group income expense (ANGIE)
accounts adjustments, and, 2.59
application of legislation, 2.48
fixed ratio debt cap, and, 2.143
interaction with CIR, 2.28
key rules, and, 2.50–2.52
Advance Thin Capitalisation Agreement (ACTA)
transfer pricing, and, 5.19
Aggregate net tax interest expense (ANTIE)
accounts adjustments, and, 2.55
application of legislation, 2.48
de minimis amount, and, 2.45
fixed ratio rule, and, 2.37
generally, 2.103–2.115
interest capacity, and, 2.136–2.137
interest allowance, and, 2.194–2.201
joint ventures, and, 2.224
key rules, and, 2.50–2.52
lease payments, and, 2.63
ratio to aggregate tax EBITDA, 2.116–2.127
Aggregate net tax interest income (ANTII)
application of legislation, 2.48
generally, 2.115
interest allowance, and, 2.192–2.193
key rules, and, 2.50–2.52
Aggregate tax EBITDA
corporate interest restriction, and, 2.50–2.52
Anti-tax avoidance
corporate interest restriction, and
EU Directive, 2.9

Anti-tax avoidance – *contd*
corporate interest restriction, and – *contd*
RAAR, 2.234
TAAR, 2.30
generally, 1.40–1.48
loss relief, and, 3.210
Arbitrage rules
capital instruments, and, 4.2
Arm's length principle
corporate interest restriction, and, 2.6
introduction, 1.31
transfer pricing, and, 5.1–5.9
Associated companies
transfer pricing, and, 5.93
Associates
controlled foreign companies, and, 6.25
Balancing payments
transfer pricing, and, 5.86–5.87
Banks
corporate interest restriction, and, 2.232
loss relief, and, 3.90–3.96
Base Erosion and Profit Shifting (BEPS)
Action Plan, 1.22–1.25
capital instruments, and, 4.17–4.22
controlled foreign companies, and, 6.1–6.3
corporate interest restriction, and, 2.1–2.10
generally, 1.14–1.21
implementation in UK, 1.26
introduction, 1.4
policy background, 1.27–1.39
transfer pricing, and
generally, 5.27–5.33
introduction, 5.5
Regulations, 5.31

225

Index

Basic interest allowance
  generally, 2.128–2.140
  introduction, 2.50–2.52
  methods, 2.132
Bifurcation
  regulatory capital, and, 4.37
'Calculate'
  corporate interest restriction, and, 2.47
Capital adequacy rules
  regulatory capital, and, 4.40–4.49
Capital instruments
  arbitrage rules, and, 4.2
  BEPS, 4.17–4.22
  deduction/non-inclusion (D/NI) mismatch
    amount, 4.30
    conditions, 4.23–4.31
    examples, 4.36
    generally, 4.11
    'ordinary income', 4.29
    related persons, 4.24
    'structured arrangement', 4.25
    'taxable profits', 4.29
    unallowable purpose test, 4.31
  double taxation agreements, and, 4.17
  general rules, 4.1
  hybrid capital instruments rules
    coupon deductibility, 4.51
    Eurobonds, 4.57
    excluded instruments, 4.55
    generally, 4.50–4.61
    introduction, 4.1
    MREL, 4.50
    'qualifying amount', 4.56
    relevant loan relationships, 4.52
  hybrid mismatch rules
    application, 4.5–4.16
    BEPS, 4.17–4.22
    CIR, and, 4.3
    conditions for D/NI mismatch, 4.23–4.31
    double deduction mismatch, 4.12
    'dual inclusion income', 4.16
    dual-resident companies, 4.13
    'financial instruments', 4.5
    financial trader exemption, 4.34
    foreign tax, 4.6
    generally, 4.2
    'hybrid entity', 4.15
    interaction, 4.3–4.4

Capital instruments – *contd*
  hybrid mismatch rules – *contd*
    introduction, 4.1
    meaning of 'hybrid mismatch', 4.2
    'mismatch amount', 4.11
    other types, 4.32–4.36
    'otherwise', 4.8
    'payment', 4.14
    payments for goods and services, 4.5
    permanent establishment, 4.13
    'quasi-payment', 4.14
    'reasonable to suppose' test, 4.7–4.9
    rent, 4.5
    royalties, 4.5
    safe harbours, 4.10
    'tax', 4.6
    transfer arrangements, 4.32–4.33
    unallowable purpose, and, 4.4
  loan relationships, and, 4.1
  multi-lateral instruments, 4.21–4.22
  regulatory capital
    bifurcation, 4.37
    capital adequacy rules, 4.40–4.49
    contingent convertibles, 4.38–4.39
    convertible bonds, 4.37
    equity notes. 4.48
    Eurobonds, 4.47
    perpetuals, 4.45–4.48
    preferred securities, 4.45–4.46
    securities convertible into shares, 4.37–4.39
  repos, 4.32–4.33
  stock lending, 4.32–4.33
  transfer pricing, and, 4.19
  unallowable purpose rule, and
    D/NI mismatch, 4.31
    hybrid mismatch, 4.4
Capitalised interest
  corporate interest restriction, and, 2.61
Captive insurance company
  controlled foreign companies, and, 6.53
Carried on 'on a commercial basis'
  loss relief, and, 3.37–3.44
Carry back relief
  loss relief, and, 3.45–3.48
Carried forward losses
  annual allowance, 3.14–3.15
  cap on relievable losses
    generally, 3.209
    targeted anti-avoidance rule, 3.210

Index

Carried forward losses – *contd*
categories, 3.21
extended losses, 3.105–3.106
extended restricted relief, 3.108
flexible relief unstreamed, 3.101–3.104
further periods, 3.105–3.106
generally, 3.97–3.99
group relief, 3.115–3.144
introduction, 3.12
later periods, 3.105–3.106
loss cap, 3.145–3.172
non-trading loan relationship deficits, 3.114
outline, 3.21–3.36
restricted relief streamed, 3.107
single company/within RM
  extended losses, 3.105–3.106
  extended restricted relief, 3.108
  flexible relief unstreamed, 3.101–3.104
  further periods, 3.105–3.106
  introduction, 3.100
  later periods, 3.105–3.106
  non-trading loan relationship deficits, 3.114
  restricted relief streamed, 3.107
  terminal loss relief, 3.109–3.113
targeted anti-avoidance rule (TAAR), 3.210
terminal loss relief, 3.109–3.113
Centrally provided services
transfer pricing, and, 5.90–5.92
Charge gateway test
captive insurance company, 6.53
generally, 6.35–6.36
introduction, 6.14
non-trading finance profits, 6.41–6.50
profits attributable to UK activities, 6.37–6.40
solo consideration, 6.54
trading finance profits, 6.51–6.52
Chargeable companies
controlled foreign companies, and, 6.12
Chargeable gains
loss relief, and, 3.34
Chargeable profits
controlled foreign companies, and, 6.56
Clogged capital losses
loss relief, and, 3.220

Compliance
loss relief, and, 3.18–3.19
transfer pricing, and, 5.97–5.98
Computation of profits
controlled foreign companies, and, 6.55–6.58
Connected
controlled foreign companies, and, 6.25
Consortium relief
generally, 3.49–3.56
introduction, 3.28
link companies, 3.57–3.67
Contingent convertibles
regulatory capital, and, 4.38–4.39
Controlled foreign companies (CFCs)
activities carried out in the UK, 6.7
'associate', 6.25
BEPS, and, 6.1–6.3
captive insurance company, 6.53
charge gateway test
  captive insurance company, 6.53
  generally, 6.35–6.36
  introduction, 6.14
  non-trading finance profits, 6.41–6.50
  profits attributable to UK activities, 6.37–6.40
  solo consideration, 6.54
  trading finance profits, 6.51–6.52
'chargeable companies', 6.12
chargeable profits, 6.56
computation of profits, 6.55–6.58
'connected', 6.25
control test, 6.18–6.25
definition, 6.15–6.17
EU law, 6.9–6.11
excluded territories exemption, 6.26–6.30
exempt period, 6.31
exemptions
  excluded territories, 6.26–6.30
  exempt period, 6.31
  introduction, 6.14
  low profit margin, 6.33
  low profits, 6.32
  tax, 6.34
finance companies, 6.5
finance profits
  non-trading, 6.41–6.50
  trading, 6.51–6.52

227

Index

Controlled foreign companies (CFCs) – *contd*
 foreign subsidiaries, 6.8
 Gateways
  captive insurance company, 6.53
  generally, 6.35–6.36
  introduction, 6.14
  non-trading finance profits, 6.41–6.50
  profits attributable to UK activities, 6.37–6.40
  solo consideration, 6.54
  trading finance profits, 6.51–6.52
 income categories, 6.30
 life insurance companies, 6.6
 low profit margin exemption, 6.33
 low profits exemption, 6.32
 low tax jurisdiction, and, 6.3
 'motive', and, 6.11
 non-trading finance profits, 6.41–6.50
 OECD recommendation, 6.2
 permanent establishment, 6.17
 profit computation, 6.55–6.58
 profits attributable to UK activities, 6.37–6.40
 qualifying net group interest expense (QNGIE), 6.4
 'relevant person', 6.15
 residence, 6.16
 solo consideration, 6.54
 'specified territory', 6.29
 tax exemption, 6.34
 territorial basis of taxation, and, 6.3
 trading finance profits, 6.51–6.52
 UK rules, 6.4–6.14
Controlled transactions
 transfer pricing, and, 5.1
Convertible bonds
 regulatory capital, and, 4.37
Corporate acquisitions
 followed by transfer of trades and assets, 3.223–3.242
Corporate interest restriction (CIR)
 accounts adjustments, 2.54–2.63
 adjusted net group income expense (ANGIE)
  interaction with CIR, 2.28
  introduction, 2.50–2.52

Corporate interest restriction (CIR) – *contd*
 aggregate net tax interest expense (ANTIE)
  generally, 2.103–2.115
  introduction, 2.50–2.52
  ratio to aggregate tax EBITDA, 2.116–2.127
 aggregate net tax interest income (ANTII), 2.50–2.52
 aggregate tax EBITDA, 2.50–2.52
 allocation of disallowances
  generally, 2.202–2.218
  introduction, 2.42
 anti-tax avoidance, and, 2.9
 application of BEPS, 2.8
 application of legislation
  diagram, 2.49
  introduction, 2.47
  stages, 2.48
 application of rules, 2.32–2.46
 arm's length principle, and, 2.6
 banks, 2.232
 basic interest allowance
  generally, 2.128–2.140
  introduction, 2.50–2.52
  methods, 2.132
 BEPS, 2.1–2.10
 'calculate', 2.47
 capitalised interest, and, 2.61
 de minimis amount, 2.45
 debt cap
  fixed ratio, 2.143–2.157
  generally, 2.38–2.39
  group ratio, 2.191
 debt financing, and, 2.1
 derivative contracts, and, 2.23
 'derive', 2.47
 diagram, 2.49
 distributions, and, 2.28
 diverted profits tax, and, 2.20
 EBITDA
  group, 2.180–2.190
  introduction, 2.2
  ratio of ANTIE to aggregate tax, 2.116–2.127
  relationship with CIR, 2.2
 economically equivalent payments, 2.43
 elections, 2.235–2.238

228

Corporate interest restriction (CIR) – *contd*
  EU Directive 2016/1164, and, 2.9
  excess debt cap, 2.50–2.52
  fair value, and, 2.56–2.60
  'find', 2.47
  fixed ratio debt cap
    generally, 2.143–2.157
    introduction, 2.50–2.52
  fixed ratio rule
    application, 2.40
    basic interest allowance, and, 2.48
    generally, 2.141–2.142
    introduction, 2.37
    use, 2.49
  foreign dividends, and, 2.12–2.13
  GAAP, and, 2.55
  gateways, 2.45
  group EBITDA
    generally, 2.180–2.190
    introduction, 2.50–2.52
  group ratio debt cap
    generally, 2.191
    introduction, 2.50–2.52
  group ratio rule
    application, 2.41
    basic interest allowance, and, 2.48
    generally, 2.158–2.165
    introduction, 2.37
    use, 2.49
  history of UK rules, 2.11–2.21
  hybrid mismatch, and
    generally, 2.24
    interaction with CIR, 2.30
  insurance business, 2.232
  interaction rules, 2.22–2.30
  interest allowance, 2.192–2.201
  interest capacity, 2.50–2.52
  interest recharacterisation, and, 2.30
  interest deduction restriction, 2.99–2.102
  joint ventures, 2.221–2.224
  key rules
    generally, 2.50–2.53
    introduction, 2.3
  lease payments, and, 2.62
  lex specialis legibus generalibus derogat, 2.22
  loan relationships, and, 2.23

Corporate interest restriction (CIR) – *contd*
  loss relief, and
    generally, 3.12
    interaction, 3.76–3.78
  methods
    fixed ratio rule, 2.141–2.142
    generally, 2.37
    group ratio rule, 2.158–2.165
  net group interest expense (NGIE), 2.50–2.52
  operation, 2.3–2.4
  outline of rules, 2.31–2.46
  purpose, 2.2
  qualifying infrastructure companies (QICs), 2.225–2.231
  qualifying net group interest expense (QNGIE)
    generally, 2.166–2.179
    introduction, 2.50–2.52
  RAAR, 2.234
  ratio of ANTIE to aggregate tax EBITDA, 2.116–2.127
  real estate investment trusts (REITs), 2.233
  related party debt, 2.1
  rules
    aggregate net tax interest expense, 2.103–2.115
    allocation of disallowances, 2.202–2.218
    basic interest allowance, 2.128–2.140
    elections, 2.235–2.238
    fixed ratio debt cap, 2.143–2.157
    fixed ratio rule, 2.141–2.142
    group EBITDA, 2.180–2.190
    group ratio debt cap, 2.191
    group ratio rule, 2.158–2.165
    interest allowance, 2.192–2.201
    interest deduction restriction, 2.99–2.102
    qualifying net group interest expense, 2.166–2.179
    ratio of ANTIE to aggregate tax EBITDA, 2.116–2.127
    special rules, 2.219–2.234
  special rules
    banks, 2.232
    insurance business, 2.232

Index

Corporate interest restriction (CIR) – *contd*
 special rules – *contd*
  introduction, 2.219–2.220
  joint ventures, 2.221–2.224
  qualifying infrastructure companies, 2.225–2.231
  RAAR, 2.234
  real estate investment trusts, 2.233
 targeted anti-avoidance rule (TAAR), and, 2.30
 tax arbitrage, and, 2.17
 thin capitalisation, and, 2.11
 transfer pricing, and
  generally, 2.19–2.20
  interaction with CIR, 2.26–2.27
 UK group company, 2.46
 unallowable purpose, and, 2.30
 worldwide debt cap (WWDC), 2.13–2.16
 worldwide group (WWG)
  accounting standards, 2.66–2.68
  consolidation rules, 2.85–2.97
  definition, 2.70
  examples, 2.98
  generally, 2.64–2.76
  'group', 2.71
  introduction, 2.45–2.46
  periods of account, 2.77–2.84
  'relevant entities', 2.75
  'subsidiary', 2.71

Corporate capital loss restriction (CCLR)
 application, 3.17
 clogged capital losses, 3.220
 generally, 3.211–3.219
 insolvent companies, 3.221
 introduction, 3.12
 pre-entry losses, 3.222

Corporate income loss restriction (CILR)
 application, 3.13–3.16
 introduction, 3.12

Corresponding adjustments
 transfer pricing, and, 5.82–5.85

Current year losses
 generally, 3.79–3.85
 introduction, 3.9–3.10
 investment company expenses, 3.84

Current year losses – *contd*
 non-trading loan relationship deficits, 3.82
 non-trading losses on intangible fixed assets, 3.83
 trading losses, 3.79–3.81
 UK property business, 3.85

De minimis amount
 corporate interest restriction, and, 2.45

Debt cap
 fixed ratio, 2.143–2.157
 generally, 2.38–2.39
 group ratio, 2.191

Debt-equity distinction
 generally, 1.54–1.60

Debt financing
 corporate interest restriction, and, 2.1

Deduction/non-inclusion (D/NI) mismatch
 amount, 4.30
 conditions, 4.23–4.31
 examples, 4.36
 generally, 4.11
 'ordinary income', 4.29
 related persons, 4.24
 'structured arrangement', 4.25
 'taxable profits', 4.29
 unallowable purpose test, 4.31

Deductions allowance
 generally, 3.152–3.167
 groups, 3.168
 introduction, 3.13
 outline of system, 3.29

Deferred tax asset
 loss relief, and, 3.10

Derivative contracts
 corporate interest restriction, and, 2.23

'Derive'
 corporate interest restriction, and, 2.47

Distributions
 corporate interest restriction, and, 2.28

Diverted profits tax (DPT)
 corporate interest restriction, and, 2.20
 generally, 5.99–5.122

Dormant companies
 transfer pricing, and, 5.96

Double taxation agreements
 capital instruments, and, 4.17
 purpose, 1.12–1.13

Index

Earnings before interest, tax, depreciation and amortisation (EBITDA)
accounts adjustments, and, 2.56–2.57
aggregate tax, 2.116–2.127
basic interest allowance, 2.132
consolidation rules, and, 2.86
fixed ratio debt cap, 2.143
fixed ratio rule, 2.141
group EBITDA, 2.180–2.190
group ratio debt cap, 2.191
group ratio rule, 2.159–2.162
introduction, 2.2
joint ventures, and, 2.221–2.223
key rules, and, 2.50–2.52
qualifying interest companies, and, 2.230
ratio of ANTIE, 2.116–2.127
relationship with CIR, 2.2

Economic substance re-characterisation
transfer pricing, and, 5.79–5.81

Economically equivalent payments
corporate interest restriction, and, 2.43

Elections
corporate interest restriction, and, 2.235–2.238

Equity notes
regulatory capital, and, 4.48

EU law
controlled foreign companies, and, 6.9–6.11
transfer pricing, and, 5.41–5.50

Eurobonds
hybrid capital instruments, and, 4.57
regulatory capital, and, 4.47

Excess debt cap
corporate interest restriction, and, 2.50–2.52

Excluded territories
controlled foreign companies, and, 6.26–6.30

Exempt period
controlled foreign companies, and, 6.31

Extended carried forward losses
loss relief, and, 3.105–3.106

Extended restricted relief
loss relief, and, 3.108

Fair value
corporate interest restriction, and, 2.56–2.60

Finance companies
controlled foreign companies, and, 6.5

Finance profits
controlled foreign companies, and
non-trading, 6.41–6.50
trading, 6.51–6.52

Financing arrangements
transfer pricing, and, 5.59–5.68

'Find'
corporate interest restriction, and, 2.47

Fixed ratio debt cap
generally, 2.143–2.157
introduction, 2.50–2.52

Fixed ratio rule
application, 2.40
basic interest allowance, and, 2.48
generally, 2.141–2.142
introduction, 2.37
use, 2.49

Flexible relief
generally, 3.86–3.89
introduction, 3.12
unstreamed, 3.101–3.104

Foreign dividends
corporate interest restriction, and, 2.12–2.13

Foreign subsidiaries
controlled foreign companies, and, 6.8

GAAP
corporate interest restriction, and, 2.55

Group EBITDA
generally, 2.180–2.190
introduction, 2.50–2.52

Group ratio debt cap
generally, 2.191
introduction, 2.50–2.52

Group ratio rule
application, 2.41
basic interest allowance, and, 2.48
generally, 2.158–2.165
introduction, 2.37
use, 2.49

Group relief
available losses, 3.131–3.144
conditions for carried-forward loss claims, 3.134–3.142
current year, 3.49–3.56
generally, 3.115–3.123
giving effect to, 3.143–3.144
'group', 3.127–3.130

231

Index

Group relief – *contd*
  introduction, 3.12
  link companies, 3.57–3.67
Guarantees
  transfer pricing, and, 5.73–5.78
Hybrid capital instruments rules
  corporate interest restriction, and
    generally, 2.24
    interaction with CIR, 2.30
  coupon deductibility, 4.51
  Eurobonds, 4.57
  excluded instruments, 4.55
  generally, 4.50–4.61
  introduction, 4.1
  MREL, 4.50
  'qualifying amount', 4.56
  relevant loan relationships, 4.52
Hybrid mismatch rules
  application, 4.5–4.16
  BEPS, 4.17–4.22
  CIR, and, 4.3
  conditions for D/NI mismatch, 4.23–4.31
  double deduction mismatch, 4.12
  'dual inclusion income', 4.16
  dual-resident companies, 4.13
  'financial instruments', 4.5
  financial trader exemption, 4.34
  foreign tax, 4.6
  generally, 4.2
  'hybrid entity', 4.15
  interaction, 4.3–4.4
  introduction, 4.1
  meaning of 'hybrid mismatch', 4.2
  'mismatch amount', 4.11
  other types, 4.32–4.36
  'otherwise', 4.8
  'payment', 4.14
  payments for goods and services, 4.5
  permanent establishment, 4.13
  'quasi-payment', 4.14
  'reasonable to suppose' test, 4.7–4.9
  rent, 4.5
  royalties, 4.5
  safe harbours, 4.10
  'tax', 4.6
  transfer arrangements, 4.32–4.33
  unallowable purpose, and, 4.4
Income
  controlled foreign companies, and, 6.30
  loss relief, and, 3.34

Income taxation
  loss relief, and, 3.3–3.8
Insurance companies
  corporate interest restriction, and, 2.232
  loss relief, and, 3.90–3.96
Interest recharacterization
  corporate interest restriction, and, 2.30
Interest allowance
  corporate interest restriction, and, 2.192–2.201
Interest capacity
  corporate interest restriction, and, 2.50–2.52
Interest deduction
  corporate interest restriction, and, 2.99–2.102
International tax
  BEPS project
    Action Plan, 1.22–1.25
    generally, 1.14–1.21
    implementation in UK, 1.26
    policy background, 1.27–1.39
  double tax treaties, 1.12–1.13
  generally, 1.5–1.11
Investment company expenses
  loss relief, and, 3.84
In-year relief
  loss relief, and, 3.45–3.48
Joint ventures
  corporate interest restriction, and, 2.221–2.224
Lease payments
  corporate interest restriction, and, 2.62
Lex specialis legibus generalibus derogat
  corporate interest restriction, and, 2.22
Life insurance companies
  controlled foreign companies, and, 6.6
Loan relationships
  capital instruments, and, 4.1
  corporate interest restriction, and, 2.23
Loss cap
  deductions allowance, 3.152–3.168
  generally, 3.145–3.150
  introduction, 3.12, 3.31
  key concepts, 3.151–3.172
  relevant deductions, 3.169–3.172
  relevant maximum, 3.189–3.208
  relevant profits, 3.173–3.188

Index

Loss relief
accounting periods, 3.68–3.75
banks, 3.90–3.96
cap on relievable carried forward losses
  generally, 3.209
  targeted anti-avoidance rule, 3.210
carried forward losses
  annual allowance, 3.14–3.15
  cap on relievable losses, 3.209–3.210
  categories, 3.21
  generally, 3.97–3.99
  group relief, 3.115–3.144
  introduction, 3.12
  loss cap, 3.145–3.172
  outline, 3.21–3.36
  single company/within RM, 3.100–3.114
carried forward losses (single company/within RM)
  extended, 3.105–3.106
  extended restricted relief, 3.108
  flexible relief unstreamed, 3.101–3.104
  further periods, 3.105–3.106
  introduction, 3.100
  later periods, 3.105–3.106
  non-trading loan relationship deficits, 3.114
  restricted relief streamed, 3.107
  terminal loss relief, 3.109–3.113
carried on 'on a commercial basis', 3.37–3.44
carry back relief, 3.45–3.48
'chargeable gains', 3.34
clogged capital losses, 3.220
compliance costs, 3.18–3.19
consortium relief
  generally, 3.49–3.56
  introduction, 3.28
  link companies, 3.57–3.67
corporate acquisitions followed by transfer of trades and assets, 3.223–3.242
corporate capital loss restriction (CCLR)
  application, 3.17
  clogged capital losses, 3.220
  generally, 3.211–3.219

Loss relief – *contd*
corporate capital loss restriction (CCLR) – *contd*
  insolvent companies, 3.221
  introduction, 3.12
  pre-entry losses, 3.222
corporate income loss restriction (CILR)
  application, 3.13–3.16
  introduction, 3.12
corporate interest restriction (CIR)
  generally, 3.12
  interaction, 3.76–3.78
current year losses
  generally, 3.79–3.85
  introduction, 3.9–3.10
  investment company expenses, 3.84
  non-trading loan relationship deficits, 3.82
  non-trading losses on intangible fixed assets, 3.83
  trading losses, 3.79–3.81
  UK property business, 3.85
deductions allowance
  generally, 3.152–3.167
  groups, 3.168
  introduction, 3.13
  outline of system, 3.29
deferred tax asset, as, 3.10
extended carried forward losses, 3.105–3.106
extended restricted relief, 3.108
flexible relief
  generally, 3.86–3.89
  introduction, 3.12
  unstreamed, 3.101–3.104
further periods, 3.105–3.106
group relief
  available losses, 3.131–3.144
  conditions for carried-forward loss claims, 3.134–3.142
  current year, 3.49–3.56
  generally, 3.115–3.123
  giving effect to, 3.143–3.144
  'group', 3.127–3.130
  introduction, 3.12
  link companies, 3.57–3.67
history of rules, 3.1–3.17
'income', 3.34
income taxation, and, 3.3–3.8

233

Index

Loss relief – *contd*
  insurance companies, 3.90–3.96
  interaction with CIR, 3.76–3.78
  investment company expenses, 3.84
  in-year relief, 3.45–3.48
  later periods, 3.105–3.106
  legislative basis, 3.20
  loss cap
    deductions allowance, 3.152–3.168
    generally, 3.145–3.150
    introduction, 3.12, 3.31
    key concepts, 3.151–3.172
    relevant deductions, 3.169–3.172
    relevant maximum, 3.189–3.208
    relevant profits, 3.173–3.188
  non-trading loan relationship deficits (NTLRD)
    current year losses, 3.82
    generally, 3.25–3.27
    single company/within RM, 3.114
  non-trading losses on intangible fixed assets (NTLIFA)
    current year losses, 3.83
    generally, 3.21
  non-trading profits
    definition, 3.36
    generally, 3.23
  outline, 3.21–3.36
  pre-entry losses, 3.222
  relevant deductions, 3.169–3.172
  relevant maximum
    companies that are members of a group, 3.205–3.208
    definition, 3.30
    generally, 3.189–3.200
    groups, 3.201–3.204
    introduction, 3.13
  relevant profits
    accounting periods 1 April 2017 to 6 July 2018, 3.183–3.185
    accounting periods from 6 July 2018, 3.186–3.188
    definition, 3.32
    generally, 3.173–3.182
    introduction, 3.13
  restricted relief streamed, 3.107
  restrictions, 3.2
  ring-fence losses, and, 3.46
  schedule system of taxation, 3.3–3.6
  sideways loss relief, and, 3.46

Loss relief – *contd*
  targeted anti-avoidance rule (TAAR), 3.210
  'taxable total profits', 3.35
  terminal loss relief, 3.109–3.113
  'total profits', 3.34
  trading income, 3.7
  trading losses
    current year, 3.79–3.81
    generally, 3.21–3.27
  trading profits, 3.23–3.24
  transitional accounting periods, 3.68–3.75
  types of business income, 3.6
  UK property business, 3.85
Low profit margin
  controlled foreign companies, and, 6.33
Low profits
  controlled foreign companies, and, 6.32
Low tax jurisdiction
  controlled foreign companies, and, 6.3
Medium-sized enterprises
  transfer pricing, and, 5.95
Multi-lateral instruments
  capital instruments, and, 4.21–4.22
Net group interest expense (NGIE)
  corporate interest restriction, and, 2.50–2.52
Non-qualifying territory
  transfer pricing, and, 5.94
Non-trading finance profits
  controlled foreign companies, and, 6.41–6.50
Non-trading loan relationship deficits (NTLRD)
  current year losses, 3.82
  generally, 3.25–3.27
  single company/within RM, 3.114
Non-trading losses on intangible fixed assets (NTLIFA)
  current year losses, 3.83
  generally, 3.21
Non-trading profits
  definition, 3.36
  generally, 3.23
  outline, 3.21–3.36
OECD Guidelines
  transfer pricing, and, 5.8

OECD Model Convention
  transfer pricing, and, 5.7
Partner enterprises
  transfer pricing, and, 5.93
Passive association
  transfer pricing, and, 5.15–5.19
Permanent establishment (PE)
  controlled foreign companies, and, 6.17
  introduction, 1.31
  transfer pricing, and, 5.33
Perpetuals
  regulatory capital, and, 4.45–4.48
'Phantom' degrouping charges
  transfer pricing, and, 5.96
Pre-entry losses
  loss relief, and, 3.222
Preferred securities
  regulatory capital, and, 4.45–4.46
Qualifying infrastructure companies (QICs)
  corporate interest restriction, and, 2.225–2.231
Qualifying net group interest expense (QNGIE)
  controlled foreign companies, and, 6.4
  corporate interest restriction, and
  generally, 2.166–2.179
  introduction, 2.50–2.52
'Qualifying territory'
  transfer pricing, and, 5.94
Qualifying infrastructure companies (QICs)
  corporate interest restriction, and, 2.225–2.231
Qualifying net group interest expense (QNGIE)
  generally, 2.166–2.179
  introduction, 2.50–2.52
RAAR
  corporate interest restriction, and, 2.234
Real estate investment trusts (REITs)
  corporate interest restriction, and, 2.233
Regime anti-avoidance rule (RAAR)
  corporate interest restriction, and, 2.234
Regulatory capital
  bifurcation, 4.37
  capital adequacy rules, 4.40–4.49

Regulatory capital – *contd*
  contingent convertibles, 4.38–4.39
  convertible bonds, 4.37
  equity notes. 4.48
  Eurobonds, 4.47
  perpetuals, 4.45–4.48
  preferred securities, 4.45–4.46
  securities convertible into shares, 4.37–4.39
Related party debt
  corporate interest restriction, and, 2.1
Relevant deductions
  loss relief, and, 3.169–3.172
Relevant maximum
  companies that are members of a group, 3.205–3.208
  definition, 3.30
  generally, 3.189–3.200
  groups, 3.201–3.204
  introduction, 3.13
Relevant person
  controlled foreign companies, and, 6.15
Relevant profits
  accounting periods 1 April 2017 to 6 July 2018, 3.183–3.185
  accounting periods from 6 July 2018, 3.186–3.188
  definition, 3.32
  generally, 3.173–3.182
  introduction, 3.13
Repos
  capital instruments, and, 4.32–4.33
Residence
  controlled foreign companies, and, 6.16
  introduction, 1.31
Restricted relief streamed
  loss relief, and, 3.107
Ring-fence losses
  loss relief, and, 3.46
Schedular system of taxation
  loss relief, and, 3.3–3.6
Securities
  regulatory capital, and, 4.37–4.39
  transfer pricing, and, 5.69–5.72
Separate entity principle
  transfer pricing, and, 5.10–5.14
Sideways loss relief
  loss relief, and, 3.46

Index

Small and medium-sized companies (SMEs)
transfer pricing, and, 5.93–5.94
Specified territory
controlled foreign companies, and, 6.29
Stock lending
capital instruments, and, 4.32–4.33
Targeted anti-avoidance rule (TAAR)
corporate interest restriction, and, 2.30
loss relief, and, 3.210
Tax
avoidance, 1.40–1.48
BEPS project
Action Plan, 1.22–1.25
generally, 1.14–1.21
implementation in UK, 1.26
policy background, 1.27–1.39
companies, on, 1.49–1.53
competition, 1.40–1.48
double tax treaties, 1.12–1.13
generally, 1.5–1.11
Tax arbitrage
corporate interest restriction, and, 2.17
Tax avoidance
generally, 1.40–1.48
Tax competition
generally, 1.40–1.48
Taxable total profits
loss relief, and, 3.35
Terminal loss relief
loss relief, and, 3.109–3.113
Territorial basis of taxation
controlled foreign companies, and, 6.3
Thin capitalisation
corporate interest restriction, and, 2.11
transfer pricing, and, 5.34–5.40
Total profits
loss relief, and, 3.34
Trading finance profits
controlled foreign companies, and, 6.51–6.52
Trading income
loss relief, and, 3.7
Trading losses
current year, 3.79–3.81
generally, 3.21–3.27
Trading profits
loss relief, and, 3.23–3.24

Transfer pricing
Advance Thin Capitalisation Agreement, 5.19
application to financing arrangements, 5.59–5.68
arm's-length principle, 5.1–5.9
associated companies, 5.93
balancing payments, 5.86–5.87
BEPS, and
generally, 5.27–5.33
introduction, 5.5
Regulations, 5.31
capital instruments, and, 4.19
centrally provided services, 5.90–5.92
compliance issues, 5.97–5.98
'controlled transactions', 5.1
corporate interest restriction, and
generally, 2.19–2.20
interaction with CIR, 2.26–2.27
corresponding adjustments, 5.82–5.85
diverted profits tax, 5.99–5.122
dormant companies, 5.96
economic substance re-characteristation, 5.79–5.81
EU context, 5.41–5.50
exemptions, 5.93–5.96
financing arrangements, 5.59–5.68
financial transactions guidance, 5.9
guarantees, 5.73–5.78
hypothesis, 5.20–5.26
meaning, 5.1
medium-sized enterprises, 5.95
'non-qualifying territory', 5.94
objective, 5.6
OECD Guidelines, 5.8
OECD Model Convention, 5.7
partner enterprises, 5.93
passive association, 5.15–5.19
permanent establishment, 5.33
'phantom' degrouping charges, 5.96
purpose of rules, 5.4
'qualifying territory', 5.94
securities, 5.69–5.72
separate entity principle, 5.10–5.14
small and medium-sized companies (SMEs), 5.93–5.94
thin capitalisation, 5.34–5.40
UK rules, 5.51–5.58
withholding tax, 5.88–5.89

Index

Transitional accounting periods
  loss relief, and, 3.68–3.75
UK group company
  corporate interest restriction, and, 2.46
UK tax
  BEPS project
    Action Plan, 1.22–1.25
    generally, 1.14–1.21
    implementation in UK, 1.26
    policy background, 1.27–1.39
  double tax treaties, 1.12–1.13
  generally, 1.5–1.11
Unallowable purpose
  capital instruments, and
    D/NI mismatch, 4.31
    hybrid mismatch, 4.4
  corporate interest restriction, and, 2.30

Withholding tax
  transfer pricing, and, 5.88–5.89
Worldwide debt cap (WWDC)
  corporate interest restriction, and, 2.13–2.16
Worldwide group (WWG)
  accounting standards, 2.66–2.68
  consolidation rules, 2.85–2.97
  definition, 2.70
  examples, 2.98
  generally, 2.64–2.76
  'group', 2.71
  introduction, 2.45–2.46
  periods of account, 2.77–2.84
  'relevant entities', 2.75
  'subsidiary', 2.71